HEINRICH HEINE:
POETRY AND POLITICS

Nigel Reeves

HEINRICH HEINE:
POETRY AND POLITICS

Paperback edition with a new preface

Libris

First published by Oxford University Press in 1974
This paperback edition first published by Libris, 1994
Copyright © Nigel Reeves, 1974, 1994
All rights reserved

Libris
10 Burghley Road
London NW5 1UE

A catalogue record for this book is available from the British Library
ISBN 1 870352 57 2

Produced by Kitzinger, London
Printed by Biddles Ltd, Guildford

For Minou

Preface to the Paperback Edition (1994)

Some twenty years have passed since this monograph was first published. In that time Heine's works have become far more firmly established as legitimate members of the German literary canon. This is not least thanks to the continued work of the Heinrich-Heine Institut in Düsseldorf, which since 1961 has published the *Heine-Jahrbuch* as a central repository for the scholarly investigation of Heine the man, his contemporaries, and especially the origins and gestation of his works. Perhaps the most significant advance since 1974 has, however, been the continuing publication of two new complete critical editions, the *Säkularausgabe* edited in the Forschungs- und Gedenkstätten der klassischen deutschen Literatur in Weimar and the Centre Nationale de la Recherche Scientifique in Paris (30 volumes, 1970–), and the *Historisch-kritische Gesamtausgabe der Werke* edited by Manfred Windfuhr (15 volumes, 1973–) for the Landeshauptstadt Düsseldorf and the Heinrich-Heine-Institut. The commentary volumes and the critical notes of these editions provide the most fundamental scholarly contribution since my study appeared, replacing the edition of the works by Ernst Elster and the edition of the *Briefe* by Friedrich Hirth which I used as the most reliable at the time. Moreover, further important background information has regularly appeared since 1981 in the series *Heine Studien: Heinrich Heines Werk im Urteil seiner Zeitgenossen* edited by Joseph A. Kruse, also on behalf of the Heinrich-Heine-Institut, Düsseldorf.

Gerhard Höhn's *Heine-Handbuch: Zeit, Person, Werk* (J. B. Metzlersche Verlagsbuchhandlung, Stuttgart, 1987) is also an invaluable reference source for biographical details, political and social background, sources of the works and a digest of secondary literature. Eberhard Galley's useful companion to Heine, also published by Metzler, has been replaced by Jeffrey L. Sammons's recent volume (1991), *Heinrich Heine* (Sammlung Metzler, Realien zur Literatur series, volume 261). Jeffrey Sammons has also published one of the most readable, yet penetrating of the Heine biographies, *Heinrich Heine: A Modern Biography* (Princeton

University Press, Princeton and Carcanet New Press, Manchester, 1979).

While Heine's poetry has generally received less attention in recent years than his prose and his political and philosophical interests, Michael Perraudin's *Heinrich Heine. Poetry in Context: A Study of the 'Buch der Lieder'* (Berg, Oxford, 1989) is of special interest in relation to this study since it builds on and indeed takes issue with my own section on the *Buch der Lieder*. Perraudin's concern is to track down Heine's use of 'received materials' from Goethe, Byron, Wilhelm Müller, *Des Knaben Wunderhorn* and the contemporary almanachs, and to show how he ironized, recreated and located himself in relation to these sources. I had stressed Heine's desire to rediscover the apparent wholeness and simplicity of the folksong and showed how Heine used caricature and self-irony to plot the failure of this venture in achieving its philosophical purpose. Perraudin rather highlights how by these same means Heine captures the complexities of the modern, self-reflective poetic sensibility. There is in fact little disagreement, however, since this is very close to my own argument in my concluding chapter, 'The Creative Personality'. What I still believe Perraudin underestimates is the persistent influence on Heine, and indeed on his almanach sources, of both the quasi-pastoral topoi and the verbal wit of rococo verse.

Heine's political affinities were of burning interest to critics in the late nineteen sixties, reflecting Heine's rediscovery as a major German literary figure who appeared to have committed himself to the political fray through defiance of Prussian censorship, merciless satire and, in the mid eighteen forties, a close association with Karl Marx. In this context Leo Kreutzer's early *Heine und der Kommunismus* (Vandenhoeck und Ruprecht, Göttingen, 1970) is useful for elucidating some of the theoretical strands in French communism at the time when Marx, Engels and Heine were together in Paris. Particularly helpful is also the section of Giorgio Tonelli's *Heinrich Heines politische Philosophie* 1830–45 (Georg Olms Verlag, Hildesheim and New York, 1975 – a translation of the Italian original) that deals specifically with the sources of Heine's political ideas. However, Tonelli's interpretation of the epics *Atta Troll* and *Deutschland, Ein Wintermärchen* is regrettably rather mechanistic and is used to illustrate Heine's ideas rather than to consider these works as poetry.

An illuminating source of information on the thought of Heine's university teachers, E. M. Arndt, K. D. Hüllmann and G. Sartorius, is provided by Walter Kanowsky's *Vernunft und Geschichte: Heinrich Heines Studium als Grundlegung seiner Welt- und Kunstanschauung* (Bouvier, Bonn, 1975) which tells us much about the origins of Heine's interpretation of European history and the intellectual foundations laid before his encounter with Hegel and with the Saint-Simonians.

Just how significant had been the relative influence of Hegel and the Saint-Simonians formed the subject of a debate between myself and Dolf Sternberger. In counter-distinction to Sternberger's argument for the primacy of the Saint-Simonian influence (in *Heinrich Heine und die Abschaffung der Sünde* – see bibliography), I argued for the pre-eminent importance of Hegel's dialectical view of history and that Heine found in the Saint-Simonians an exciting confirmation and extension of his own early ideas. My article, 'Heinrich Heine – Politics or poetry? Hegel or Enfantin?' *Modern Language Review*, 75 [1], 1980) offered the opportunity to demonstrate that the concept of reunifying the sensual and sexual with the spiritual had been a central theme of Heine's *Almansor* as early as 1820 and could be traced through to the *Reise von München nach Genua* (1829) before Enfantin had even formulated his principal ideas.

Jean Pierre Lefebvre, *Der gute Trommler: Heines Beziehung zu Hegel* (Hoffmann und Campe, Hamburg, 1986) and Eduard Krüger, *Heine und Hegel: Dichtung, Philosophie und Politik bei Heinrich Heine* (Scriptor Verlag, Kronberg, 1977) both explore the Hegelian dimension further, but Krüger in particular raises an issue central to this study: how did Heine reconcile the competing demands of poetic freedom and commitment to political action? Albrecht Betz, *Ästhetik und Politik. Heinrich Heines Prosa* (Carl Hanser Verlag, Munich, 1971) had identified a stylistic match in the prose between Heine's use of juxtaposition, contrast and characteristic miniature scenes and the disappearance of an organic social structure in the years of early industrialization. Betz argues for art's reflective role rather than any role as a stimulus to action. It is a view close to that represented in Benno von Wiese's *Signaturen: Zu Heinrich Heine und seinem Werk* (Erich Schmidt Verlag, Berlin, 1976) both in von Wiese's tracing of the dance image in Heine as a device for giving shape to a reality defying definitive understanding (in the chapter entitled 'Das tanzende Universum'), and in the argument (in 'Zum Problem der politischen Dichtung Heinrich Heines') that in Heine political issues are transformed into poetic motifs subordinate to the aesthetic purpose.

My own re-examination of *Atta Troll*, 'Atta Troll and his Executioners. The Political Significance of Heinrich Heine's Tragi-Comic Epic' (*Euphorion*, 73 [1979], pp. 388–409) comes to a similar conclusion. It first argues against previous views of the huntsman Laskaro's symbolical role as a representative of Carlism or Communism (indeed the bulk of commentators had offered no interpretation) and provides evidence that he is a figure standing for the demonic pagan forces that had survived the onslaught of Christianity and which Heine highlighted in *Elementargeister* and *Zur Geschichte der Religion und Philosophie*. But beyond that allegorical significance the entire epic is a satirical reversal of *La Chanson de Roland* and Immerman's *Das Tal von Ronceval*, framed in a tragi-comic verse setting that plays with political, literary and biographical elements alike and in the final analysis relativizes them all aesthetically.

Heine's brilliant use of the miniature scene or complex of images to symbolize a key idea and then to lock that idea into a poetic and artistic kaleidoscope is a central characteristic of his epics and his prose, highlighted, as we saw, by Betz. But this aesthetic effect is never far from satirical intention, and Heine's supreme art as a caricaturist has been brilliantly captured by two scholars from Oxford to whom I owe a profound debt in the development of my own ideas, S. S. Prawer and T. J. Reed. I refer to Prawer's monumental and penetrating study *Heine's Jewish Comedy: A Study of his Portrait of Jews and Judaism* (Clarendon Press, Oxford, 1983) and his lecture on Heine's caricature of England as the early exemplar of industrialization and urbanization, published as *Coal smoke and Englishmen. A Study of Verbal Caricature in the Writings of Heinrich Heine* (Institute of Germanic Studies, London, 1984), which led to the longer study *Frankenstein's Island: England and the English in the Writings of Heinrich Heine* (Cambridge University Press, 1986). T. J. Reed pursued Heine the verbal cartoonist for whom society, religion, and philosophy as well as politics, offered subject matter for an insatiable satirical appetite in his 'History in Nutshells; Heine as a

Cartoonist' (1991), in P. U. Hohendahl and S. L. Gilman (eds), *Heinrich Heine and the Occident: Multiple Identities, Multiple Receptions* (University of Nebraska Press, Lincoln and London, 1991, pp. 163–86) having previously traced Heine's taste for food images in 'Heines Appetit' (*Heine-Jahrbuch*, 1983).

But my own lasting image of Heine, which I mapped in 'Heimat aus der Ferne. Gedanken zu einem Leitmotiv in Heines Dichtung' (in *Heimat im Wort*, ed. R. Görner, iudicium verlag, Munich, 1992, pp. 72–89) is that of the wanderer in search of a Utopia, the pilgrim in search of a religion, the futility of whose search for a spiritual home spurs insight into the absurdity of human endeavours and prompts both the wry smile and the biting wit of the satirist. From the *Buch der Lieder* to the embittered and often frightening tales of *Romanzero*, Heine's works plot this quest and record the intellectual process behind it. What has survived Heine's voyage through post-Napoleonic Prussia and France was not of course the poet protagonist, the Juan Ponce de León of 'Bimini', who thought he could locate the island of eternal youth in the ocean of time, but the ship's log-book, Heine's poetry.

Aston University and Great Malvern
April 1994

CONTENTS

INTRODUCTION

CONTRADICTION seems to be the very stuff of Heine's thought and works. In 1822, five years before the publication of the *Buch der Lieder*, he enjoined Karl Immermann to follow him to battle and abandon poetry: 'Kampf dem verjährten Unrecht, der herrschenden Thorheit und dem Schlechten! Wollen Sie mich zum Waffenbruder in diesem heiligen Kampfe, so reiche ich Ihnen freudig die Hand. Die Poesie ist am Ende doch nur eine schöne Nebensache.'[1] Yet some nine years later and seven months after the July Revolution Heine was still writing *Lieder*. The prologue to *Neuer Frühling* depicts him as a warrior who has fallen foul not of his enemy but of a host of unwanted cupids.[2] It is not chains of iron that have ensnared him but chains of flowers:

> In Gemälde-Galerieen
> Siehst du oft das Bild des Manns,
> Der zum Kampfe wollte ziehen,
> Wohlbewehrt mit Schild und Lanz'.
>
> Doch ihn necken Amoretten,
> Rauben Lanze ihm und Schwert,
> Binden ihn mit Blumenketten,
> Wie er auch sich mürrisch wehrt.
>
> So, in holden Hindernissen,
> Wind' ich mich mit Lust und Leid,
> Während andre kämpfen müssen
> In dem großen Kampf der Zeit.[3]

Shortly before his death in 1856 he described the inner dissonance of his early youth in words that have been applied to his entire life:[4]

Mein Leben glich damals einem großen Journal, wo die obere

---

[1] *Heinrich Heine: Briefe*, ed. Friedrich Hirth, Mainz, 1950, i. 51 f. (= *Br*).
[2] The Baroque and Rococo motif of Love and War.
[3] *Heines sämtliche Werke*, ed. Ernst Elster, Leipzig, 1887–90, i. 203 (= E).
[4] Cf. Laura Hofrichter, 'Heines Entwicklung als Dichter', Diss., Toronto, 1954, pp. 88 f. See also id., *Heinrich Heine*, Oxford, 1963, p. 2.

Abteilung die Gegenwart, den Tag mit seinen Tagesberichten und Tagesdebatten, enthielt, während in der unteren Abteilung die poetische Vergangenheit in fortlaufenden Nachtträumen wie eine Reihenfolge von Romanfeuilletons sich phantastisch kundgab. (E vii. 477)

His production similarly seems to be divided, ranging from *Traumbilder* and songs in the *Buch der Lieder* to satire and the proclamation of freedom in the later *Reisebilder*, from caricature to an intoxicated absorption in nature within *Die Harzreise* itself, from the dream sequences and 'Protest gegen die Plebiscita der Tagestribünen' in *Atta Troll*[5] to the biting attacks of *Deutschland. Ein Wintermärchen*, to name just a few obvious examples. And it was a cruel irony that the man who had preached the rehabilitation of the flesh, the gladiator whom the *Idee* had driven into the arena of world events,[6] had to be reduced to the pitiful Lazarus of the mattress grave, unable to leave the confinement of his room and restricted to the spectres of his own mind for the last eight years of his life.

Heine's contemporaries were fascinated and perplexed by this remarkable human phenomenon. For Théophile Gautier he was not simply Faustian in his inner discord but the child of Faust and Helen, born of the untiring search for the infinite and of the finite perfection of classical beauty:

Jamais nature ne fut composée d'éléments plus divers que celle de Henri Heine; il était à la fois gai et triste, sceptique et croyant, tendre et cruel, sentimental et persifleur, classique et romantique, Allemand et Français, délicat et cynique, enthousiaste et plein de sang-froid; tout, excepté ennuyeux. A la plastique grecque la plus pure il joignait le sens moderne le plus exquis; c'était vraiment l'Euphorion, enfant de Faust et de la belle Hélène.[7]

The college of Prussian censorship saw in him a threat to the proper belief in religion and the crown.[8] And yet Börne, with whom he was readily associated as one of the few and most outspoken critics of post-Napoleonic Germany, found in him not an ally, not

---

[5] E ii. 353.   [6] E iv. 14 (Vorrede to *Salon* I, 1833).
[7] Théophile Gautier, *Portraits et Souvenirs littéraires*, Paris, 1875, pp. 121 f.
[8] Cf. H. H. Houben, *Verbotene Literatur von der klassischen Zeit bis zur Gegenwart*, Berlin, 1924, 'Heine' pp. 385–429. He was, for example, accused of 'gemeingefährliche Schandreden über den Charakter des deutschen Volkes, die politisch-sozialen Institute Deutschlands und ins Besondere auf die brutalsten Ausfälle auf die geheiligte Person des diesseitigen Staatsoberhauptes' (p. 417).

a revolutionary at all—but an effete and wanton aesthete, who only loved the truth when it chanced also to be beautiful.[9] In the early 1840s Friedrich Engels would have accepted Börne's judgement. He himself had seen in Börne the John the Baptist of the new Socialism that issued from Hegel[10]—and in Heine an introspective *Weltschmerzler*,[11] an exhausted *Tannhäuser*,[12] whose essay on Börne was one of the basest works ever written in the German language.[13] But by 1844, when Heine had become the personal friend of Karl Marx, and like him a collaborator in *Vorwärts*, Engels proclaimed him as the leading German poet of the day, a major figure in the upsurge of Socialism, and published a translation of his poem on the Silesian weavers to prove it.[14] To add to the confusion, however, Heine was by his own declaration a convinced monarchist and fearful of the egalitarianism preached by Jacobin and Communist alike.[15]

Nevertheless Heine has remained a firm favourite in the Socialist countries of the East to the present day. His works are listed in Marxian histories of literature under the category 'Cultural Heritage'[16] and recent years have seen a considerable number of academic studies and monographs from East Germany,[17] which all have in common the basic interpretation of Heine as the herald of a new post-Goethean, politically committed literature, a role that Heine claimed for himself in works immediately preceding and following the July Revolution of 1830.[18] It is the period from the late 1820s to 1848 that forms their primary or

---

[9] Cf. *L. Börnes sämtliche Werke*, ed. Inge and Peter Rippmann, Düsseldorf, 1964, iii. 810 f. (*Briefe aus Paris*, 25 Feb. 1833). Quoted by Heine, E vii. 137.
[10] Marx/Engels, *Werke*, Institut für Marxismus-Leninismus beim ZK der SED, Berlin, 1957 ff., i. 438 (= MEW).
[11] Ibid., Ergänzungsband 2, p. 438 (1839/40?).   [12] Ibid. p. 118 (1841).
[13] Ibid. i. 440, 441 (1842).   [14] Ibid. ii. 512 f.
[15] See for example E iii. 420 (1831); v. 37 (1833); iv. 223 (1834); vi. 41 ff. (1854); vi. 571 ff. (1855).
[16] Cf. Ludwig Marcuse, 'Heine and Marx: A History and a Legend', *Germanic Review*, 30 (1955), 113.
[17] W. Dietze, *Junges Deutschland und deutsche Klassik*, Berlin, 1957; K. Emmerich, *Heinrich Heines 'Reisebilder'*, Diss., Berlin (Humboldt), 1965; Hans Kaufmann, *Politisches Gedicht und klassische Dichtung*, Berlin, 1958; id., *Heinrich Heine. Geistige Entwicklung und künstlerisches Werk*, Berlin and Weimar, 1967; Hans Pfeiffer, *Begriff und Bild. Heines philosophische und ästhetische Ansichten*, Rudolstadt, 1958; G. Schmitz, *Über die ökonomischen Anschauungen in Heines Werken*, Weimar, 1960.
[18] E vii, esp. 255 ('*Die deutsche Litteratur*' von Wolfgang Menzel, 1828); iv. 72 f. (*Französische Maler*, 1831); v. 253 f. (*Die romantische Schule*, 1833–6).

even exclusive concern and naturally the closest attention has been focused on the work that Heine wrote in his year of collaboration with Marx, *Deutschland. Ein Wintermärchen*.[19] But it would be wrong to imply that Heine has long stood as a representative of the struggle against social injustice and political oppression in Marxist circles alone. As early as 1865 Matthew Arnold called Heine 'the most important German successor and continuator of Goethe in Goethe's most important line of activity. And which of Goethe's lines of activity is this?—His line of activity as "a soldier in the war of liberation of humanity"'.[20] This view of Heine as a poet as worthy of attention as Goethe and above all as the great German humanist of the nineteenth century has undoubtedly encouraged and helped to shape interest in Heine in the English-speaking countries to the present.[21] It has ensured a tradition of Heine criticism even at times when his works were proscribed in Germany.[22]

It was a rather different Heine that began to fascinate French critics and poets from soon after his arrival in Paris.[23] In his report on the Salon of 1831 he not only spoke of a new, post-classical age of literature: he defended the paintings of Decamps as examples of a deliberately non-realistic art, an art that transforms its subject in the mirror of the artist's soul. Other images, more mystical still, may derive from the soul itself, he adds, appearing as symbols of innate ideas. This was a passage that fascinated the critic Sainte-Beuve sufficiently for him to reproduce it in his review of *De la France* of 1833: 'En fait d'art, dit excellemment M. Heine, je suis *surnaturaliste*. Je crois que l'artiste

---

[19] See esp. Hans Kaufmann, *Politisches Gedicht und klassische Dichtung*, a study devoted to this work. Significantly his recent monograph on Heine ends with a discussion not of the last lyrics but of the *Wintermärchen*.

[20] Matthew Arnold, 'Heinrich Heine', in *Complete Prose Works*, ed. R. H. Super, Ann Arbor, 1962, iii. 108. Arnold's phrase is, of course, Heine's own epitaph, E iii. 281.

[21] A proper account of Heine criticism in England could not neglect George Eliot's shrewd essay of nine years before (1856). Chiefly an appreciation of Heine as a humorist and wit it also sees him as Goethe's successor and an ardent lover of freedom. 'German Wit: Heinrich Heine', in *Essays and Leaves from a Note-book*, Edinburgh, 1884, pp. 79–144. Cf. also S. L. Wormley, *Heine in England*, Chapel Hill, 1943, pp. 108–16 (on Eliot and Arnold).

[22] See Eberhard Galley, *Heinrich Heine* (3rd edn.), Stuttgart, 1971, pp. 73 f.

[23] Cf. Kurt Weinberg, *Henri Heine, 'Romantique défroqué'. Héraut du symbolisme français*, New Haven and Paris, 1954; Oliver Boeck, *Heines Nachwirkung und Heine-Parallelen in der französischen Dichtung* (Göppinger Arbeiten zur Germanistik 52), Göppingen, 1972.

ne peut trouver dans la nature tous ses types, mais que les plus remarquables lui sont révélés dans son âme comme la symbolique innée d'idées, et au même instant.'[24] In his turn the young Baudelaire referred to these same words in his own *Salon de 1846*.[25] Nine years earlier Gautier had already characterized the Heine of *Reise von München nach Genua* as a pagan sculptor-poet: 'on croirait voir un chœur de statues antiques polies par les baisers amoureux de vingt siècles.'[26] Thus Heine begins to appear as the forerunner not simply of art for art's sake but of the philosophy that saw in art a magic realm of beauty to which life and health must be sacrificed in the search for poetic material. His remarks in the essays of the thirties were matched eventually by the poems that emerged from the mattress grave, poems exploring the agonies of approaching death, written while Heine was tormented by pain or stimulated by the morphine with which he hoped to deaden his suffering. We are, then, hardly surprised to find Baudelaire asking in connection with Heine why a poet should not be 'un broyeur de poisons aussi bien qu'un confiseur, un éleveur de serpents pour miracles et spectacles, un psylle amoureux de ses reptiles, et jouissant des caresses glacées de leurs anneaux en même temps que des terreurs de la foule?'[27] In his youngest days as a poet Heine had been dubbed in the Berlin salons the German Byron.[28] Some seventy years later this quality seemed new and fascinating:

C'est une nature moderne, une de ces natures de nos derniers temps, malades, tant elles sont spirituelles! (Car c'est encore Heine qui a dit le premier que tous les grands spirituels étaient malades, qu'ils avaient tous au flanc — plus ou moins — la plaie éternelle.) C'est enfin un de ces sublimes Ennuyés de la vie, un de ces Antées de la jouissance humaine qui ont touché et mordu cette poussière, et, à cause de cela, doivent un jour remonter vers Dieu![29]

Barbey d'Aurevilly was not blind to Heine the philosopher and political thinker, but that he could choose Hegel as his mentor

[24] Sainte-Beuve, *Premiers Lundis*, Paris, 1874, ii. 256 f. (First published 8 Aug. 1833.)

[25] In 'Curiosités esthétiques', *Œuvres complètes de Charles Baudelaire*, ed. Jacques Crépet, Paris, 1923, ii. 108.

[26] In *Br* v. 231.

[27] 'Lettre à Jules Janin' (1865) in *Œuvres posthumes, juvenilia, reliquiae*, ed. Crépet, Paris, 1939, i. 231.

[28] H. H. Houben ed., *Gespräche mit Heine*, Frankfurt, 1926, pp. 33 f.

[29] Barbey d'Aurevilly, *Littérature étrangère*, (XIXᵉ Siècle. Les Œuvres et les Hommes. Deuxième série, xii.) Paris, 1890, p. 155.

baffled him. This was a monstrous betrayal of poetry and religion. How could Heine have been attracted to this, the arch anti-poet?[30] But Heine was himself fully aware of a fundamental antipathy between the abstract thinker and the poet. If he learnt from Hegel, he did not hesitate to satirize him also,[31] while the hostility between intellect and art is a central component in the clash between Nazarene and Hellene which he documents in *Ludwig Börne. Eine Denkschrift*. Engels, as we saw, detested this essay as a piece of vile polemic. To a writer who belonged to the generation that followed the French *fin de siècle* the work was attractive precisely because it depicted the supreme detachment of the artist and the profound conflict between spirit and art. In his *Notiz über Heine* Thomas Mann states that *Ludwig Börne* is his favourite work by Heine. For Mann, and this completes my rapid survey of the interpretation of Heine as an aesthete, this essay was neither a mere polemic, nor simply an exposé of Nazarene psychology: it was a work of art, an expression of aesthetic freedom:

Ach, nur wer das selig zerstreute Lächeln versteht, mit dem er den Freunden, die ihm warnend die menschliche, persönliche, politische Anstößigkeit des Buches vorhielten, zur Antwort gab: 'Aber ist's nicht schön ausgedrückt?' — nur der begreift, welch eine denkmalswürdige Erscheinung dieser Künstlerjude unter den Deutschen gewesen![32]

How can one possibly accommodate these incongruous and, it would seem, mutually exclusive traditions of Heine interpretation? How is it conceivable that a writer could be *both* the supreme aesthete and decadent *and* the warrior in the cause of the poor, the poet of the proletariat, the champion of humanism?

Two years after Thomas Mann's note had appeared, Karl Kraus published an article in *Die Fackel* which sought to provide the answer to this riddle, an answer that would also take into account the reputation that Heine had enjoyed through much of the nineteenth century as Germany's finest lyric poet next to Goethe— in short that Heine who was the darling of the very Philistines whom he had so despised. What for Mann had almost certainly been one of Heine's shrewdest insights into the nature of artists— 'diese sind Meister des Wortes, handhaben es zu jedem beliebigen

[30] Barbey d'Aurevilly, xii. 158 f.
[31] See, for example, E iii. 381 ff., and his view on Hegel in *Geständnisse*, E vi. 51.
[32] Thomas Mann, *Gesammelte Werke*, Frankfurt, 1960, x. 839.

Zwecke, prägen es nach Willkür, schreiben objektiv, und ihr Charakter verrät sich nicht in ihrem Stil'[33]—is taken by Kraus as one of Heine's few genuine confessions, the confession of a pseudo-artist or of a journalist. Kraus feels no surprise at the notorious *Stimmungsbrechungen* of the early lyric for the simple reason that there was no lyrical mood, no state of *Ergriffenheit* for Heine to disrupt. An experience or an idea was just so much material with which he could play as a virtuoso of language. He is the 'lust- und leidgeübte Techniker, prompte Bekleider vorhandener Stimmungen', whose verse is 'ein skandierter Journalismus, der den Leser über seine Stimmungen auf dem Laufenden hält', and whose prose has the doubtful merit of being the grandfather of modern commercial feuilletonism.[34] In short Heine manufactured his works as goods to be sold to as large a market as possible, if we are to bring Kraus's metaphors up to date as Theodor Adorno has done.[35] Kraus is the most vehement representative, then, of that third tradition of Heine criticism which has its founder in Ludwig Börne, and has been echoed in the academic world by detailed studies of Heine's inconsistency and cunning such as Margaret Clarke's examination of *Französische Zustände*[36] and Artur Weckmüller's *Heines Stil*,[37] and in the broader public by the general charge that Heine is consistent only in his insincerity.

Thus we are faced with three completely divergent schools of Heine interpretation. The two first are compatible only if we see Heine as what amounts to a schizophrenic, two separate men in one. Certainly this was the manner in which Heine frequently pictured himself. Nevertheless, it seems only a makeshift solution, an attempt to understand the incomprehensible; its psychology is too facile to satisfy, and it leaves us with two divorced bodies of work, that of the lyrical poet and that of the thinker, while certain

[33] E vii. 134 (*Ludwig Börne*).

[34] 'Heine und die Folgen', in *Untergang der Welt durch schwarze Magie*, Vienna and Leipzig, 1922, pp. 200–35. Quotations, pp. 212 f., 216. The inconsistency of Kraus's own position, indeed its similarity to the picture that Kraus drew of Heine, is emphasized in Mechthild Borries's *Ein Angriff auf Heinrich Heine. Kritische Betrachtungen zu Karl Kraus*, Stuttgart etc., 1971.

[35] Theodor Adorno, 'Die Wunde Heine', in *Noten zur Literatur*, Frankfurt, 1958, 144–52. Adorno tries to go beyond Kraus to an appreciation of Heine's lyric even in its very inauthenticity.

[36] *Heine et la monarchie de juillet*, Paris, 1927.

[37] Breslau, 1934. 'Die Sprache ist wie Wachs in seinen Händen — oder wie Geld: man kann sich alles dafür kaufen' (p. 72). Otherwise the study is the most valuable analysis of his language and style to the present.

major works such as the *Reisebilder* seem to defy both categories. On the other hand, the third school kills Heine entirely, removing him from literature and thought alike and reducing his work and influence to a mere sociological phenomenon.

What other approaches to Heine's production have been adopted? The straightforward chronological account of his life and works naturally has a long tradition,[38] but the problem with which we are concerned here is not of central importance to it. Other critics have tried to make watertight compilations of his ideas[39] but have had to neglect or have even rejected the works in which they appear as art.[40] Others again have concentrated on the verse alone,[41] while it is only recently that the form of the prose has been taken at all seriously.[42] It is also only in recent years that an attempt has been made to find some link between the lyrical poet

[38] Adolf Strodtmann's *Heinrich Heines Leben und Werke*, 2 vols., Berlin, 1867, was the first standard biography and is still useful. The most important modern account is Manfred Windfuhr's *Heinrich Heine. Revolution und Reflexion*, Stuttgart, 1969. It raises the question of unity in Heine's work but is restricted by the very nature of the study to a series of suggestive remarks in the last section, pp. 281–93. Indispensable is Eberhard Galley's introduction and select bibliography, *Heinrich Heine*, op. cit.

[39] See, for example, H. Lichtenberger, *Henri Heine penseur*, Paris, 1905; Kurt Sternberg, *Heinrich Heines geistige Gestalt und Welt*, Berlin, 1929; E. L. Evans, 'Heinrich Heine's Attitude to Tradition' Diss., Swansea, 1954; W. Rose, *Heinrich Heine. Two Studies of his Thought and Feeling*, Oxford, 1956; P. K. Kurz, *Künstler, Tribun, Apostel. Heinrich Heines Auffassung vom Beruf des Dichters*, Munich, 1967.

[40] Erich Loewenthal in *Studien zu Heinrich Heines 'Reisebildern'*, Palaestra 138, Berlin and Leipzig, 1922, states specifically that unity is provided in these works only by their content: 'Die Einheit der Tendenz macht die Einheit der "Reisebilder" aus' (p. 3). This is echoed by Karl Emmerich, op. cit., p. 2.

[41] This has produced some of the most successful studies on Heine: cf. Jules Legras, *Henri Heine poète*, Paris, 1897; Charles Andler, *La Poésie de Heine*, Lyons and Paris, 1948; S. S. Prawer, *Heine: Buch der Lieder*, London, 1960; id., *Heine. The Tragic Satirist. A Study of the Later Poetry, 1827–1856*, Cambridge, 1961.

[42] Ernst Feise's 'Form and Meaning of Heine's "Die Nordsee"', *Monatshefte*, 34 (1942), 223–34 (reprinted in: *Xenion: Themes, Forms and Ideas in German Literature*, ed. Werner Neuse, Baltimore, 1950, pp. 90–104) was something of a pioneering effort. The most notable recent work has come from Jeffrey Sammons: 'Heine's *Rabbi von Bacherach*: The Unresolved Tensions', *German Quarterly*, 37 (1964), 26–38; 'Heine's Composition: *Die Harzreise*', *Heine-Jahrbuch 1967*, pp. 40–7, and his monumental work, *Heinrich Heine. The Elusive Poet*. New Haven and London, 1969. See also Peter Bürger, *Der Essay bei Heine*, Diss., Munich, 1959; A. I. Sandor, *The Exile of Gods. Interpretation of a Theme, a Theory, and a Technique in the Work of Heinrich Heine*, The Hague and Paris, 1967, pp. 147–58; Jürgen Jacobs, 'Zu Heines *Ideen. Das Buch Le Grand*', *Heine-Jahrbuch 1968*, pp. 3–11.

and the satirist,[43] the writer of prose and of verse,[44] the creative writer and the thinker.[45] Each of these works has illuminated aspects of the problem. None has directly tackled the problem of how it was possible for a poet to be so divided against himself. Hofrichter, for example, sees a dialectical movement in Heine's development. He progresses, she claims, from the untameable fantasies of the *Traumbilder* to an overriding concern with the outside world in his prose works. A synthesis is then achieved in the lyric of *Romanzero*, where mood is dictated not by the poet but by the subject-matter. Nevertheless the changes from lyric to prose and back to lyric do not explain the often glaring contradictions in the arguments, themes, and vision of the world that can appear in a single work. Sandor has sought continuity in the single central theme and experience of exile, Heine's related theory of man's alienation through Christian–Judaic spiritualism, and his fundamental creative mode, which is determined by the creative intellect as opposed to the creative imagination. These are interesting ideas, yet they raise further problems. How, for example, can we correlate the view that Heine's primary aesthetic value is form with his professed ideal of the engaged writer? Sammons's interpretations tackle the question of unity by examining the poetic *personae* which Heine creates, and set a precedent by treating prose and verse alike as works of art. But the political and critical writings are not examined and central contradictions in Heine's thought remain unexplained. The problem demands a study of how Heine's ideas evolved to see whether their inner contradictions are evidence of a mental duality or perhaps spring from a common source. Heine was supremely aware of the cultural situation of his day, and it is vital to trace his thought back to its roots. An examination of his position in the history of German literary and intellectual

---

[43] See S. S. Prawer's valuable account, *The Tragic Satirist*, cited above.

[44] See Hofrichter, works cited; Sandor, op. cit.; Sammons, *Heinrich Heine*, cited above, and Barker Fairley's fascinating examination of Heine's imagery, *Heinrich Heine. An Interpretation*, Oxford, 1954. His discovery of a complex of repeated 'social' images throughout Heine's works irrespective of their genre certainly dispels the views that Heine's art can be treated in isolation from his political and critical writings. But this 'vaudeville' (see title of Fairley's article in the *University of Toronto Quarterly*, Jan. 1934) of song, dance, music, costume, and procession marks essentially 'an order of the imagination' (*Heinrich Heine*, p. 161), and given the anomalies in Heine's thought one can still see why for some he was an aesthete and for others a revolutionary.

[45] See especially Sandor, op. cit.

development may throw new light on the curious dichotomy in his work with which we are presented. This does not involve a search for verifiable sources and influences in the spirit of the positivist school of the turn of the century, a school for which Heine was a happy hunting-ground.[46] Nevertheless their findings can be suggestive to a non-mechanical interpretation also. On the other hand an analysis simply of Heine the thinker would neglect him as an artist and must inevitably tend to reduce his work to a store-house of ideas, which waits to be plundered. If we are to relate the products of the imaginative writer to those of the political thinker the prose must be considered potentially as worthy of aesthetic interpretation as the lyric, while we can no less afford to lose sight of how Heine's art evolved than of how his thought developed.

This study cannot claim to present Heine's work in its entirety. It simply seeks to disentangle some of the major strands of Heine's thought and poetic production and attempts to follow apparently contradictory elements back to their origin, which often proves to be less in Heine than in the transitional intellectual situation of the day. Since the formative periods of Heine's development are particularly illuminating in this context, the greatest emphasis is on the products of the early and middle years. Further, I have not tried to enforce any preconceived division between Heine's views on the role and nature of art and the artist and those of a revolutionary and political kind. Certainly Heine himself did not always distinguish between these realms and this itself is a cause of major confusion. Instead I have followed a broadly chronological course, except where the continuity of the poet's thought and aspirations throughout his lifetime suggested otherwise. As the study works out from Heine's ideas and ideals, the mechanics of analysis have forced me frequently to separate these from the works in which they are embedded. This is perhaps inevitable but can only be justified if the works themselves are also taken seriously

---

[46] Some examples: R. Goetze, *Heinrich Heines 'Buch der Lieder' und sein Verhältnis zum deutschen Volkslied*, Diss., Halle, 1895; Otto zur Linde, *Heine und die deutsche Romantik*, Diss., Freiburg, 1899; Friedrich Marcus, *Jean Paul und Heinrich Heine*, Diss., Marburg, 1919; F. Melchior, *Heines Verhältnis zu Lord Byron*, Diss., Leipzig, 1902; J. S. Nollen, 'Heine und Müller', *Modern Language Notes*, 17 (1902), 206–19, 261–76; P. Santkin, *Ludwig Börnes Einfluß auf den jungen Heine*, Diss., Berne, 1905; W. Siebert, *Heinrich Heines Beziehungen zu E. T. A. Hoffmann*, Marburg, 1908.

as art, which I have attempted as far as was practicable. Indeed, in a significant number of cases it is only when ideas are seen in the context of a work's aesthetic structure that apparent anomalies and complexities can be understood. In Heine more than in many poets any separation of thought from the poetic work tends to be artificial. Far from being distinct areas they are concentric circles in the production of a single creative personality—and it was this personality which Heine succeeded in portraying above all else.

I

SIMPLICITY AND WHOLENESS

A. *The ideal of an organic culture*

HEINE's first prose writing was a short essay, written in response to an article whose author is today quite forgotten, and it based its arguments on largely borrowed material. Nevertheless 'Die Romantik' of 1820 contains *in nuce* ideas that were to continue to shape Heine's thought for the remainder of his life. Its purpose was to dismiss the distinction that a certain Wilhelm von Blomberg had made between the plastic imagery of Greek Antiquity and the nebulous imagery of Romanticism in a satirical article that had appeared earlier in the year in a Rhineland journal. Heine's chief argument is that the imagery of Romantic poetry should be as clearly moulded in 'bestimmt gezeichneten Konturen' as that of the Ancients. The two great modern exponents of this art are, he claims, Goethe and August Wilhelm Schlegel. What distinguishes Classical imagery from that of the moderns, or Romantics as he terms them, is that the Greeks intended their images only as a direct representation of visible finite reality. The Romantics, however, seek to symbolize and to evoke a sense of the infinite. This awareness of a world beyond the empirically perceptible was awakened in Europe by Christianity.[1] European cultural history is broadly divided into two epochs, the one in which men's thought, feeling, and literature were absorbed in the world of objects surrounding them, and the modern Christian age, in which feeling for the infinite is expressed in spiritual love. Such views are not, as Heine claims, purely personal but those of his teacher in Bonn, August Wilhelm Schlegel.[2] For Schlegel the epithet Romantic was synonymous with modern and designated the approach of those who saw the sterility of imitating Classical models in an age of an altogether different character

[1] E vii. 150.
[2] In addition to attending Schlegel's lectures on the history of the German language he submitted poems to Schlegel for criticism (cf. *Br* i. 11 f., 18).

from that in which the Greeks lived. Admittedly Greek culture represented a high point in human achievement:

Die Bildung der Griechen war vollendete Naturerziehung. Von schönem und edlem Stamme, mit empfänglichen Sinnen und einem heitern Geiste begabt, unter einem milden Himmel, lebten und blühten sie in vollkommener Gesundheit des Daseins, und leisteten durch die seltenste Begünstigung der Umstände alles, was der in den Schranken der Endlichkeit befangene Mensch leisten kann. Ihre gesammte Kunst und Poesie ist der Ausdruck vom Bewußtsein dieser Harmonie aller Kräfte. Sie haben die Poetik der Freude ersonnen.[3]

But as is apparent from the quotation, Schlegel is at pains to point out the limitations of their joy and harmony. Their feeling of self-sufficiency and desire to seek nothing beyond their own powers blinded them to God and eternal life after death. This awareness of a new metaphysical dimension did not begin, as we have seen Heine also argued, until the advent of Christianity:

Bei den Griechen war die menschliche Natur selbstgenügsam, sie ahndete keinen Mangel, und strebte nach keiner andern Vollkommenheit, als die sie wirklich durch ihre eigenen Kräfte erreichen konnte. Eine höhere Weisheit lehrt uns, die Menschheit habe durch eine große Verirrung die ihr ursprünglich bestimmte Stelle eingebüßt, und die ganze Bestimmung ihres irdischen Daseins sei, dahin zurückzustreben, welches sie jedoch, sich selbst überlassen, nicht vermöge.[4]

Schlegel now goes on to show that the harmony enjoyed by the Greeks is an impossibility for modern men just because they have seen that the gap between themselves and the infinite is unbridgeable in life itself. The inner discord which characterizes the modern age Schlegel terms 'die innere Entzweiung'.[5] As we shall see, this and Schlegel's fundamental historical categories made an indelible impression on Heine. But even in 'Die Romantik' it is plain that any attraction Heine felt for the medieval world of Roman Catholicism and a feudally structured society was, to say the least, ambiguous. With all the boisterous patriotism of a *Burschenschafter*[6] Heine dismisses the view that Romantic literature need still be linked inextricably with its medieval religious and social origins:

Deutschland ist jetzt frei; kein Pfaffe vermag mehr die deutschen

[3] A. W. Schlegel, *Sämmtliche Werke*, ed. E. Böcking, Leipzig, 1846, v. 12 f.
[4] Ibid., p. 15. [5] Ibid., p. 17.
[6] Cf. O. F. Scheuer, *Heinrich Heine als Student*, Bonn, 1922, p. 19.

Geister einzukerkern; kein adeliger Herrscherling vermag mehr die deutschen Leiber zur Fron zu peitschen, und deshalb soll auch die deutsche Muse wieder ein freies, blühendes, unaffektiertes, ehrlich deutsches Mädchen sein und kein schmachtendes Nönnchen und kein ahnenstolzes Ritterfräulein. (E vii. 151)

With this declaration Heine establishes two central elements in his political thought, elements which derive directly from the ideals of the French Revolution[7] and bring him closest to the aims of the German Republican Liberals, namely his unrelenting hostility towards the Roman Catholic Church and priesthood and towards the aristocracy. Whenever Heine later speaks of freedom or equality he always has in mind the idea that these essentially medieval institutions were to blame for the political backwardness of Germany. It is they that maintain the principles of 'Servilism' (as opposed to Liberalism) in the review of Menzel's *Die deutsche Litteratur*;[8] they are the embodiment of all that is reactionary which the German revolution will have to overthrow in *Einleitung zu 'Kahldorf über den Adel'*,[9] a revolution which began with the invention of printing[10] and the subsequent Reformation.[11] These are ideas which find their fullest expression in *Zur Geschichte der Religion und Philosophie in Deutschland* with its eulogy of Martin Luther and his campaign against priest and aristocrat.[12] At the same time the optimism with which Heine hoped to sever Romantic literature from its ties with the aristocracy and priesthood was to disappear. In *Die romantische Schule* of 1833-6 he defines German Romanticism as the poetic revival of medieval inequality, a movement that is in league with a religion, 'die ebenfalls durch die Lehre von der Verwerflichkeit aller irdischen Güter, von der auferlegten Hundedemut und Engelsgeduld die erprobteste Stütze des Despotismus geworden' (E v. 217).

This trend towards a rejection of Schlegel's sympathies whilst retaining his analysis of the two ages of European man becomes far more striking in Heine's first drama, *Almansor*, which he began in the autumn of 1820 only a few months after writing 'Die Romantik'. The setting of this play is Spain at the end of the fifteenth century, a time when two epochs such as Schlegel

---

[7] Cf. E iii. 498, 508.   [8] E vii. 253 (1828).

[9] E vii. 282 (1831); cf. also *Reise von München nach Genua* (1830), iii. 275 f.; *Die Stadt Lucca* (1831), iii. 420, 421, 429.

[10] *Englische Fragmente* (1831), E iii. 495.   [11] Ibid., pp. 495 f.

[12] E iv, esp. pp. 188 ff. (1834).

described were in collision. The concerted efforts of the two Christian kingdoms of Aragon and Castille have succeeded in conquering the Muslim kingdom of Granada and in expelling most of the Moorish population. For Schlegel the Romantic epoch had flowered in the days of chivalry, when Christianity and the heroic temperament of the former Germanic tribes fused to produce a culture that celebrated love, honour, and religion in its poetry.[13] It is in similar terms that the chorus in Heine's play depicts the achievements of Cordova and Granada after the secession of Spanish Mohammedanism from the North African empire:

> Da wehte jetzt ein reinrer Lebensgeist,
> Als in des Orients dumpfigen Haremen. . . .
> Wo sonst nur lärmte Tamburin und Zimbel,
> Erhob sich jetzt beim Klingen der Chitarre,
> Der Wehmutsang, die schmelzende Romanze;
> Wo sonst der finstre Herr, mit strengem Blick,
> Die bange Sklavin trieb zum Liebesfrohn,
> Erhub das Weib jetzund sein Haupt als Herrin,
> Und milderte, mit zarter Hand, die Roheit
> Der alten Maurensitten und Gebräuche,
> Und Schönes blühte, wo die Schönheit herrschte.
> Kunst, Wissenschaft, Ruhmsucht und Frauendienst,
> Das waren jene Blumen, die da pflegten
> Der Abderrhamen königliche Hand. (E ii. 290)

It is, then, a society that still broadly resembles the ideal picture of the Middle Ages which the Romantics held, and maintains the same chivalric values that Heine celebrated in his *Minnelieder* written before he even met Schlegel.[14] But the *Frauendienst* of Granada means the rule of beauty and so Heine's Moorish kingdom is close to Schlegel's view of Greece. Furthermore, this paradise is not Christian but Muslim—indeed it is Christianity that destroyed it. When the hero of the tragedy returns to his father's ruined palace in what had been Granada he discovers in Christianity all that is hostile to life, to joy, to love. On his pilgrimage home Almansor has chanced to enter one of the churches that have replaced the former mosques. What he sees is a grotesque vision of a religion of blood and death:

> Und überall, wohin mein Auge sah,
> Aus jeder Nische nickte mir entgegen

---

[13] Schlegel, *Werke*, v. 14 f.   [14] Cf. E i. 47 f.; ii. 111 f.

Dasselbe Bild, das ich hier wiedersehe.
Doch überall sah schmerzenbleich und traurig
Des Mannes Antlitz, den dies Bildnis darstellt.
Hier schlug man ihn mit harten Geißelhieben,
Dort sank er nieder unter Kreuzeslast,
Hier spie man ihm verachtungsvoll ins Antlitz,
Dort krönte man mit Dornen seine Schläfe,
Hier schlug man ihn ans Kreuz, mit scharfem Speer
Durchstieß man seine Seite, — Blut, Blut, Blut
Entquoll jedwedem Bild. Ich schaute gar
Ein traurig Weib, die hielt auf ihrem Schoß
Des Martermannes abgezehrten Leichnam,
Ganz gelb und nackt, von schwarzem Blut umronnen —
Da hört' ich eine gellend scharfe Stimme:
'Dies ist sein Blut', und wie ich hinsah, schaut' ich
                    Schaudernd
Den Mann, der eben einen Becher austrank.   (E ii. 284 f.)

It is a picture of Christianity that Heine did not modify until the days of his own slow death. The Italian *Reisebilder* may be said to pivot on the themes of death, mortification of the flesh, sickness, and life amid a decaying culture, phenomena which are all seen to be caused by the stranglehold of Christianity and petty despotism on society.[15] In *Zur Geschichte der Religion und Philosophie* this religion is called an infectious disease, bearing the germs of Spiritualism, the doctrine that seeks to kill off the flesh.[16] Its symbol according to *Die romantische Schule* is the passion flower, in which one can see the impression of the instruments of torture and execution used on Christ.[17] Finally in *Ludwig Börne. Eine Denkschrift* the asceticism common to both Judaism and Christianity, an essential connection already adumbrated in the last two named works,[18] forms the basis of his analysis of the two fundamental types of human temperament, that of the Nazarene and that of the Hellene, of the spiritualist and of the sensualist.[19]

---

[15] See esp. *Die Stadt Lucca*, chs. 5–6, iii. 389–98.   [16] E iv. 169, 219 ff.
[17] Ibid. v. 217.   [18] Ibid. v. 218 f.; iv. 219 f.
[19] Ibid. vii, esp. 23 f., 46 f. It is this continuity in Heine's critique of Christianity and in his hedonist philosophy that Dolf Sternberger seems to miss in his interesting recent study of Heine's Utopian sensualism, *Heinrich Heine und die Abschaffung der Sünde*, Hamburg and Düsseldorf, 1972. For Sternberger the decisive influence is the Saint-Simonian doctrine, which Heine is unlikely to have encountered before early 1831 (cf. *Br* i. 475) and see below pp. 79 ff.). The eschatological pattern of Heine's thought can be seen to derive not from

To return to Heine's drama, where these themes are already contained in embryonic form: Almansor's purpose in revisiting the land of his fathers and of his youth is not as might have been expected to lead a rebellion against the Christian conquerors. This is the objective that Almansor's former servant, Hassan, together with a small band of the faithful have set themselves and which they hope Almansor will organize. The young man has, however, come to seek his beloved, Zuleima, to whom he had been betrothed before the Conquest. She is now a convert to Christianity, and this itself makes her unwilling to elope with her lover. For her Christianity is a religion not of death but of love, which promises a new existence *after* death, when sins committed on earth will be forgiven.[20] She thus presents views that reflect A. W. Schlegel's position, and in the tension between her and Almansor's interpretations of love we see clearly how Heine redefines the Romantic ideal of reunification with the beloved in death as the ideal of unification in life.

In Novalis's *Heinrich von Ofterdingen*, the hero meets a beautiful Arabian girl, whose home has been destroyed by the crusaders, whose Oriental culture is presented as somehow more meaningful than the crude desire for conquest that motivates the Christian warriors, and who has also been separated from her relatives and brought up in a Christian castle. Her name is—Zulima.[21] The coincidences are too great for us not to suppose that Heine used the episode from Novalis's work as his conscious model. But of greater interest is the contrasting treatment of this material. Zulima is but one stage in Heinrich's progress towards the Realm

Saint-Simon but from Schlegel, Novalis, and then his teacher in Berlin, Hegel. It is, of course, true that this pattern must have been reinforced by his encounter with the Saint-Simonians.

[20] E ii. 286.

[21] *Novalis Schriften. Die Werke Friedrich von Hardenbergs*, ed. P. Kluckhohn and R. Samuel, 2nd edn., Stuttgart, 1960, i. 234 ff. 'Vorzüglich hielt sie sich bei dem Lobe ihrer Landsleute und ihres Vaterlandes auf. Sie schilderte den Edelmut derselben, und ihre reine starke Empfänglichkeit für die Poesie des Lebens und das wunderbare, geheimnisvolle Anmut der Natur. Sie beschrieb die romantischen Schönheiten der fruchtbaren arabischen Gegenden, die wie glückliche Inseln in unwegsamen Sandwüsteneien lägen, wie Zufluchtsstätte der Bedrängten und Ruhebedürftigen, wie Kolonien des Paradieses, voll frischer Quellen, die über dichten Rasen und funkelnde Steine durch alte, ehrwürdige Haine rieselten, voll bunter Vögel mit melodischen Kehlen und anziehend durch mannigfaltige Überbleibsel ehemaliger denkwürdiger Zeiten' (p. 236). Zulima, in turn, is closely modelled on Goethe's Mignon.

of Poetry, a world in which life and death are no longer divorced. Novalis's plans for the continuation of the fragment suggest that Zulima is a manifestation of Mathilde, with whom he will live eternally. Almansor on the other hand identifies religious love with erotic fulfilment. His religion is strictly temporal. When Zuleima's unshaken faith balks his plans for an elopement, he decides to abduct her. For a brief moment, perched on a high rock and protected from their pursuers, the lovers are able to enjoy bliss. Zuleima believes that she is in fact dead and that this is the Christian paradise promised to her. For Almansor their embrace is the realization of heaven on earth:

> Wir sind im Himmel, und die Engel singen,
> Und rauschen drein mit ihren seidnen Flügeln, —
> Hier wohnet Gott im Grübchen dieser Wangen, —
> (E ii. 309)

But the outcome of the drama is tragic precisely because they are still on earth. Almansor's rapture is allowed but these three lines before the enemy approach from below. Almansor with his bride, his heaven, in his arms plunges to death.

If we look aside from the play's histrionic gesture, we must admit that *Almansor* occupies a significant position in the evolution of Heine's thought. Heine has largely accepted Schlegel's definition of Christianity as the religion of longing for life after death—'das Leben ist zur Schattenwelt und zur Nacht geworden, und erst jenseits geht der ewige Tag des wesentlichen Daseins auf.'[22] But it is this that makes Christianity repellent and Satanic.[23] Instead, heaven, the third stage in the pattern that both Schlegel and Novalis adopt, must be created on earth, while Heine's ideal age is essentially a version of Schlegel's portrait of Greek culture. Here is a further constant in Heine's philosophy and it is ironic that *Die romantische Schule*, a writing which makes the fullest use of these elements of Schlegelian thought, begins with an attack on Mme de Staël for reproducing Schlegel's insidious views.[24] Heine has simply reversed his mentor's sympathies.

Almansor is condemned to death because the age in which his heaven could exist has not been born. But his solution is not merely tragic for himself and Zuleima: in order to carry out his abduction

---

[22] Schlegel, *Werke*, v. 16.   [23] Cf. E ii. 309.   [24] E v. 216.

he has to use Hassan's men. The lovers escape but Hassan is killed and his men are routed. Almansor's purely individualistic plan thus leads in effect to the extinction of any remaining chances for the Moorish kingdom to be re-established. It is in more senses than one that with Almansor Granada perishes. This source of further dramatic and tragic material is not, however, exploited. Nevertheless the tension between the personal fulfilment of an ideal and its realization on a social scale continues to characterize the whole of Heine's mature thought.

William Ratcliff, Heine's only other venture into drama, written in January 1822, is equally interesting in this respect. The tragedy is in the tradition of the fate-drama which was in vogue at the time.[25] The hero is again a disappointed lover, but as in the *Traumbilder* and so much of the early lyric his rejection is not apparently related to religious or social causes so much as to the cruel indifference of the girl.[26] Ratcliff has sworn, and the Fates must have heard his oath, to prevent any other man from marrying Maria. Time and again he kills them in duels the night before the wedding. Yet at the same time, to drown his sorrows, he has become an outlaw pledged to the cause of the poor against the rich. He lives amongst highwaymen and footpads, defying the protective wall of the law that the propertied classes have built around them:

> O seht mir doch die klugen, satten Leute,
> Wie sie mit einem Walle von Gesetzen,
> Sich wohlverwahret gegen allen Andrang
> Der schreiend überläst'gen Hungerleider!
> Weh' dem, der diesen Wall durchbricht!
> Bereit sind Richter, Henker, Stricke, Galgen, —
> Je nun! manchmal gibt's Leut', die das nicht scheun.
>
> TOM [landlord of the thieves' tavern]:
> So dacht' ich auch, und teilte ein die Menschen

---

[25] In December 1821 he saw a performance of Grillparzer's *Die Ahnfrau* (cf. Elster, 2nd. edn., Leipzig, 1925, iii. 254). In the same month he wrote to Adolf Müllner to express his admiration for *Die Schuld* (*Br* i. 35.) The motifs of the Lord's Prayer and the Edward ballad are borrowed from Zacharias Werner's *Der 24. Februar.* (Cf. also H. Mutzenbecher, *Heine und das Drama*, Diss., Bonn, 1914, pp. 41 f.). William and Grillparzer's Jaromir are both robbers pursued by their forebears and united with their beloved only in death. (Cf. Mutzenbecher, op. cit., pp. 39 f.) The figure of Margareta, the mad servant woman, comes from Brunhilde in Müllner's *König Yngard* (for passing ref., cf. W. Ochsenbein, *Die Aufnahme Lord Byrons in Deutschland und sein Einfluß auf den jungen Heine*, Diss., Berne, 1905, p. 215).

[26] E ii. 327.

In zwei Nationen, die sich wild bekriegen;
Nämlich in Satte und In Hungerloider
Weil ich zu letzterer Partei gehörte,
So mußt' ich mit den Satten oft mich balgen.   (E ii. 323)

But it would not be true to say that Ratcliff the Socialist and
Ratcliff the lover are entirely disparate figures. Maria and her
intended bridegrooms all belong to the Scottish ruling classes, the
same whom the highwayman robs.[27] More significantly there is
an implied parallel between the compulsion with which Ratcliff
murders his rivals and that which drives the robbers on despite
the threat of death by hanging. Both are victims of circumstances
beyond their control. As we have seen, their crimes result from
their poverty, and this in turn is enforced by the law established by
the rich. They cannot resist temptation, as we learn when the
landlord's little son tries to recite the Lord's Prayer but always
stumbles at the line 'Führe uns nicht in Versuchung'. Tom
scolds him, but Ratcliff, the demented lover and outlaw, inter-
cedes on the boy's behalf:

> Laßt nur den Buben gehn. Auch ich hab' nie
> Im Kopf behalten können diese Stelle.
> *Schmerzlich*
> 'Führe uns nicht in Versuchung!'   (E ii. 321)

Only a few scenes later Tom himself cannot resist picking the
pockets of two of his 'guests'. Thus the same line of the Lord's
Prayer which is the motto of Zacharias Werner's fate tragedy
Der 24. Februar is given radical social implications. Within the
economy of the play the link between Socialist ideas and love is
contrived and dramatically unconvincing. Nevertheless it remains
an attempt at least. We might compare it with *Traumbild* 8, where
each of the disappointed lovers who comes to sing in the graveyard
at midnight has died through a combination of rebuff and social
injustice. A tailor's apprentice dies of a broken heart for the master
tailor's daughter; a robber chief, Ratcliff's obvious forerunner, is
left to die love-sick in prison; a student commits suicide when a
professor's lovely daughter is married off to a Philistine; a youth
is hanged for trying to abduct a Count's daughter.[28] Slight though

---

[27] But they are not caricatured as are the fops who surround Zuleima; cf. ii.
271 ff.
[28] E i. 23 ff. (Dated 1821 by P. Beyer, *Der junge Heine*, Berlin, 1911, pp.
146 ff.)

the material may be, there is evidence here, and still more plainly so in *Ratcliff*, that Heine wishes to make disappointed love both a symptom and symbol of an unjust social order. The obverse to this is that *Frauendienst* lies at the heart of Granada's cultural ethos, and although *Almansor* was the earlier work the association of love, religion, and society is more clearly established. In both plays the 'private' interests of the hero lead to catastrophe and thus to the end of any continued activity on a social level. Almansor is responsible for Hassan's defeat. Ratcliff's *Doppelgänger* compels him to murder even Maria and then to join her in death.

Die Harzreise, which Heine wrote in the closing months of 1824, takes these same themes one stage further. As in *Almansor*, two essentially different societies are again drawn, existing side by side, the one, however, being all that remains of an earlier, happier age. This is the world that is found, as in *Almansor*, away from the cities up in the mountains. This contrast provides the basic theme and structure of the work. Satiated with the superficial polish and empty-headedness of polite society, the narrator seeks the genuine feeling of a simpler, more natural world:

> Schwarze Röcke, seidne Strümpfe,
> Weiße, höfliche Manschetten,
> Sanfte Reden, Embrassieren —
> Ach, wenn sie nur Herzen hätten!

> Herzen in der Brust, und Liebe,
> Warme Liebe in dem Herzen —
> Ach, mich tötet ihr Gesinge
> Von erlognen Liebesschmerzen.

> Auf die Berge will ich steigen,
> Wo die frommen Hütten stehen,
> Wo die Brust sich frei erschließet,
> Und die freien Lüfte wehen. (E i. 150; iii. 15)

He encounters this world in the cottages of the Harz silver-miners. In their lives these simple folk are entirely at one with their environment. Indeed so intimate is their relationship with the inanimate that they imbue it with life:

So stillstehend ruhig auch das Leben dieser Leute erscheint, so ist es dennoch ein wahrhaftes, lebendiges Leben. Die steinalte, zitternde Frau, die, dem großen Schranke gegenüber, hinterm Ofen saß, mag dort schon ein Vierteljahrhundert lang gesessen haben, und ihr Denken und Fühlen ist gewiß innig verwachsen mit allen Ecken dieses Ofens und allen Schnitzeleien dieses Schrankes. Und Schrank und Ofen leben, denn ein Mensch hat ihnen einen Teil seiner Seele eingeflößt. (E iii. 32) This union with their surroundings finds spontaneous expression in fairy-tales:

Nur durch solch tiefes Anschauungsleben, durch die 'Unmittel-barkeit' entstand die deutsche Märchenfabel, deren Eigentümlichkeit darin besteht, daß nicht nur Tiere und Pflanzen, sondern auch ganz leblos scheinende Gegenstände sprechen und handeln. Sinnigem, harmlosen Volke, in der stillen, umfriedeten Heimlichkeit seiner niedern Berg- oder Waldhütten offenbarte sich das innere Leben solcher Gegenstände, diese gewannen einen notwendigen, konsequenten Charakter, eine süße Mischung von phantastischer Laune und rein menschlicher Gesinnung .... (E iii. 32)

And the examples that follow, the needle and pin that get lost in the dark, the straw and lump of coal that try to cross the brook, and others are all taken directly from the *Kinder- und Hausmärchen* collected by the Brothers Grimm, which had appeared in a new augmented edition in 1822. Like the Grimms Heine regarded this peasant culture as one of innocence and childlike simplicity. But he adds a further dimension, supposing there to be an episte-mological difference between our own intellectually sophisticated society and that of folk cultures: theirs is a life in which experience and knowledge are visual and open, ours is abstract and selective:

... Aus demselben Grunde ist unser Leben in der Kindheit so unend-lich bedeutend, in jener Zeit ist uns alles gleich wichtig, wir hören alles, wir sehen alles, bei allen Eindrücken ist Gleichmäßigkeit, statt daß wir späterhin absichtlicher werden, uns mit dem Einzelnen ausschließlicher beschäftigen, das klare Gold der Anschauung für das Papiergeld der Bücherdefinitionen mühsam einwechseln und an Lebensbreite gewin-nen, was wir an Lebenstiefe verlieren. (E iii. 32)

One of the manuscript scraps which Heine preserved for later utilization, and which were published by Strodtmann as *Gedanken und Einfälle* (without regard to chronology, incidentally) again speaks of a culture that perceives and experiences in a visual and synthetic manner, not in the analytical manner of Europe. This culture is the Indian, to which he had also been introduced by August Wilhelm Schlegel.[29]

[29] Cf. *Br* iv. 94. The *Mahabharata* had been translated by another of his teachers, Franz Bopp, in 1824 and Heine had himself been requested to write a

Der Indier konnte nur ungeheuer große Gedichte liefern, weil er nichts aus dem Weltzusammenhang schneiden konnte, wie überhaupt der Anschauungsmensch. Die ganze Welt ist ihm ein Gedicht, wovon der Mahabarata nur ein Kapitel. — Vergleich der indischen mit unserer Mystik: diese übt den Scharfsinn an Zerteilung und Zusammensetzung der Materie, bringt es aber nicht zum Begriff. — Anschauungsideen sind etwas, das wir gar nicht kennen. Die indische Muse ist die träumende Prinzessin der Märchen. (E vii. 417)

For brief moments in *Die Harzreise* the poet is also able to share in such life. The most striking occasion is that magic evening together with the beautiful young niece of one of the miners, when the fairy-tale world, in which the girl believes, seems to come true. In a scene reminiscent of the celebrated conversation between Faust and Gretchen on religion, the poet tries to calm the girl's fear of evil spirits by telling her of the Holy Trinity. As a grown man he now believes in the Holy Ghost, but it soon becomes apparent that he is speaking less in Christian terms than symbolically. It is the force of *reason* that will break the rule of feudality and death and introduce a new age:

'Jetzo, da ich ausgewachsen,
Viel gelesen, viel gereist,
Schwillt mein Herz, und ganz von Herzen
Glaub' ich an den heil'gen Geist.

'Dieser that die größten Wunder,
Und viel größre thut er noch;
Er zerbrach die Zwingherrnburgen,
Und zerbrach des Knechtes Joch.

'Alte Todeswunden heilt er,
Und erneut das alte Recht:
Alle Menschen, gleichgeboren,
Sind ein adliches Geschlecht.

'Er verscheucht die bösen Nebel,
Und das dunkle Hirngespinst,
Das uns Lieb' und Lust verleidet,
Tag und Nacht uns angegrinst.' (E iii. 46)

The Holy Ghost has dispatched a thousand warriors to carry out this task—and he is himself one of their number. But the girl is not

review of it. His work on *Die Harzreise* prevented him from doing so. Cf. *Br* i. 177, 188.

convinced and speaks of the wicked witch who has cast a spell on their home, which was once a palace— beneath the fairy-tale language we are back in the now familiar historical progression from a Golden Age to a period of present misery caused by the aristocracy and by Christian superstition, a period that will finally yield to a new age of harmony. The poet goes on to conjure up the scene in that magic palace of long ago and depicts himself as the prince who has come to claim his fairy princess. Love triumphs and the evil spell is broken. The 'Berg-Idylle' has thus been described as both the spiritual and structural summit of the work.[30] Here, high in the mountains, the narrator's search for love and the simple life would seem to be satisfied. And yet, when we reflect that for all its evident symbolism this poem contains nothing but a dream of a different existence couched in the language of an Uhland ballad, and that the palace does not actually materialize even within the terms of reality imposed by the poem, it gains a distinct ambiguity.

There is a parallel to this moment during the narrator's descent from the mountain. As he watches the mountain stream leaping and tumbling down the slope in all its 'Fröhlichkeit, Naivetät und Anmut', he has a dream-like vision of the Ilse legend. The fairy princess who inhabits the waters of the stream calls him to her enchanted palace, and again the fairy-tale level is reflected in the use of verse. The poet immediately associates this momentary experience of union with nature with the theme of non-reflective life:

Unendlich selig ist das Gefühl, wenn die Erscheinungswelt mit unserer Gemütswelt zusammenrinnt, und grüne Bäume, Gedanken, Vögelgesang, Wehmut, Himmelsbläue, Erinnerung und Kräuterduft sich in süßen Arabesken verschlingen. Die Frauen kennen am besten dieses Gefühl, und darum mag auch ein so holdselig ungläubiges Lächeln um ihre Lippen schweben, wenn wir mit Schulstolz unsere logischen Thaten rühmen, wie wir alles so hübsch eingeteilt in objektiv und subjektiv, wie wir unsere Köpfe apothekenartig mit tausend Schubladen versehen, wo in der einen Vernunft, in der andern Verstand, in der dritten Witz, in der vierten schlechter Witz und in der fünften gar nichts, nämlich die Idee, enthalten ist. (E iii. 72 f.)

---

[30] Cf. Karl Emmerich's interesting analysis, op. cit., pp. 104 ff. But it runs the danger, through a forced political interpretation, of reducing the poem to mere allegory.

But such moments are fleeting, and the simple life is threatened. The narrator sets out to escape from Philistines and to laugh at them from above only to find that he has to laugh at them face to face. Thus *Die Harzreise* has a carpet-like structure in which strands of reflection and magic are interwoven with the comic and satirical depiction of the Philistine on holiday. The burlesque counterpart to the 'Berg-Idylle' is the high jinks on the Brocken and at the inn. Where there should have been beauty and peace there is the buffoonery of pseudo-Ossians and that rapturous response to the setting sun, 'Wie ist die Natur doch im allgemeinen so schön!'[31] The Philistine represents the dry logic that divides modern man from true experience, from 'Unmittelbarkeit'.

B. '*Intellectus archetypus*'

This same pattern of themes, the ideal of an organic age, the dissonance of the present and the role of aristocrat, priest, and Philistine in maintaining it, the suspicion of the intellect, and the desire for a new, healthy age all recur in *Die Nordsee* III, written two years later in 1826.

The characteristic feature of the fisher-folk of Norderney is the non-literate immediacy of their lives. Although the narrator is fully aware of the primitive nature of their mental development, their ability to communicate emotion throws into relief the isolation and alienation of educated man. Heine's feeling of divorce from any genuine social experience, the thought that the intellect separates a man from his spiritual home and sets him at odds with himself here finds poignant expression:

Was diese Menschen so fest und genügsam zusammenhält, ist nicht so sehr das innig mystische Gefühl der Liebe als vielmehr die Gewohnheit, das naturgemäße Ineinander-Hinüberleben, die gemeinschaftliche Unmittelbarkeit. Gleiche Geisteshöhe oder, besser gesagt, Geistesniedrigkeit, daher gleiche Bedürfnisse und gleiches Streben; gleiche Erfahrungen und Gesinnungen, daher leichtes Verständnis untereinander; und sie sitzen verträglich am Feuer in den kleinen Hütten, rücken zusammen, wenn es kalt wird, an den Augen sehen sie sich ab, was sie denken, die Worte lesen sie sich von den Lippen, ehe sie gesprochen worden, alle gemeinsamen Lebensbeziehungen sind ihnen im Gedächtnisse, und durch einen einzigen Laut, eine einzige Miene, eine einzige stumme Bewegung erregen sie untereinander so viel Lachen oder

[31] E iii. 56.

Weinen oder Andacht, wie wir bei unseresgleichen erst durch lange Expositionen, Expektorationen und Deklamationen hervorbringen können. Denn wir leben im Grunde geistig einsam; durch eine besondere Erziehungsmethode oder zufällig gewählte besondere Lektüre hat jeder von uns eine verschiedene Charakterrichtung empfangen; jeder von uns, geistig verlarvt, denkt, fühlt und strebt anders als die andern, und des Mißverständnisses wird so viel, und selbst in weiten Häusern wird das Zusammenleben so schwer, und wir sind überall beengt, überall fremd und überall in der Fremde.   (E iii. 92)

But Heine immediately switches to a sharp attack on the Christian medieval world, which enforced a similar identity of thought and feeling by blinkering men's minds. This was not the first occasion on which he had rejected a harmony bought at the price of spiritual bondage: in *Die Harzreise* the narrator goes down a mine only to learn that in one of the galleries the Duke of Cambridge often held parties, which the miners attended with song and music. The contrast between this 'benevolence' and the harsh discomfort of working in dark, wet, and often stifling shafts strikes the narrator as a remarkable example of unshakeable German loyalty.[32] But the Harz silver-mines are so deep that in them some thought one could hear voices from the New World, voices crying 'Hurrah, Lafayette!'[33]. In *Die Nordsee* III we remain firmly in the Old World, for the narrator has to concede that the Renaissance brought with it all the frustration and dissatisfaction which derive from the capacity of enlightened men to reflect. Are people any happier for the assault on the hegemony of Roman Catholicism? The vast majority are not, he decides, but contents himself with the thought that there are brief moments of god-like ecstasy awaiting the free-thinking man. And as the narrator switches from envy of the simplicity and wholeness of ages and societies that do not reflect on their condition to his protest against the effective intellectual servitude that they entail, he discovers in his mixed response an example of what he terms the 'Zerrissenheit der Denkweise unserer Zeit'. What were the origins of this celebrated term in Heine's thought?

In the language of the turn of the century 'zerrissen' described a

[32] E iii. 30 f.
[33] Ibid., p. 20. These sentiments are in distinct, and very probably deliberate contrast to those expressed by the aged miner whom Heinrich von Ofterdingen meets and admires. The miner praises his profession's piety, loyalty, and joyous acceptance of poverty. Cf. Novalis, op. cit., esp. pp. 243 ff.

state of emotional disturbance, most obviously a 'broken' heart. Adelung's dictionary gives the figurative meaning: 'Jemandes Herz zerreißen, ihm den lebhaftesten Schmerz verursachen' and quotes as an example Weiße's line: 'Habe Mitleiden mit diesem Herzen, das du zerreißest.' *Zerrissenheit* is not listed.[34] One of Heine's *Fresko-Sonetten* of 1821 uses the word in this established sense:

Und wenn das Herz im Leibe ist zerrissen,
Zerrissen und zerschnitten und zerstochen,
So bleibt uns doch das schöne gelle Lachen! (E i. 39)

The letter in which the poem first appeared[35] continues: 'Ja, wenn die weitklaffende Todeswunde meines Herzens sprechen könnte, so spräche ich: ich lache.' He is referring to his most recent catastrophic visit to Hamburg to see his unnamed and cold-hearted love, whom most critics assume to have been his cousin, Amalie. But he also used the term to describe a more general sense of emotional malaise without reference to any specific occasion. In a letter of November 1820 he wrote that he wished his 'tolles, zerrissenes und verwildertes Gemüth' could be healed.[36] Two years later in the correspondence the word describes his feeling of estrangement from society, suspicion of all friends, and burning desire to leave Germany, to find some paradise where the world is different. We find ourselves in familiar territory:

Aussitôt que ma santé sera rétablie je quitterai l'Allemagne, je passerai en Arabie, j'y menerai une vie pastorale, je serai homme dans toute l'étendue du têrme, je vivrai parmis des chameaux qui ne sont pas étudiants, je ferai des vers arrabes, beau comme le Moalaccat, enfin je serai assi sur le rocher sacré, où Mödschnun a soupiré après Leila. O Christian, wüßtest Du, wie meine Seele nach Frieden lechzt, und wie sie doch täglich mehr und mehr zerrissen wird. Ich kann fast keine Nacht mehr schlafen. Im Traum seh ich meine sogenannten Freunde, wie sie sich Geschichtchen und Notizchen in die Ohren zischeln, die mir wie Bleytropfen in's Hirn rinnen. Des Tags verfolgt mich ein ewiges Mißtrauen, überall hör' ich meinen Namen und hinterdrein ein höhnisches Gelächter. (*Br* i. 38)

In *Die Nordsee* III, *Zerrissenheit* refers to that sense of alienation and division which characterizes modern society. It is in short

---

[34] Johann Christoph Adelung, *Grammatisch-kritisches Wörterbuch der hochdeutschen Mundart*, Vienna, 1811.
[35] *Br* i. 27 f.   [36] Ibid. 21.

Heine's version of A. W. Schlegel's 'innere Entzweiung'. Schlegel saw modern man suspended between memories of a past Golden Age and a yearning for the true existence of life after death.[37] For Heine the yearning is for a new Golden Age on earth and it is man's intellect that forever seems to balk a satisfying union with our earthly surroundings. Heine's values, as we have seen, are the exact opposite of Schlegel's. But for both men this inner dissonance is the product of a specific historical situation; it is the malaise of the age, not just the state of mind of some lovesick poet. The narrator of *Die Bäder von Lucca* argues the point in a well-known passage:

Ach, teurer Leser, wenn du über jene Zerrissenheit klagen willst, so beklage lieber, daß die Welt selbst mitten entzweigerissen ist. Denn da das Herz des Dichters der Mittelpunkt der Welt ist, so mußte es wohl in jetziger Zeit jämmerlich zerrissen werden. Wer von seinem Herzen rühmt, es sei ganz geblieben, der gesteht nur, daß er ein prosaisches weitabgelegenes Winkelherz hat. Durch das meinige ging aber der große Weltriß, und eben deswegen weiß ich, daß die großen Götter mich vor vielen anderen hoch begnadigt und des Dichtermärtyrtums würdig geachtet haben.

Einst war die Welt ganz, im Altertum und im Mittelalter,[38] trotz der äußeren Kämpfe gab's doch noch immer eine Welteinheit, und es gab ganze Dichter. Wir wollen diese Dichter ehren und uns an ihnen erfreuen; aber jede Nachahmung ihrer Ganzheit ist eine Lüge, eine Lüge, die jedes gesunde Auge durchschaut, und die dem Hohne dann nicht entgeht. (E iii. 304)

The passage clearly refers to Heine's own early lyric with its notorious *Stimmungsbrechung* and raises the question of the relationship between this love lyric and Heine's historical and social analysis of his age. The examination of *Almansor*, *Ratcliff*, and *Die Harzreise* has already suggested that the theme of disappointed love cannot be separated from Heine's social thought, and we shall return to the problem later.

Die Nordsee III is built around the experience of dissonance, of

---

[37] A. W. Schlegel, op. cit. v. 16 f.

[38] The reader may already have noticed the inconsistency in Heine's interpretation of the Middle Ages. When he speaks of the rise of Spiritualism and man's resultant sickness, these were times of inner discord, cf. E iv. 169 ff. (*Zur Geschichte* . . .), v. 217 ff. (*Die romantische Schule*). When he thinks of the authority of the One Church and its restriction of free thought, as in *Die Nordsee* III, and here, they are times of unity, even if enforced.

Zerrissenheit.[39] Two figures emerge gradually from the association of ideas on which the essay's narrative technique is based, as prototypes of a wholeness that transcends the dissonance felt by their contemporaries. These men are Goethe and Napoleon. Both are characterized by their exceptional powers of perception. As in 'Die Romantik' Goethe is regarded as a poet who sees and represents the world with the clarity of an Ancient Greek and does not distort it with his own subjective judgements. The Romantics, on the other hand, who here stand for the rest of modern culture, are now sick, a distinction that runs counter to A. W. Schlegel's view, but of which Goethe himself would certainly have approved.[40]

Das ist ein Verdienst Goethes, das erst spätere Zeiten erkennen werden; denn wir, die wir meist alle krank sind, stecken viel zu sehr in unseren kranken, zerrissenen, romantischen Gefühlen, die wir aus allen Ländern und Zeitaltern zusammengelesen, als daß wir unmittelbar sehen könnten, wie gesund, einheitlich und plastisch sich Goethe in seinen Werken zeigt. (E iii. 99)

In Goethe, then, is realized what distinguishes all Heine's ideal, organic cultures, an intuitive, non-abstract grasp of life, 'das Vermögen des plastischen Anschauens, Fühlens und Denkens.'[41] Such individuals are not, however, restricted to specific historical periods. There are chains of monumental figures stretching down through the ages, understanding one another far better than we them. One such outstanding individual is Napoleon, and we recognize in the ensuing description the same features as Heine finds in Goethe. He uses Kantian vocabulary with which to depict Napoleon's mind, showing that the ultimate level at which he understands the problem of harmony and dissonance is epistemological. But this does not mean that Heine was entirely familiar with Kant in the original. He admits that he found the quotation not in the *Kritik der Urteilskraft* but in an essay by Goethe himself. It had appeared in an article entitled 'Anschauende Urteilskraft' in Goethe's periodical *Zur Morphologie* in 1820.[42] Heine begins with Mme de Staël's grudging recognition that for

[39] Cf. Feise, op. cit., pp. 96 ff.

[40] Cf. Goethe's famous remark to Eckermann (2 Apr. 1829), *Gedenkausgabe der Werke*, ed. E. Beutler, Zürich, 1949, xxiv. 332. He may even have had this passage in mind.

[41] E iii. 99.

[42] *Goethes Werke*, Weimar, 1893, section II, vol. 11, part I, pp. 54 f.

all his faults Napoleon possessed a mind too remarkable to be assessed by normal standards:

Ein solcher Geist ist es, worauf folgende Worte Kants, die ich un-längst in der Morphologie erwähnt sah, hinzuweisen scheinen: 'Wir können uns einen Verstand denken, der, weil er nicht wie der unsrige diskursiv, sondern intuitiv ist, vom synthetisch Allgemeinen, der Anschauung eines Ganzen als eines solchen, zum Besonderen geht, das ist, von dem Ganzen zu den Teilen. Hierbei ist gar nicht nöthig zu beweisen, daß ein solcher intellectus archetypus möglich sei, sondern nur daß wir in der Dagegenhaltung unseres diskursiven, der Bilder bedürftigen Verstandes (intellectus ectypus) und der Zufälligkeit einer solchen Beschaffenheit, auf jene Idee eines intellectus archetypus geführt werden, diese auch keinen Widerspruch erhalte.' Ja, was wir durch langsames Nachdenken und lange Schlußfolgen erkennen, das hatte jener Geist im selben Momente angeschaut und tief begriffen. Daher sein Talent, die Zeit, die Gegenwart zu verstehen, ihren Geist zu kajolieren, ihn nie zu beleidigen und immer zu benutzen. (E iii. 113 f.)[43]

Such a mind can perceive the external world with the immediacy of an entirely non-reflective man and yet grasp and understand it without resort to analysis or the processes of logical thought. We may question the accuracy of the description as applied to Napo-leon; Goethe, on the other hand, would certainly have liked to apply it to himself and this tiny article illuminates one of Goethe's principal ambitions—to show that the distinction between abstract thought and direct perception was false and damaging.[44]

It was not by chance that Heine was attracted to Goethe's quotation from Kant. He recognized the clear affinity between his own ideal and Goethe's mode of thinking and feeling. A second article in the same volume of Goethe's periodical reflected his attitude towards systematic philosophy. 'Für Philosophie im eigentlichen Sinn hatte ich kein Organ', he writes,[45] and when his friends discussed with reference to Kant 'wie viel unser Selbst und wie viel die Außenwelt zu unserem geistigen Dasein beitrage', he found their analysis irrelevant. 'Ich hatte beide niemals gesondert, und wenn ich nach meiner Weise über Gegenstände philosophirte,

---

[43] Including restored passage from original *Reisebilder* version, E iii. 524 f. (spelling standardized).

[44] Cf. Erich Heller, 'Goethe and the Idea of Scientific Truth', *The Disinherited Mind*, Cambridge, 1952, p. 5.

[45] 'Einwirkung der neueren Philosophie', *Werke*, II, vol. 11, part I, p. 47.

so tat ich es mit unbewußter Naivetät und glaubte wirklich, ich sähe meine Meinungen vor Augen.'[46] Heine echoes these words in an oblique reference to another article by Goethe that appeared in a later volume of *Zur Morphologie*. Goethe, he says, does not notice the immediacy and plasticity of his perceptive powers: '. . . in seiner naiven Unbewußtheit des eignen Vermögens wundert er sich, wenn man ihm "ein gegenständliches Denken" zuschreibt' (E iii. 99). Goethe had found this description of himself in a manual of anthropology[47] and it leads in his essay 'Bedeutende Fördernis durch ein einziges geistreiches Wort'[48] to a fresh self-interpretation. In a particularly felicitous formulation of his own powers of thinking and perceiving we find what might well stand as a motto for Heine's ideal of the 'Anschauungsmensch', which we have been pursuing. He defines Heinroth's phrase as meaning: '. . . daß mein Denken sich von den Gegenständen nicht sondere, daß die Elemente der Gegenstände, die Anschauungen in dasselbe eingehen und von ihm auf das innigste durchdrungen werden, daß mein Anschauen selbst ein Denken, mein Denken ein Anschauen sei.'[49]

What Heine said of Napoleon thus applies rather to Goethe and supplements his earlier comments on him in the same essay. Indeed it might be claimed that the central pattern of themes was directly inspired by his reading Goethe's periodical. Why, then, did he use this material to describe Napoleon at all? This question becomes still more pertinent when we discover that in the second, 1831 edition of the work, the edition that we read today, the reference to Goethe as the source of the Kantian quotation is suppressed. This not only leads the reader to believe that Heine had himself perused Kant's works but removes the possibility of directly linking the two monumental figures. As association of ideas forms the basic narrative technique of the essay, we can sense in this alteration a shift of Heine's sympathies away from the artistic genius to the political genius. As he worked on the essay the political perspective must have become increasingly important to him, and the close reflects this.

Sir Walter Scott had announced his intention to publish a book

[46] Ibid., pp. 48 f.
[47] Johann Christian Heinroth's *Lehrbuch der Anthropologie*, Leipzig, 1822.
[48] *Werke*, II, vol. 11, part I, pp. 58–64.
[49] Ibid., p. 58.

on Napoleon. In Scott Heine sees an elegy not only for the disappearance of Scotland's traditional customs: he captures the mood
as older, more organic cultures are destroyed by the advance of the
modern, rational world. It is Heine's old theme from *Almansor* and
Die Harzreise and he even compares the profound effect of Scott's
works with the nostalgia and desperation an ancient Moorish song
never failed to awake in Spanish Granada.[50] Heine's own fascination with the defeated and dead Emperor is itself part of a lament
for an age that had been stamped out ruthlessly by the Restoration.
Small wonder that he goes on to compare Philippe Paul Ségur's
Histoire de Napoléon et de la grande armée pendant 1812 with the
great epics of world literature, the *Edda*, the *Nibelungenlied*—and
the *Mahabharata*. What they all have in common, he says, is that
they sing of the decline and fall of a heroic epoch. But unlike the
melancholy aroused by Scott, Ségur 'weckt nicht die Liebe zu
längst verschollenen Tagen der Vorzeit, sondern es ist ein Ton,
dessen Klangfigur uns die Gegenwart gibt, ein Ton, der uns für
eben diese Gegenwart begeistert'.[51] Here lies the crux of Heine's
shift in sympathy. The age of harmony is no longer to be mourned:
it is to be created in the future. Napoleon was a man of action who
employed his archetypal intellect to make history:

> Zur verwickelten, langsamen Intrige neigen sich kleine, analytische
> Geister, hingegen synthetische, intuitive wissen auf wunderbar geniale
> Weise die Mittel, die ihnen die Gegenwart bietet, so zu verbinden, daß
> sie dieselben zu ihrem Zwecke schnell benutzen können. Erstere
> scheitern sehr oft, da keine menschliche Klugheit alle Vorfallenheiten
> des Lebens voraussehen kann und die Verhältnisse des Lebens nie
> lange stabil sind; letzteren hingegen, den intuitiven Menschen, gelingen
> ihre Vorsätze am leichtesten, da sie nur einer richtigen Berechnung des
> Vorhandenen bedürfen und so schnell handeln, daß dieses durch die
> Bewegung der Lebenswogen keine plötzliche, unvorhergesehene Ver-
> änderung erleiden kann.   (E iii. 114)

What Napoleon tried to achieve is still a possibility, Heine
implies. And to suggest what the immediate task for Germany is
without incurring trouble from the censors he simply goes on to
complain about German *Zerrissenheit*, but this time extending the
term still further to refer to the political fragmentation of the country into dozens of principalities and dukedoms, a fragmentation

which the reader knew to have been partly abolished by Napoleon's conquests only to be re-established after his defeat.[52] We now understand his choice of motto for the essay from Varnhagen von Ense's *Biographische Denkmale*, a motto that Heine did not have printed but merely referred to:

Die Gemütskraft und Geistesstärke des Einzelnen mag noch so groß sein, die der Nation, verteilt und belebt in ihren getrennten Gliedern, steht mächtiger daneben, und verwehrt die großen freien Bahnen, die wir bei andern Völkern jedem Außerordentlichen so bald und leicht eröffnet sehn. Unsre Litteratur wie unsre Politik sind reich an Beispielen dieser Eigenheit; unsre Helden in beiden, unsre Fürsten, Feldherren, Staatsmänner, Reformatoren, Bildner in Kunst und Leben, alle mußten ihre größten Gaben, ausgestattet für Vollgewinn, um geringeren verwenden, der selbst nur um jenen Preis erreichbar wurde. Auch Luther und Friedrich der Große, gerüstet und berufen für die Gesamtheit des Vaterlandes, konnten in dessen Vielgestalt und Zersplitterung, wie mächtige Werke sie auch darin gebildet, nicht das Ganze vereinigend umfangen. (E iii. 90)

It is not hard to connect Heine's criticism of the German political structure with his attack on feudalism, with which we are already familiar. Feudalism and the Church had both been overthrown in the French Revolution and it is as the embodiment of the Revolution that Heine admired Napoleon. In the *Reisebild* that follows *Die Nordsee* III Heine uses the figure of Le Grand, the French drum-major, to symbolize Napoleon's achievement and then his fall. When Napoleon's armies march across Europe they take with them their revolutionary tunes, the Marseillaise and the guillotine march, which Le Grand beats out on his drum. Heine sees Napoleon's conquest of Europe as the continuation of the Revolution in anachronistic countries. If this seems extraordinary to us, we need only think of the civil liberties for Jews that accompanied Napoleon's occupation of Heine's own home town, Düsseldorf.[53] Under French law there were no special clauses restricting the places where Jews could live or the trades and

[52] E iii. 120 f. Cf. Agatha Ramm, *Germany, 1789–1919. A Political History*, London, 1967, pp. 60 ff., 139 ff. The Federative Act of 1815 produced thirty-eight quite sovereign states with no central authority, in the true sense of the word, a *Staatenbund* not a *Bundesstaat*.

[53] Cf. for example, Eberhard Galley, op. cit., pp. 7 f., Agatha Ramm, op. cit., p. 83, and Isaiah Berlin, *Karl Marx. His Life and Environment*, London, 1963, pp. 25 ff.

professiono they could pursue. It would be wrong, furthermore, to assume that only the Jewish population admired the French system and preferred it to Prussian rule. When the Rhineland came under Prussian jurisdiction, this primarily Roman Catholic and French-looking area deeply resented control from the east.[54] For decades it continued to revere the '*Code Napoléon*', and while there were liberalizing tendencies in Prussia, too, where for example, Jews had also been emancipated, these tendencies were to a large extent obstructed by Metternich from Austria. It was Metternich who came to dominate German politics, and his power was confirmed and symbolized by the Karlsbad decrees of 1819 following the assassination of Kotzebue. As a result the *Burschenschaften* were banned, professors dismissed, free speech suppressed, and rigid press and book censorship introduced. All writings of under twenty printers' sheets (i.e. 320 octavo pages) had to be submitted to the censors if published anywhere within the German Confederation.[55] It is against the spirit of this arch-conservative and dictatorial Germany of the 1820s[56] that we must judge Heine's hatred of the aristocracy and Church as symbols of regression, and at the other extreme his almost religious love of Napoleon.

Two years after *Ideen. Das Buch Le Grand* Heine wrote that every age has its task and that the task of the present age is emancipation, the emancipation of the Irish, Greeks, Jews, West Indian Negroes, and the whole of Europe. Man has reached the age of majority, and again it is Napoleon who is invoked as the spirit of modern times, Napoleon the general, that is: the Emperor is now rejected as a secret aristocrat and traitor to freedom.[57] As dawn comes to the scene of the French general's victory at Marengo, the rising sun brings with it the promise of a new and totally different epoch. It is Heine's vision of wholeness, of an organic society, transported into the future when hereditary privilege will have disappeared like the birds of the night at daybreak:

'Es wird ein schöner Tag werden', rief mein Reisegefährte aus dem Wagen mir zu. Ja, es wird ein schöner Tag werden, wiederholte leise mein betendes Herz und zitterte vor Wehmut und Freude. Ja, es wird

[54] Cf. Hans Kohn, *The Mind of Germany*, London, 1961, pp. 100 f.
[55] Cf. Hajo Holborn, *A History of Modern Germany, 1648–1840*, London, 1965, pp. 465 ff., and Ramm, op. cit., pp. 148 f. Ramm mistranslates 'Bogen', writing 'pages' for 'printers' sheets'.
[56] Cf. the vivid account of the period in Isaiah Berlin, op. cit., pp. 24 f.
[57] E iii. 273 f.

ein schöner Tag werden, die Freiheitssonne wird die Erde glücklicher wärmen als die Aristokratie sämtlicher Sterne; emporblühen wird ein neues Geschlecht, das erzeugt worden in freier Wahlumarmung, nicht im Zwangsbette und unter der Kontrolle geistlicher Zöllner; mit der freien Geburt werden auch in den Menschen freie Gedanken und Gefühle zur Welt kommen, wovon wir geborenen Knechte keine Ahnung haben — O! sie werden ebensowenig ahnen, wie entsetzlich die Nacht war, in deren Dunkel wir leben mußten, und wie grauenhaft wir zu kämpfen hatten mit häßlichen Gespenstern, dumpfen Eulen und scheinheiligen Sündern! (E iii. 280 f.)

But he foresees that, like his hero Almansor, he will but enjoy a glimpse of what could be, and himself die a victim of the contemporary dark world. He completes his reflections with the epitaph he should like to see on his warrior's grave:

Ich weiß wirklich nicht, ob ich es verdiene, daß man mir einst mit einem Lorbeerkranz den Sarg verziere. Die Poesie, wie sehr ich sie auch liebte, war mir immer nur heiliges Spielzeug oder geweihtes Mittel für himmlische Zwecke. Ich habe nie großen Wert gelegt auf Dichterruhm, und ob man meine Lieder preiset oder tadelt, es kümmert mich wenig. Aber ein Schwert sollt ihr mir auf den Sarg legen; denn ich war ein braver Soldat im Befreiungskriege der Menschheit. (E iii. 281)

And in the same year as this virtual disavowal of his songs as irrelevant to the political issues of the day, as playthings that he adored, revered even, but which had no bearing on the world of here and now, he also declared that the whole era which was dominated by Goethe and the idea of the primacy of art had come to a close.[58]

Does not this new concern with political action furnish an eloquent argument for the view of Heine as the divided man, the man who swung between lyrical introspection and revolutionary fervour? So far the evidence has been against such a conclusion. We have seen Heine's thought evolve directly along the historical lines established by August Wilhelm Schlegel with the important distinction that Heine's third ideal age is non-metaphysical, an age to be realized on earth. It is the constant ideal of a harmonious culture as opposed to the discordant time Heine felt he lived in, a discord created by the tyranny of the intellect. Modern man's intellect has alienated him from his social roots and from his sensual being. Heine sees alienation spreading from the erotic to

[58] 'Die deutsche Litteratur' von Wolfgang Menzel, E vii. 245 f., 255 f.

the political level, from the religious to the epistemological. Equally constant has been his attack on those social forces that he recognized as instrumental in causing this malaise, the feudal hierarchy, the priesthood and authority of the Roman Church, and the Philistine. As his understanding of the price at which primitive people bought their inner unity grows, so too has his interest in the future. Again the development is linear. Yet his growing interest in Napoleon at the expense of Goethe and his suspicion of his own lyrical activities still suggest a rift between Heine the poet and Heine the warrior. Must we also condemn Heine's early lyric as the outpourings of a consumptive *Mondscheinheld*, to use Ratcliff's term of abuse,[59] divorced from the more serious preoccupations of the *Reisebilder*? To answer this question more closely we must examine Heine's early lyric and relate Heine's own view of its purpose to his later work and ideals.

[59] E ii. 325

II

THE VOICE OF THE PEOPLE

A. 'Volkslied' or 'Kunstlied'?[1]

EVEN today Heine's fame, and for that matter notoriety, rest chiefly on the volume of collected verse, the *Buch der Lieder*, which he published in 1827. Probably no other German poet of the nineteenth century produced a lyrical work which has enjoyed such great popularity: within his own lifetime it already ran to thirteen editions. Its success, however, has obscured the essentially experimental nature of its verse. The bulk of the songs in this collection were written in the short period from 1821 to 1824 and form only one type of verse among several at which Heine tried his hand. This is most clearly evident in the *Junge Leiden* section based on his first volume of verse, *Gedichte*, of 1822. Here we find, alongside songs, the wild visions of *Traumbilder* which derive from folk-tale and superstition, from Bürger and from Hoffmann, ballads in which the influence of *Des Knaben Wunderhorn* is apparent, *Minnelieder* inspired by Uhland, sonnets that A. W. Schlegel prompted. It is easily forgotten, moreover, that Heine did not confine himself to verse even in these early years. We have seen that he wrote two tragedies and in 1824 turned to travel literature. He had already gained some experience in the latter when writing reports on the social and cultural life of Berlin for a Rhineland newspaper in 1822. In addition he also attempted a novel. Were his songs, then, a mere lyrical interlude between works of more obvious religious and social relevance as the title of his *Tragödien nebst einem lyrischen Intermezzo* of 1823 suggests? This is the impression one gains from reading the preface to the third edition of the *Buch der Lieder* of 1839:

O Phöbus Apollo! sind diese Verse schlecht, so wirst du mir gern verzeihen. . . . Denn du bist ein allwissender Gott, und du weißt sehr gut, warum ich mich seit so vielen Jahren nicht mehr vorzugsweise mit

[1] This section is largely based on my article 'The Art of Simplicity: Heinrich Heine and Wilhelm Müller', *Oxford German Studies*, 5 (1970), 48–66.

Maß und Gleichklang der Wörter beschäftigen konnte . . . Du weißt, warum die Flamme, die einst in brillanten Feuerwerkspielen die Welt ergötzte, plötzlich zu weit ernsteren Bränden verwendet werden mußte. . . . Du weißt, warum sie jetzt in schweigender Glut mein Herz ver-zehrt. . . . Du verstehst mich, großer schöner Gott, der du ebenfalls die goldene Leier zuweilen vertauschtest mit dem starken Bogen und den tödlichen Pfeilen. . . . (E i. 10)

However, if we read Heine's account of the folk-song in *Die romantische Schule*, written some ten years after *Lyrisches Inter-mezzo*, it becomes plain that while he may no longer have written songs himself[2] and even spoke out against them as in-appropriate for the times, he continued to admire the genuine and original folk-song without reservation. In discussing Clemens Brentano he comes naturally to the subject of *Des Knaben Wunder-horn*, which he recommends to his French readers with a warmth that surprises. Elsewhere in his essay Heine is anxious not only to introduce the foreign reader to the beauties of German Romantic literature but also to warn him of the Romantics' pernicious desire to resurrect feudalism. Taking Arnim and Brentano's collection of folk-songs as an unadulterated expression of popular, artless culture, he praises them above all else for their spontaneity. These, he says, are the improvised, anonymous creations of his country's journey-men, and he insists that their attraction lies precisely in the fact that no poet has had to brood over them, write and rewrite, alter and polish:

Fragt man nun entzückt nach dem Verfasser solcher Lieder, so antworten diese wohl selbst mit ihren Schlußworten:

> Wer hat das schöne Liedel erdacht?
> Es haben's drei Gäns' übers Wasser gebracht,
> Zwei graue und eine weiße.[3]

Gewöhnlich ist es aber wanderndes Volk, Vagabunden, Soldaten, fahrende Schüler oder Handwerksburschen, die solch ein Lied gedich-tet. Es sind besonders die Handwerksburschen. Gar oft auf meinen Fußreisen verkehrte ich mit diesen Leuten und bemerkte, wie sie zuweilen, angeregt von irgend einem ungewöhnlichen Ereignisse, ein Stück Volkslied improvisierten oder in die freie Luft hineinpfiffen.

---

[2] The *Neuer Frühling* cycle of 1831 remains an 'erratic block' in his production and was written at the special request of Albert Methfessel, the composer, to be set to music.

[3] *Des Knaben Wunderhorn*, ed. Willi Koch, Darmstadt, 1963, p. 144.

Das erlauschten nun die Vögelein, die auf den Baumzweigen saßen; und kam nachher ein andrer Bursche mit Ränzel und Wanderstab vorbeigeschlendert, dann pfiffen sie ihm jenes Stücklein ins Ohr, und er sang die fehlenden Verse hinzu, und das Lied war fertig. Die Worte fallen solchen Burschen vom Himmel herab auf die Lippen, und er [sic] braucht sie nur auszusprechen, und sie sind dann noch poetischer als all die schönen poetischen Phrasen, die wir aus der Tiefe unseres Herzens hervorgrübeln. (E v. 314 f.)

Here we experience, he claims, the true spirit of the German people, 'all seine düstere Heiterkeit, all seine närrische Vernunft'.[4] Of his favourite image for Germany, 'der deutsche Michel', with his night-cap pulled down over his eyes and ears, there is no mention.

The belief that in folk-culture and particularly in the folk-song one finds the genuine character of a people, a character which has been distorted and overlaid by the inauthentic cultural accretions of later more reflective, prosaic, and eclectic ages derives in Germany from Herder. We have already encountered the tradition in *Die Harzreise* and *Die Nordsee* III. At the heart of Herder's theory lay the same deep-rooted suspicion of the intellect and of reflection that Heine came to inherit.[5] A radical dissatisfaction with the spirit and achievements of the *Aufklärung* with its heavy reliance on analytical reason and on the cultural example set by France is patent in Herder's writings. He had fervently hoped that the rediscovery of what remained of the poetic age in more primitive 'uneducated' layers of society and particularly in the songs that they still sang would help to revitalize German culture. That Heine was familiar at least with Herder's essay on Ossian and the folk-song is strongly suggested by his use of the Edward ballad in *William Ratcliff*, echoes of the same in 'Die Grenadiere',[6] his adaptation of 'Wenn ich ein Vöglein wär' in *Lyrisches Intermezzo* 53, and later his debt to *Der Webegesang der Valkyriur* for the refrain of his famous song on the Silesian weavers.[7]

---

[4] E v. 311.

[5] See, e.g., 'Über Ossian und die Lieder alter Völker' in *Sämtliche Werke*, ed. Bernhard Suphan, Berlin, 1877 ff., v. 182 f. See also i. 153 ff.

[6] Compare 'Was schert mich Weib, was schert mich Kind! / Ich trage weit beßres Verlangen; / Laß sie betteln gehn, wenn sie hungrig sind, / Mein Kaiser, mein Kaiser gefangen!' with Herder's 'Und was soll werden dein Weib und Kind, / Wann du gehst über Meer — O! / Die Welt ist groß! laß sie betteln drinn . . .'.

[7] Heine: 'Deutschland, wir weben dein Leichentuch, / Wir weben hinein

No one contributed more decisively to this philosophy in later years, however, than Arnim and Brentano with their collection of folk-songs, *Des Knaben Wunderhorn*, that Heine so loved. Like Herder their interest in the folk-song was far from directly antiquarian: their songs had the specific function of rejuvenating German literature and the German people.[8]

Heine did not collect folk-songs but we can see from a review which dates from 1823, a time when he was actively engaged in writing *Lieder*, that he equally saw cultural rejuvenation as the role of the modern poet, or more specifically in this case, of the modern composer. He felt that Albert Methfessel, for whom he was later to write the *Neuer Frühling* cycle, was a man who possessed this ability to recreate the genuine spirit of the folk-song:[9]

Wahrlich, man kann jene Komponisten nicht genug ehren, welche uns Liedermelodieen geben, die von der Art sind, daß sie sich Eingang bei dem Volke verschaffen und echte Lebenslust und wahren Frohsinn verbreiten. Die meisten Komponisten sind innerlich so verkünstelt, versumpft und verschroben, daß sie nichts Reines, Schlichtes, kurz nichts Natürliches hervorbringen können — und das Natürliche, das organisch Hervorgegangene und mit dem unnachahmlichen Stempel der Wahrheit Gezeichnete ist es eben, was den Liedermelodieen jenen Zauber verleiht, der sie allen Gemütern einprägt und sie populär macht. (E vii. 222 f.)

The chief characteristics of the folk-song for Heine are, then, immediacy and simplicity. Like the fairy-tale, of which he speaks in *Die Harzreise*, it grows naturally as an organic expression of men's thoughts and feelings. The act of creation is an unconscious process. Still more important, it is possible for modern individuals to revive this spontaneity and purity of expression through themselves creating works that capture the mood of the folk-song.

Viewed against this background neither the interest of the Romantics in collecting folk-songs nor Heine's own attempts to write poems emulating their artless *naïveté* were just a lyrical pastime. It was an active step both towards making the life of the

den dreifachen Fluch — / Wir weben, wir weben!' Herder: 'Wir weben, wir weben / Schlachtgewebe!'

[8] Cf. Achim von Arnim, 'Von Volksliedern' in *Des Knaben Wunderhorn*, ed. cit., pp. 885 f.

[9] This could well explain why Heine was willing to turn back to the song as late as 1830: an old ideal was being revived. The frequency of the *Stimmungsbrechung* shows that in practice the ideal could not be realized.

educated man more organic and towards bringing German culture as a whole closer to its native roots, which still survived in the unreflective *Anschauungsleben* of peasant communities. Thus Heine's love of the folk-song cannot properly be considered independently of the ideals which I have already analysed in his plays and prose of the same period. His experiment with the folk-song may be regarded as a conscious response to the cultural and social alienation which he felt dominated his age; rather than being dismissed as a mere *Intermezzo* his early lyric would be more accurately described in the words that Willi Koch uses of *Des Knaben Wunderhorn*[10] as 'eine politische Angelegenheit'.

So much for Heine's ideal. From the outset, however, it was a venture which, in practical terms, was beset with difficulties. In another review dating from 1823, which discusses the lyric of a young contemporary, Heine argues that it is vital to seize the spirit of the folk-song and not be content merely to imitate its external forms. It was because the song was the product of an uncomplicated state of mind, a mind untrammelled by artificial rules and abstract thinking, that the folk-song was attractive in the first place:

Es kömmt darauf an, den Geist der Volksliedformen zu erfassen und mit der Kenntnis desselben nach unserem Bedürfnis gemodelte, neue Formen zu bilden. Abgeschmackt klingen daher die Titulaturvolkslieder jener Herren, die den heutigsten Stoff aus der gebildeten Gesellschaft mit einer Form umkleiden, die vielleicht ein ehrlicher Handwerksbursche vor zweihundert Jahren für den Erguß seiner Gefühle passend gefunden. Der Buchstabe tötet, doch der Geist macht lebendig.

(E vii. 220)

Heine's own most characteristic device for capturing that spirit of simplicity is to reduce typical folk-song motifs to an absolute minimum in scope, removing anything that might seem extraneous and allowing, as it were, no room for the language and feeling of modern sophisticated society. An excellent illustration of this process can be seen in the very first poem of the 'Lieder' group in *Junge Leiden*.[11] It consists of no more than two stanzas, each of four lines with a regular *abab* rhyme scheme:

> Morgens steh' ich auf und frage:
> Kommt feins Liebchen heut'?

---

[10] 'Nachwort' to *Des Knaben Wunderhorn*, ed. cit., p. 909.
[11] For Heine's source cf. Robert Goetze, op. cit., p. 7.

Abends sink' ich hin und klage:
Ausblieb sie auch heut',

In der Nacht mit meinem Kummer
Lieg' ich schlaflos, wach;
Träumend, wie im halben Schlummer,
Wandle ich bei Tag. (E i. 30)

Heine has taken the central motifs of this song from a longer poem
entitled 'Gruß' which had appeared in *Des Knaben Wunderhorn*.[12]
This had started far more elaborately than Heine's version:

Soviel Stern am Himmel stehen,
Soviel Schäflein, als da gehen
In dem grünen Feld,

Soviel Vögel als da fliegen,
Als da hin und wider fliegen,
Sovielmal sei du gegrüßt!

Soll ich dich dann nimmer sehen?
Ach, das kann ich nicht verstehen,
O du bittrer Scheidens Schluß.

A few verses later we come to the lines which probably form the
core of Heine's poem:

Was für Wellen, was für Flammen
Schlagen über mir zusammen,
Ach, wie groß ist meine Not.

Mit Geduld will ich es tragen,
Alle Morgen will ich sagen:
O mein Schatz, wann kommst zu mir?

Alle Abend will ich sprechen,
Wenn mir meine Äuglein brechen:
O mein Schatz, gedenk an mich!

Ja, ich will dich nicht vergessen,
Wann ich sollte unterdessen
Auf dem Todbett schlafen ein.

[12] Ed. cit., pp. 429 f.

Heine has sharpened the antithetical structure of the whole by repeating the morning/evening contrast in each stanza, and by expanding the sleep motif to include its opposite, but at the time of day when it is least expected, so that the normal order of waking and sleeping is reversed. The 'folksy' flavour of the language has even been carefully developed by employing elisions, the stock form of endearment 'feins Liebchen', and a syntactical curiosity in the inversion of subject and verb in the fourth line.

Heine was not, however, satisfied with such attempts. The decisive stimulus to writing *Lyrisches Intermezzo* seems to have been his reading Wilhelm Müller's *Siebenundsiebzig Gedichte aus den hinterlassenen Papieren eines wandernden Waldhornisten*, which appeared in November 1820. When Heine had published his cycle in 1823 he sent Müller a dedicated copy. But by far the most revealing document in this respect is the letter which accompanied a volume of *Reisebilder* sent to Müller three years later. Here Heine openly admits that it was Müller who showed him how it was possible for the modern poet to recapture the all-important spirit of simplicity that already fascinated him in the folk-song:

Ich bin groß genug, Ihnen offen zu bekennen, daß mein kleines 'Intermezzo'-Metrum nicht bloß zufällige Ähnlichkeit mit Ihrem gewöhnlichen Metrum hat, sondern daß es wahrscheinlich seinen geheimsten Tonfall Ihren Liedern verdankt, indem es die lieben Müllerschen Lieder waren, die ich zu eben der Zeit kennen lernte, als ich das 'Intermezzo' schrieb. Ich habe sehr früh schon das deutsche Volkslied auf mich einwirken lassen; späterhin, als ich in Bonn studirte, hat mir August Schlegel viel metrische Geheimnisse aufgeschlossen, aber ich glaube erst in Ihren Liedern den reinen Klang und die wahre Einfachheit, wonach ich immer strebte, gefunden zu haben. Wie rein, wie klar sind Ihre Lieder, und sämmtlich sind es Volkslieder.

(*Br* i. 270)

If Heine had a delicate ear for metre, and he was indeed profoundly influenced by Müller's example, as has been shown,[13] he was no less concerned with language. We have seen that he feared the danger of merely imitating archaic expressions without seizing the essentially artless mood of the song. In the early Heine song that I have discussed he tried both to achieve simplicity and to maintain the appropriate linguistic forms. In Müller he felt that he had discovered a poet who could write unaffectedly without

[13] Cf. Nollen, op. cit., pp. 212 ff.

resorting to a mode of expression that struck the modern reader less as artless than as downright crude. His letter continues:

> Ja, ich bin groß genug, es sogar bestimmt zu wiederholen, und Sie werden es mahl [*sic*] öffentlich ausgesprochen finden, daß mir durch die Lektüre Ihrer 77 Gedichte zuerst klar geworden, wie man aus den alten vorhandenen Volksliedformen neue Formen bilden kann, die ebenfalls volksthümlich sind, ohne daß man nöthig hat, die alten Sprachholperigkeiten und Unbeholfenheiten nachzuahmen.[14]

From the time when Heine becomes acquainted with Müller his songs begin to rely less on linguistic borrowings from earlier works and more exclusively on their images and motifs. A significant proportion of the songs in *Des Knaben Wunderhorn* and in Müller's work draw on an established set of motifs which appear over and over again in different variations and combinations. In this absence of emphasis on originality they bear the imprint of an earlier attitude to art which sought its objective less in novelty than in the skilful rearrangement of conventionally accepted material. One such motif is that of tears which, on falling to the ground, spring up again as flowers. A striking use of this is to be found in a poem by Spee which Arnim and Brentano reproduced in their folk-song anthology. To them a work of pre-Enlightenment origin of this kind seemed to be adequately termed a folk-song. 'Der Herr am Ölberg und der Himmelsschäfer'[15] takes the form of a dialogue between a shepherd and the moon, symbolizing Christ in the Garden of Gethsemane before the Passion. The moon leaves its flock of stars to graze while it seeks to console 'Daphnis' and one stanza in its total of nineteen reads:

> Weidet, meine Schäflein, weidet,
> Niemand hat's gezählet gar,
> Niemand hat es ausgekreidet,
> Wie die Zahl der Tropfen war,
> Nur der Boden, wohl erquicket
> Durch den weiß und roten Trank,
> Dankend ihm entgegenschicket
> Rosen rot und Lilien blank.

The poem then explores the motif for one further stanza, in which

---

[14] Cf. E v. 350 f., where in *Die romantische Schule* Heine kept his promise and made public his admiration for Müller's poetic language.

[15] *Des Knaben Wunderhorn*, ed. cit., pp. 196 ff.

more drops of blood fall on to the flowers as if baptizing them. After that the poet turns to the shepherd's sighs.

A song by Wilhelm Müller entitled 'Thränen und Rosen' takes up this motif of tears and flowers, where it is developed together with the popular image of the beloved sitting at a window at night, to form a poem in its own right.[16] The girl's suitor picks a rose and throws it into her window. We then learn that this rose has sprung up from tears she shed while waiting for him. In Heine we find this same process in which motifs are freed from their earlier secondary position within the narrative chain and themselves made the virtual subject of the new poem. But Heine achieves a still higher degree of compression. He was already close to this in 'Morgens steh' ich auf und frage'. In the second poem of *Lyrisches Intermezzo* he employs the motifs of the tears transformed to flowers and the girl at the window and then fuses them with another common folk-song motif, that of the nightingale as the bearer of messages of love,[17] to form a song of a mere eight lines:

> Aus meinen Thränen sprießen
> Viel blühende Blumen hervor,
> Und meine Seufzer werden
> Ein Nachtigallenchor.
>
> Und wenn du mich lieb hast, Kindchen,
> Schenk' ich dir die Blumen all,
> Und vor deinem Fenster soll klingen
> Das Lied der Nachtigall. (E i. 66)

Is this written in the spirit of simplicity? Such a poem is clearly contrived and a second look at the lover's words with their condescending 'Kindchen', which has come to replace the more awkward 'feins Liebchen', confirms our suspicions. One can hear the voice of the socially sophisticated, reproducing the favourite images of the folk-song: beneath the rosy cheeks of the peasant boy are the weary eyes and drawn features of the worldly-wise. The *Kunstlied*, for this it is that Heine and Müller write, is a distillation of the folk-song and less spontaneous expression than conscious construction. Heine's very statement that Müller had captured

---

[16] The parallels are pointed out in Nollen's list, op. cit., p. 271. For Müller's poem see *Gedichte*, ed. J. T. Hatfield (Deutsche Literaturdenkmale 137), Berlin, 1906, pp. 64 f.

[17] *Des Knaben Wunderhorn*, ed. cit., pp. 432 f., 691 ff. Compare pp. 277 f.

the *naïveté* of the spirit of the folk-song without its clumsy form reveals the paradoxical view that the modern poet can 'improve' on the original song. This is trimmed and cut to shape so that it will fit the interpretation of its 'true' nature, which is said to lie in the immediacy of its expression. Yet here we find a poet, or rather a succession of poets, deliberately polishing and repolishing in order to produce something more obviously artless. Far from recreating a naïve state of mind the latter-day folk-poet reached a new level of refinement.

The poetic age which Herder postulated marked the childhood of culture and preceded the appearance of philosophical reflection. Heine's longing for such innocence was a reaction against an already established age of reflection. A return to the literature of simplicity could not mean the rebirth of spontaneous expression but was at best a search for what had not yet been reduced to the merely stereotyped. Heine implies as much when, in passing, he gives a résumé of the origins of the genres in a review of 1821. He has adjusted Herder's theory to his own situation:

Lyrik ist die erste und älteste Poesie. Sowohl bei ganzen Völkern als bei einzelnen Menschen sind die ersten poetischen Ausbrüche lyrischer Art. Die gebräuchlichen Konvenienzmetaphern scheinen hier dem Dichter zu abgedroschen und kalt, und er greift nach ungewöhnlichen, imposanteren Bildern und Vergleichen, um sowohl seine subjektiven Gefühle als auch die Eindrücke, welche äußere Gegenstände auf seine Subjektivität ausüben, lebendig darzustellen.   (E vii. 153)

It did not take Heine long to realize that the folk-song, far from offering an alternative to cliché, was itself artificial and hackneyed. Some months before this review he had enclosed in a letter to his friend Heinrich Straube a poem, later published in *Gedichte* of 1822, which is of considerable interest:

Wenn der Frühling kommt mit dem Sonnenschein,
Dann knospen und blühen die Blümlein auf;
Wenn der Mond beginnt seinen Strahlenlauf,
Dann schwimmen die Sternlein hintendrein;
Wenn der Sänger zwei süße Äuglein sieht,
Dann quellen ihm Lieder aus tiefem Gemüt;
Doch Lieder und Sterne und Blümelein,
Und Äuglein und Mondglanz und Sonnenschein,
Wie sehr das Zeug auch gefällt,
So macht's doch noch lang' keine Welt.   (E i. 55)

The poem falls into two distinct though related parts, the first ending significantly with 'Gemüt', the second beginning with 'Doch' and revealing the true nature of the poetic frame of mind. The initial section presents us with a list of all the ingredients used in the folk-song recipe; the second shows how insipid they are. They may be superficially pleasing but they have little to do with reality. We are already prepared for this rejection of the outworn images of the *Kunstlied*, however, by the deliberately contrived structure of the preceding lines, in which the repeated 'wenn/dann' construction demonstrates the purely mechanical nature of the all-too-familiar song.[18]

The correspondence between reality and art, between experience and the image, has been lost. This was still clearer in the original version, where the last lines read:

> Wie sehr das Zeug auch gefällt,
> Ist es doch noch lang nicht die Welt. (*Br* i. 26)

The letter then continues to bring out the gap between the world of the poet and the world of business and money. The altered line makes the application of the poem's sentiments more far-reaching: it now suggests that such images cannot make up a self-sufficient poetic world. Reality dismisses the world of the song as dreams vanish when we awake.[19] And so, far from the modern poet's songs being able to recreate the longed-for simplicity of mind that Heine admired in more primitive peoples and in certain exceptional individuals of his own day like Goethe and Napoleon, these songs are rendered meaningless by the existence of modern unpoetic reality.

The situation is, however, still more critical. In the first place the date of the poem, 5 February 1821, shows that Heine already sensed the futility of his experiment with the song *before* he had written his main song cycles. Furthermore, a comparison with a poem by Müller that had appeared three months before in his *Siebenundsiebzig Gedichte*[20] reveals that Heine's work might well

[18] Cf. Walther Killy, ' "Mein Pferd für'n gutes Bild." Heine und Geibel', in *Wandlungen des lyrischen Bildes* (2nd edn.), Göttingen, 1958, pp. 94–115; Susanne Teichgräber, *Bild und Komposition in Heinrich Heines 'Buch der Lieder'*, Diss., Freiburg, 1964, esp. p. 24.

[19] The central structural motif of the early '*Traumbilder*' had been the passage from dream vision back to life and daylight. See in this context Walther Killy, 'Nachwort' to *Buch der Lieder*, Frankfurt a. M., 1961, p. 185.

[20] p. 12.

be a parody of Müller's *Kunstlied*, despite the words of praise he
directed to him personally five years later. And certainly Straube,
as editor of the poetic journal *Die Wünschelrute*, in which Müller
had already published,[21] would have been the first to understand
such a hidden reference. 'Thränenregen' in the *Schöne Müllerin*
cycle opens:

> Wir saßen so traulich beisammen
> Im kühlen Erlendach,
> Wir schauten so traulich zusammen
> Hinab in den rieselnden Bach.

> Der Mond war auch gekommen,
> Die Sternlein hinterdrein,
> Und schauten so traulich zusammen
> In den silbernen Spiegel hinein.

> Ich sah nach keinem Monde,
> Nach keinem Sternenschein,
> Ich schaute nach ihrem Bilde,
> Nach ihren Augen allein.

> Und sahe sie nicken und blicken
> Herauf aus dem seligen Bach,
> Die Blümlein am Ufer, die blauen,
> Sie nickten und blickten ihr nach.

We can now see the comic echo in Heine's lines with their
'little' stars, flowers, and eyes, and why these stars should come
'floating along behind' the moon.[22] And where in Müller's poem
the boy weeps and his tears fall into the stream, in Heine's work
the tears reappear as songs welling up in the poet's imagination.
We are left with a mere accumulation of folk-song motifs and
images. Indeed Heine's parody may have been suggested by the
tone of self-mockery in which 'Thränenregen' itself seems to end.
The last stanzas read:

> Und in den Bach versunken
> Der ganze Himmel schien
> Und wollte mich mit hinunter
> In seine Tiefe ziehn.

[21] 'Auszug', 'Auf der Landstraße', ibid., pp. 32 f.
[22] Cf. Nollen's list of parallel passages, op. cit., pp. 261 f., where Müller's
poem and Heine's 'Wahrhaftig', lines 3–4, are placed side by side without
comment.

Und über den Wolken und Sternen,
Da rieselte munter der Bach
Und rief mit Singen und Klingen:
'Geselle, Geselle, mir nach!'

Da gingen die Augen mir über,
Da ward es im Spiegel so kraus;
Sie sprach: 'Es kommt ein Regen,
Ade, ich geh nach Haus.'

In the context of the cycle this ironic ending adumbrates the
miller's suicide by drowning and makes his blind love for the girl,
to whom he believes the stream has benevolently guided him,
seem a cruel deception. Read in isolation the close of the poem
seems deliberately frivolous and to be related to Heine's *Stimmungsbrechung* technique, a technique that already begins to
emerge in the second section of 'Wahrhaftig'. To what extent was
Müller aware of his folk-poem as a flimsy fiction? A number of his
poems are distinctly humorous, but their bantering tone is usually
closer to the humour of the folk-song proper than to Heine's
parodies. 'Große Wanderschaft', for example, ends:

Heute blond und morgen braun,
Ist mein Schätzchen anzuschauen,
Wandern, wandern!
Kalt und warm, und schlicht und kraus,
Bienenschwarm und Schneckenhaus,
Wandern, wandern!
Heute hab' ich dies Lied erdacht,
Morgen wird es ausgelacht,
Wandern, wandern![23]

'Thränenregen' seems to be of a different order and our suspicions
are confirmed when we read the prologue and epilogue in which
Müller enclosed *Die schöne Müllerin*. The cycle had resulted from
a series of home entertainments in which Müller and some friends
took part, each performing an appropriate role. Müller's part was,
one imagines, determined by his surname.[24] In the prologue the
'poet' steps forward to introduce his work:

Ich lad' euch, schöne Damen, kluge Herren,
Und die ihr hört und schaut was Gutes gern,

[23] *Gedichte*, p. 32.   [24] Ibid., pp. 450 f.

Zu einem funkelnagelneuen Spiel
Im allerfunkelnagelneusten Styl;
Schlicht ausgedrechselt, kunstlos zugestutzt,
Mit edler deutscher Roheit aufgeputzt,
Keck wie ein Bursch im Stadtsoldatenstrauß,
Dazu wohl auch ein wenig fromm für's Haus:
Das mag genug mir zur Empfehlung sein,
Wem die behagt, der trete nur herein.[25]

For a moment Müller has dropped the mask and we, the audience,
are shown the essential theatricality that lies behind the revival of
the artless by the sophisticated.[26] A few lines later we hear:

Auch ist dafür die Szene reich geziert,
Mit grünem Sammet unten tapeziert,
Der ist mit tausend Blumen bunt gestickt,
Und Weg und Steg darüber ausgedrückt.
Die Sonne strahlt von oben hell herein
Und bricht in Thau und Thränen ihren Schein,
Und auch der Mond blickt aus der Wolken Flor
Schwermütig, wie's die Mode will, hervor.

Here surely is the material that prompted Heine's 'Wahrhaftig',
and following Müller's example, in the *Buch der Lieder* Heine
removed the poem from among the *Sonette und vermischte Gedichte*
and placed it at the end of the song and ballad sections. This
confirms his practice of completing his cycles with poems that
refer not only to his beloved but to the cycle or the poems as such,
implying that the irony we find in his work is not only the expression of bitter disappointment in love but should be understood on
another level as the ironic questioning of the song medium itself.[27]

Both Heine and Müller found themselves having to put on
a show of *naïveté* in their folk-songs which neither they nor their
readers possessed. Though, as we have seen, Heine must have
recognized this in Müller, he preferred not to pursue the point.
Instead he told him in the letter of 1826 that the real difference
between their works was that his own songs were only folk-like in

[25] Ibid., p. 3.
[26] A. Cottrell's failure to observe Müller's fundamental sophistication and
conscious manipulation of naïve poetic statements vitiates the picture he presents
of the poet in *Wilhelm Müller's Lyrical Song-Cycles. Interpretations and Texts*,
Chapel Hill, 1970.
[27] Cf. 'Die alten, bösen Lieder', *Lyrisches Intermezzo* 65, E i. 92, and the
'Büchlein' referred to in *Die Heimkehr* 88, ibid., p. 134.

their form while their content was society life, 'der Inhalt gehört der convenzionellen Gesellschaft'.[28] Müller in contrast, he claimed, had succeeded in reproducing the inner simplicity of song without repeating its external forms. Heine was, then, fully aware that his method for capturing the innocence of the genuine folk product, the compression of folk-song motifs and images to a new level of concision and clarity, was only a method. It was the creation of a highly self-conscious poet, who still sought to express his own feelings and experience beneath the folk costume. And the letter to Müller makes it clear that this realization was the immediate reason for Heine abandoning the song and turning to prose: 'Mit mir selbst, wie gesagt, steht es schlecht und hat es als Liederdichter wohl ein Ende, und das mögen Sie selbst fühlen. Die Prosa nimmt mich auf in ihre weiten Arme . . .' (*Br* iii. 270). His search for a solution to the sick age in which he felt he lived was carrying him to new spheres of activity.

A full analysis of the song in the *Buch der Lieder* would now have to establish the various ways in which Heine tried both to resuscitate the folk-song and to parody it in the *Kunstlied*, to find new unworn and exotic imagery, and to satirize the Philistines who in fact read these songs of love.[29] It would draw attention to a song like 'Der Tod, das ist die kühle Nacht' (*Die Heimkehr* 87) as a remarkable example of how Heine still managed to rescue a genuine and unbroken feeling of artless simplicity from highly organized and already over-familiar material. It would run through the gamut of *Stimmungsbrechungen* in which the true nature of his beloved is revealed, ranging from the frequent theme of the cold heart beneath the beautiful and innocent appearance to the mischievous suggestion that she is really a lady of professionally easy virtue (*Die Heimkehr* 70). It would trace the parody of the typical figures and language of song which underlies these disruptions of mood on another level, making these poems ultimately songs about song and not just about love. But such a task would go well beyond the scope of this study.[30] What remains to be stressed

---

[28] *Br* i. 270.
[29] Cf. the particularly effective 'Sie saßen und tranken am Teetisch', E i. 84 f.
[30] Valuable in this respect is the work by Killy and Teichgräber, and S. S. Prawer's *Heine: Buch der Lieder*, which provides an excellent account of how Heine poked fun both at himself and at his readers—see especially chs. 2, 6–8.

is that Heine's experiment with the song did not only fail because
it was an art form that was already played out by Heine's time, as
has been argued.[31] His suspicion and parody of the *Kunstlied*
struck at one of the dearest ambitions of the Romantic movement,
an ambition which he himself had shared, namely that it was
possible for the trend towards ever greater cultural refinement in
Germany with its subsequent loss of spontaneity and immediacy
of feeling to be reversed. Especially the second generation of
Romantics had hoped to achieve this by reviving a dying folk-
culture:

Kunstpoesie, das heißt die mit Bewußtsein und Absicht gedichtete, ist
in ihrer Idee ebenso vortrefflich als Natur- und Nationalpoesie, denn
wenn sie echt ist, setzt sie diese nur fort, das heißt, wo diese untergeht
und sich nicht mehr erzeugt, da bildet sie zum Beispiel durch Belesen-
heit erworbenen Stoff in dem Geist der Nation mit all dem, was ihr
eigenthümlich ist, um, damit es einheimisch werden kann.[32]

It was in this belief that Arnim and Brentano, and Arnim in
particular, had felt little or no compunction about altering, re-
writing, and even adding to the poems they published in the
Wunderhorn.[33] They realized that if they were to capture the
imagination of a modern public they would have to make the archaic, awkward, and obscure appeal. Heine clearly did not know
of their activities. Ironically the very strophe he selects in *Die
romantische Schule* to illustrate the anonymity of the folk-song:

> Wer hat das schöne Liedel erdacht?
> Es haben's drei Gäns' übers Wasser gebracht,
> Zwei graue und eine weiße.

was in fact Arnim's own creation.[34] On the other hand his interpretation of Müller's poems as genuine folk-songs was wishful
thinking—or self-deception—for, as we have seen, it was probably
Müller's own poetry which first suggested to him the fiction on

[31] Cf. Killy, works cited.
[32] Wilhelm Grimm, 'Über die Entstehung der altdeutschen Poesie und ihr
Verhältnis zu der nordischen', in *Kleinere Schriften*, ed. Gustav Hinrichs,
Berlin and Gütersloh, 1881–7, iv. 114 f.
[33] Cf. Karl Bode, *Die Bearbeitung der 'Vorlagen in Des Knaben Wunderhorn'*
(Palaestra 76), Berlin, 1909, esp. pp. 296 ff. and 733 ff. Bode concludes that
the *Wunderhorn* is less a document that bears the authentic stamp of folk-
culture than Arnim's personal achievement. Brentano was far more cautious.
[34] Cf. ibid., pp. 730 f.

which the modern *Kunstlied* rests. His apparently unshaken admiration of Müller shows how he was divided between an uncritical longing for artlessness and the knowledge that this was a prize not to be won by conscious intention. His own bitter experience had proved that the *Kunstlied* was less naïve than synthetic: 'Die Kunstpoeten wollen diese Naturerzeugnisse nachahmen, in derselben Weise, wie man künstliche Mineralwässer verfertigt. Aber wenn sie auch durch chemischen Prozeß die Bestandteile ermittelt, so entgeht ihnen doch die Hauptsache, die unzersetzbare sympathetische Naturkraft.' (*Die romantische Schule*, E v. 311.) Other poets had less conscience and produced what their age demanded. The genuine folk-song to which Heine contrasted such concoctions was 'Zu Straßburg auf der Schanz'. It was highly popular in Heine's day, its author was Brentano, and it has been called the most notorious forgery of the entire *Wunderhorn*.[35]

B. *Ballad, folklore, legend*

Heine's enthusiasm for what he believed to be original folk-song was not dampened by the failure of would-be folk-poets to create a new unreflective culture. In later years he continued to be fascinated by folk literature and to interpret its significance in social, political, and religious terms. If the modern poet could not rejuvenate German culture and thus Germany itself, the slumbering forces of a German nation could still be heard in the legends and ballads of the people.

One of the most attractive characteristics of the folk-song for Heine was its anonymity. It was not the creation of a particular individual but grew round the successive improvisations of a whole series of unknown singers. It was in this sense that Heine could regard it as the product and voice of the German people.[36] A major factor in the crisis of the *Kunstlied* that Heine recognized and explored was the inevitable discrepancy between the modern poet and this anonymous or collective first person of the folk-song, a discrepancy that I have indicated in the case of *Lyrisches Intermezzo* 2. Again Heine's difficulty lay in his historical situation.

If any one German poet can be said to have created the *Kunstlied*, it was Goethe, and Heine admired him for it. He did not

---

[35] Bode, op. cit., p. 318.   [36] Cf. E v. 311.

forgot to tell Müller in his letter of 1826 that he was his favourite
writer of songs 'apart from Goethe'.[37] In *Zur Geschichte der
Religion und Philosophie in Deutschland* his brief but poignant
description of Goethe's songs throws further light on why he
recognized in Goethe a mind that transcended modern analytical
thought, being gifted with intuitive perception and undivided
creativity. These songs, he says, are 'so zart ätherisch, so duftig
beflügelt. Ihr Franzosen könnt euch keinen Begriff davon machen,
wenn ihr die Sprache nicht kennt. Diese Goetheschen Lieder
haben einen neckischen Zauber, der unbeschreibbar. Die harmo-
nischen Verse umschlingen dein Herz wie eine zärtliche Geliebte;
das Wort umarmt dich, während der Gedanke dich küßt.'[38] But
Goethe was also the decisive influence in the emergence of the
Erlebnislyrik, and though Herder was able to publish his 'Heiden-
röslein' as a folk-song, it is *the* commonplace of German literary
criticism to point out the new and direct connection between
personal experience and its artistic expression in Goethe's early
songs. True, the poetry that he inspired had imbibed the magic
spontaneity of the folk-song, but it was a vehicle for conveying the
most subtle personal emotions and quite the opposite of a collective
creation. Müller helped himself out of this dilemma by placing his
songs in the mouths of fictitious journeymen. The equivalent to
this technique in Heine's production is the use of the ballad. In
the ballad the first person is excluded and the poem restricted to a
narration of events. Its content may be supernatural or mysterious
and indeed seem incredible to the modern sceptical reader, but all
such events are presented impassively, as if there were no question
of their not having occurred. In his brief analysis of the major
genres in the review of Smets's *Tassos Tod* Heine lists the ballad
as a transitional form between the subjective lyric and the more
objective epic and drama.[39] As a poet grows more mature, his
argument runs, he will seek progressively less personal forms of
expression, and certainly ballads rank among the finest achievements of Heine's early production just because he can avoid a
problematic relationship with the medium. In a work like 'Belsat-
zar', for example, his ability to condense material and to shape it
with a dramatic intensity lacking in the original finds an outlet
denied to him in the song proper. The story of Belshazzar's feast

[37] *Br* i. 270.   [38] E iv. 274.
[39] E vii. 155, where, as in *Junge Leiden*, he terms the ballad 'Romanze'.

in Daniel 5 is essentially moralistic in tone and hinges on Daniel's interpretation of the letters that appear on the wall. The king's days are numbered because his way of life has been displeasing to Jehovah. After the prophet's lengthy admonitions it seems almost incidental that Belshazzar's enemies should overrun his country and that he should die that night. Heine's ballad builds up with mounting tension from a panoramic view of Babylon at midnight to Belshazzar's frenzied outburst of blasphemy, and then moves with unrelenting rapidity to his death at the hands of his own retainers. Daniel does not even appear. In short, this, like so many *Kunstlieder*, is a conscious 'improvement' on an early, relatively unsophisticated piece of literature, but because the narrative form provides distance we do not experience any clash between subject-matter and presentation. Since the narrator is hidden, the question of the ballad's religious significance is not raised: we simply read it as a moving story. And so in the ballad Heine can use his sense of irony as a powerful device within the narrative itself and not as a means to arouse reflection about the poem as a poem. The violent turn taken by Belshazzar's fate is but one example of this type of irony. Equally ironic is the effect of Donna Clara's invocation of God in the midst of her wild dance with Don Ramiro in the ballad of that name. As the vision vanishes our terrible suspicions are confirmed: the bride has been dancing not with her former suitor but with his ghost. Whether we are to accept her vision as a real experience or as the figment of her guilty conscience is left entirely open. The ballad form does not require that we *should* decide and it is in this capacity to depict the inner life of non-sceptical, 'innocent' ages and layers of society in concrete form that it comes closest to Heine's ideal of the *Volkslied*. When Heine originally published 'Die Wallfahrt nach Kevlaar' in 1822 he accompanied it with a note explaining that he had himself heard the story of miracle healings performed by the Virgin at Kevlaar when he was a young boy living in Düsseldorf. A friend, who had suffered an unhappy love affair, told him he would take a wax heart to the Virgin to be healed. Later Heine saw him, pale and wan, with his mother in the procession of pilgrims who were making their way to Kevlaar and singing the well-known song with its refrain 'Gelobt sey'st du, Maria!'[40] Heine has, of course, sharpened the material with the introduction of the boy's mysterious—and for the modern

[40] E i. 527 f.

reader ambiguous—death. But the ballad does not read as a covert polemic against Christianity. It remains a powerful depiction of the simple and unshaken faith of Rhineland folk.

It is in this form of popular legend and superstition that Heine maintains his interest in folk culture after the crisis in the *Kunstlyrik* of the *Buch der Lieder*. This is nowhere more apparent than in the work he entirely devoted to German folklore, *Elementargeister*. In December 1835 the German Federal Diet had decreed a ban on the further publication and distribution of works by a group of authors it called 'Junges Deutschland', which included Heine.[41] It might therefore be assumed that Heine's folklore book, which first appeared in Germany in 1837, when the total ban had been relaxed, was a mere triviality with which Heine hoped to regain access to the German market. Even in his correspondence he suggests to his German publisher, Campe, that this new section of the *Salon* might be entitled 'Das stille Buch' or 'Das Mährchen'.[42] The first part of the work had already been published in French, however, in 1835 before the decree. Furthermore it forms a logical sequel to *Zur Geschichte der Religion und Philosophie in Deutschland* of 1834, in which Heine's opposition to Christianity, and particularly to the Roman Church, was at its most articulate. The first book of this work had described how Christianity failed to stamp out the pantheist religion of heathen Germany and was compelled to accept the existence of its gods in the imagination of the populace. To break their influence it reinterpreted them as devils and evil spirits.[43] But knowledge of the former gods was still preserved in popular tales and legends. What had been religious faith might have degenerated into superstition but it survived.

Why was Heine so concerned with this earlier pantheist religion of Germany? He explains that because Christian spiritualism, a direct descendant from Judaism, neglected the body and material things, it was content to deprecate political absolutism in words alone. This proved ineffectual, however, and when the priesthood saw the slavery of its flock beneath the rule of Caesar and of money it both accepted the need for compromise and even allied itself with the forces of oppression.[44] A religion, on the contrary,

---

[41] The ban on Young Germany (Gutzkow, Laube, Wienbarg, and Mundt) had already been passed on 14 Nov. 1835. It was expressly extended to Heine on 10–11 Dec. Cf. H. H. Houben, *Verbotene Literatur*, cited above, pp. 391, 405, 408, etc. Elster reproduces the decree, vii. 545 f.

[42] *Br* ii. 119 (Mar. 1836).   [43] E iv. 173 f.   [44] Ibid., pp. 220 f.

whose gods inhabit the earth and whose values are embodied in the physical world, cannot bend to the yoke of political despotism. Slavery would be the very denial of its *raison d'être*. Thus the re-emergence of the former German national religion would be a phenomenon of revolutionary significance. Later in the treatise Heine surveys the affinities between this religion and the philosophies of Spinoza and the young Schelling. Goethe is depicted as the pantheist of contemporary literature. In these men we find in modern guise the ancient German tradition, which refuses to be crushed by the forces of spiritualism, and it is not hard to see in this interpretation of German religious and philosophical history a development of views expressed in the early *Reisebilder*. There is a close relationship between the *Anschauungsleben* of the Harz miners with its animation of the inanimate in the fairy-tale and the pantheistic worship of divine forces in nature. And again, Goethe stands out as one of those exceptional men who still possess that wholeness of perception which in earlier, happier ages had been the property of all men.

In the third and last book of the work Heine turns from history to prophecy. Seeing in the development of German philosophy since Kant an intellectual equivalent of the political upheaval caused by the French Revolution, he conjures up a vision of the day when Germany will be convulsed by a revolution in which the ancient slumbering forces of pantheism that Christianity has failed to extinguish will reawake and together with the neo-Kantians, Fichtians, and their brethren the nature philosophers, will erupt in a horrifying apocalypse: 'Die alten steinernen Götter erheben sich dann aus dem verschollenen Schutt und reiben sich den tausendjährigen Staub aus den Augen, und Thor mit dem Riesenhammer springt endlich empor und zerschlägt die gotischen Dome.' (E iv. 294.) The essential difference between this theory of revolution and that of the French Revolution, Heine takes pains to point out,[45] is that its principles are not derived from a shallow utilitarianism but from a far deeper source, from the very nature of the German people. In short Heine claims an *organic* origin for the future German revolution, an origin that renders its coming inevitable and its course inexorable.

Thus to trace the vestiges of this earlier German religion that live on in folk legend is to provide evidence of latent revolutionary

[45] E iv. 211.

forces and anything but non-political. Of course, from the point of view of avoiding censorship such an approach was ideal, but this cannot be regarded as the primary reason for Heine's interest in folklore. The opening lines of *Elementargeister*, written before the Bundestag resolution, take up this thread quite plainly, plainly that is if we are familiar with the preceding part of the *Salon*:

— Wie man behauptet, gibt es greise Menschen in Westfalen, die noch immer wissen, wo die alten Götterbilder verborgen liegen; auf ihrem Sterbebette sagen sie es dem jüngsten Enkel, und der trägt dann das teure Geheimnis in dem verschwiegenen Sachsenherzen. In Westfalen, dem ehemaligen Sachsen, ist nicht alles tot, was begraben ist. Wenn man dort durch die alten Eichenhaine wandelt, hört man noch die Stimmen der Vorzeit, da hört man noch den Nachhall jener tiefsinnigen Zaubersprüche, worin mehr Lebensfülle quillt als in der ganzen Litteratur der Mark Brandenburg. Eine geheimnisvolle Ehrfurcht durchschauerte meine Seele, als ich einst, diese Waldungen durchwandernd, bei der uralten Siegburg vorbeikam. 'Hier', sagte mein Wegweiser, 'hier wohnte einst König Wittekind', und er seufzte tief. Es war ein schlichter Holzhauer, und er trug ein großes Beil.

Ich bin überzeugt, dieser Mann, wenn es drauf ankömmt, schlägt sich noch heute für König Wittekind; und wehe dem Schädel, worauf sein Beil fällt!   (E iv. 381)

Heine's modified view of primitive or non-reflective cultures as an expression less of wholeness and simplicity than of a state of political oppression was not entirely new. It had, of course, been foreshadowed in the passages on the servitude of the miners and fisher-folk in *Die Harzreise* and *Die Nordsee* III. Another striking variant of the same theme had occurred in the Italian *Reisebilder*, in which Heine presents the music of the *opera buffa* and *commedia dell'arte* farces as a secret demonstration of the Italian people's political bondage and suffering. Here, too, a rudimentary form of expression also serves to defeat the scrutiny of the censors. The esoteric call for liberation escapes the ears of the exoteric guards.[46] The esoteric voice that speaks through folk legend is that of pantheism, and for Heine in the 1830s the theme of demonization, the transformation of the gods of the Greeks and of the Ancient Germans into devils, constitutes *the* principal component of folk culture.

---

[46] E iii. 251. The terms 'esoteric' and 'exoteric' were later adopted by Marx in his thesis and applied to Hegel in the spirit of *Zur Geschichte der Religion und Philosophie in Deutschland*. Cf. Reeves, 'Heine and the Young Marx', *Oxford German Studies*, 7 (1972–3), 53 ff.

As usual Heine did not collect his own source material. He found it above all in the collections of the Brothers Grimm[47] and in a work otherwise forgotten today, Friedrich von Dobeneck's *Des deutschen Mittelalters Volksglauben und Heroensagen*.[48] It is in Dobeneck that we find a description of how Charlemagne tried in vain to stamp out paganism in Saxony and of the people's wild dances and rites in the Harz mountains at night when they worshipped and sacrificed to their gods once more.[49] Alongside this account there is much that was to reappear in Heine's work—whole chapters on the spirits of the elements, the stories of Ogier the Dane and Fata Morgana, of Diana and the wild hunt, details of the early Faust chapbooks, and the legend of Kaiser Friedrich's vigil in the Kyffhäuser mountain. Heine does more than reproduce, however. He uses Dobeneck's simple narrations to exemplify his theory of pandemonism. Let us take the tale of the Basle nightingale, with which Heine makes his first striking illustration of Christianity's hostility towards beauty and the senses in *Zur Geschichte*. In Dobeneck's version the scholars (not priests as in Heine) are fearful of the bird's wonderful song and exorcize the wretched creature, in which is the soul of a damned man, awaiting trial on Judgement Day. Later the scholars die and the tale demonstrates the injuriousness of the spirits of the air. Heine introduces the scholastic discussion, makes the bird defiant, intensifies the conflict with Christianity, and turns the death of the priests into the revenge of suppressed beauty and sensuality on asceticism.[50]

When Heine comes to the elemental spirits with tales of dwarfs or gnomes from the earth, elves from the air, nixies from water and salamanders, the spirits of fire, he points to their origins in the gods of stones, trees, and rivers that the Ancient Germanic tribes worshipped. One rapidly gains the impression, however, that Heine's interest has been aroused merely by the sometimes comic, sometimes purely bizarre quality of the legends. Unfortunately we still read the German version of the section, which was specially prepared for the censor. The original French version leaves no doubt that these curious tales are intended as part of his survey of

[47] *Deutsche Sagen*, Berlin, 1816–18, and Wilhelm Grimm, *Altdänische Heldenlieder, Balladen und Märchen*, Heidelberg, 1811.
[48] Berlin, 1815.   [49] Op. cit., pp. 60 f. and 93.
[50] Heine: iv. 172 f. Dobeneck: op. cit., pp. 102 f.

dormant revolutionary forces. This version of the essay closes with a question. Who will finally liberate Germany from the oppression and influence of the Middle Ages? Who will be 'le dieu de la révolution'? Heine's provisional answer refers to another figure of legend, Barbarossa, who is said to be sleeping in the Kyffhäuser for a thousand years until the time comes for him to emerge in triumph, though not to claim the Holy Sepulchre as in Dobeneck's version. In Heine, he will create a new kingdom, a kingdom not unlike Granada in *Almansor*:

Ce n'est pas un tombeau, la froide couche d'un mort, mais une brillante demeure pour les vivans que veut conquérir le vieux Barbe-rousse, un chaud royaume de lumière et de plaisir où il puisse régner joyeusement, tenant dans sa main le sceptre divinatoire de la liberté, et portant sur sa tête la couronne impériale sans croix.   (E iv. 618)

This sets, or rather should set, the tone for the entire work, which continues in the second section with the theme of the exile of the Greek gods from Olympus and their new lowly existence as devils who can only dance their frenzied bacchanalia and hunt with Diana at midnight in ghostly form. It is, as Sandor shows in his detailed account,[51] a central theme in Heine's production and can be found as early as 1823 in 'Götterdämmerung' and as late as his ballet scenario *Die Göttin Diana* published in 1854. Sandor's study makes it unnecessary to render a full account of the reappearance of these now familiar motifs in works like *Atta Troll* or *Deutschland*. One should, however, be wary of taking the motifs of the gods, their exile, and their longed-for return too literally, as if Heine really believed in the elemental spirits or actually expected Barbarossa or Venus to rule again in person. The appeal of such material was twofold: in the first place these tales corresponded closely in pattern to the tripartite theory of cultural history with which Heine had been acquainted since his days in Bonn under A. W. Schlegel. Secondly their source in popular culture made them the apparent expression of the way the people had suffered since Greek or pantheist harmony was destroyed by the rise of Christianity; they were thus independent evidence of Heine's view of history. What mattered to him was the quality of life, and the expulsion from Olympus served as a useful symbol, but only symbol, of the deterioration in this quality since Greek or Ger-

[51] Op. cit.

manic times. Heine wished that the *spirit* of Greece could emerge
again, not its gods. He called this Greek spirit Hellenism.[52]

For Heine world history is dominated by the conflict between
two antagonistic modes of civilization. The first, which is his ideal,
welcomes man's physical existence and believes that life is worth
living for its own sake. Its principal value is beauty. The second,
which stems from Judaism and incorporates Christianity, sees
man's true reality in his soul; this has constantly to fight against
and rise above his animal nature, which is a temporary, earthly
obstacle to the attainment of spiritual fulfilment in life after death.
In *Zur Geschichte der Religion und Philosophie* he termed these two
modes Sensualism and Spiritualism, taking care to point out that
they are not simple parallels to the two philosophical schools,
Materialism and Idealism.[53] Nor are they only historical and
social phenomena. True, Heine's evidence for the survival of
pantheism in folk-culture is presented in a historical framework,
from which he derives his prediction of the coming revolution in
German culture. Nevertheless, he calls both movements 'Denkweisen'[54] and the manuscript of *Zur Geschichte* provides a clearer
explanation of what he means. These forces are rooted in the very
temperament and physical constitution of the individual:

> Auch diese zwei Systeme stehen sich seit Menschengedenken ent-
> gegen! denn zu allen Zeiten giebt es Menschen von unvollkommener
> Genußfähigkeit, verkrüppelten Sinnen und zerknirschtem Fleische,
> die alle Weintrauben dieses Gottesgartens sauer finden, bei jedem
> Paradiesapfel die verlockende Schlange sehen, und im Entsagen ihren
> Triumph und im Schmerz ihre Wollust suchen. Dagegen giebt es zu
> allen Zeiten wohlgewachsene, leibesstolze Naturen, die gern das Haupt
> hoch tragen; allen Sternen und Rosen lachen sie einverständlich ent-
> gegen, sie hören gern die Melodien der Nachtigall und des Rossini, sie
> lieben das schöne Glück und das Titian'sche Fleisch, und dem kopf-
> hängerischen Gesell, dem Solches ein Ärgernis, antworten sie wie der
> Shakespeare'sche Narr: Meinst du, weil du tugendhaft bist, solle es
> keinen süßen Sekt und keine Torten auf dieser Welt geben?
>
> (E iv. 584 f.)

If this is so, then Heine's optimism that the spirit of Greece can

[52] E iv. 422 f.
[53] Ibid. 208. I cannot follow how Sandor can relate pantheism to Idealism (op.
cit., p. 55).
[54] E iv. 185, 422.

return and create a lasting civilisation seems to rest on shaky
ground, for the antagonism between these two attitudes must inevitably be permanent and not a passing historical phenomenon.
In *Ludwig Börne* of 1840 this conclusion is consciously drawn.
This essay documents the clash between two such antithetical
natures, men whom one would have expected to be kindred spirits,
co-operating to promote political freedom in Germany. Both were
emancipated Jews, both lived in exile yet were passionately involved in the fate of their homeland, both were articulate exponents of liberal thinking, and yet from the moment of Heine's arrival
in Paris a vehement sense of antipathy and hostility developed
between them. This was an experience in direct contradiction to
Heine's view of the two attitudes as the expression of particular
cultures and the product of particular historical constellations.

Elementargeister ends, appropriately in the present context, with
two ballads, or rather two versions of the same ballad about
Tannhäuser and the Mountain of Venus. The first is a reproduc-
tion of the work published in *Des Knaben Wunderhorn* but which
Heine claims to have come across previously in the seventeenth-
century treatise *Mons Veneris* by Heinrich Kornmann.[55] Again
Heine recognizes that essential spirit of simplicity which so fascinated him in folk literature: 'Es war mir, als hätte ich in einem
dumpfen Bergschacht plötzlich eine große Goldader entdeckt, und
die stolzeinfachen, urkräftigen Worte strahlten mir so blank ent-
gegen, daß mein Herz fast geblendet wurde von dem unerwarte-
ten Glanz.' (E iv. 432.) Furthermore, its theme is the familiar
conflict between erotic love and Christian morality. It tells of
Tannhäuser's attempt to escape from the life of permanent sin and
sensuality in which he is ensnared in Venus's mountain refuge, of
his pilgrimage to the Pope to ask for absolution, and of the latter's
outright denunciation of his life as devilish. The Pope declares
there is no more possibility of Tannhäuser being absolved than of
the papal sceptre bursting into leaf. Tannhäuser returns to the
mountain to await Judgement Day and it is in vain that the Pope's
emissaries search for him after the sceptre has miraculously
burgeoned. The second version, for which Heine also claims
'eine gewisse Wahrheit des Gefühls', is, of course, of his own
authorship and as his first major innovation in verse since the
North Sea cycles of 1825-6 it marks a turning-point in his poetic

---

[55] Frankfurt a. M., 1614.

career.[56] Unlike the earlier ballads that I have discussed it is not an attempt to reproduce the anonymous distance of the folk ballad or the beliefs and feelings of simple peasants. Tannhäuser is weary of Venus. Sated with pleasure this hedonist seeks different sensations, the sensations afforded by pain and asceticism. In Rome he waxes lyrical over his love for Venus, the delights of her eyes and her lips, and the rushing torrent of his passion. This, he tells the Pope unconvincingly, is the 'Höllenqual' to which he is condemned. The Pope refuses Tannhäuser absolution and the knight returns to the mountain after a rapid tour of Germany. This provides the opportunity for a series of satirical sallies, in which Heine pillories the thirty-six 'kings' of Germany, the Swabian school of poets, life in Weimar with Eckermann and without Goethe, and more. The value of the journey motif to furnish material for a satirical survey of a country, its customs, foibles, and political developments (or rather lack thereof) had, of course, been plain to Heine since the *Reisebilder* and before that the *Briefe aus Berlin* of 1822. Here it finds a new and particularly effective mode of employment, for what is lost of the breadth of prose satire is gained in the bite of the rapid metre, concentrated four-line stanzas, and the closely knit rhyme scheme (*abcb*), all of which Heine found in the original ballad and was to carry over intact into *Deutschland*.

'Und als ich auf dem Sankt Gotthard stand,
Da hört' ich Deutschland schnarchen,
Es schlief da unten in sanfter Hut
Von sechsunddreißig Monarchen.

'In Schwaben besah ich die Dichterschul'
Doch thut's der Mühe nicht lohnen;
Hast du den größten von ihnen besucht,
Gern wirst du die kleinen verschonen.

'Zu Frankfurt kam ich am Schabbes an
Und aß dort Schalet und Klöse;
Ihr habt die beste Religion,
Auch lieb' ich das Gänsegekröse . . .' (E iv. 437 f.)

---

[56] In the meantime he had written *Neuer Frühling* for Albert Methfessel and a number of songs of 'niedere Minne' ('Verschiedene' in *Neue Gedichte*), to which I shall return below. For a valuable account of these years cf. Prawer, *Heine, Tragic Satirist*, pp. 12–46. Laura Hofrichter's depiction of Heine's poetic experiments and development is also interesting in this context, cf. *Heinrich Heine*, pp. 80 ff.

But the satire of the poem is not confined to Heine's favourite religious and political targets. Equally the narrator pokes fun at life in the Venusberg. Tannhäuser's satiety is one aspect of this: another is the transformation Venus has undergone on his return. Like the gods of the North Sea poems[57] she now appears as a middle-class housewife and rather the worse for wear. As she awakes her nose starts bleeding and when Tannhäuser goes to bed straight away without a word she brings him some soup, washes his feet, and combs his hair. Like the stranger on the beach in 'Die Nacht am Strande' he turns out to be the opposite of a hero: his life with Venus, now literally 'Frau Venus, seine schöne Frau', is neither passionate nor infernal. It is the everyday monotony of bourgeois life, and his decision to leave seems in retrospect the result of a matrimonial squabble. Thus both modes of life, the sensual and the spiritual, are caricatured. Was perhaps Heine's intention to direct his irony at the ballad form itself, using the second poem as a parody of the first in the same way as he parodied and thus undermined the *Kunstlied* in the *Buch der Lieder*? Does *Tannhäuser* mark the reopening of an earlier poetic struggle? Rather the opposite is true. Heine has at last come to terms with the difference between the modern poet and the anonymous creators of the genuine folk-song. He now uses their external techniques unashamedly for his own purposes without wishing to detract from the value of the original in any way.[58] In Heine's view both ballads must have had their source in the same fundamental situation, the Christian subjection of body to mind. The negative light in which Tannhäuser and Venus appear in the second is not

---

[57] Cf. 'Sonnenuntergang', 'Poseidon', 'Untergang der Sonne'.

[58] The mature Heine's awareness of the essential differences in the approach of the two writers, medieval and modern, is beautifully formulated in the 1855 French version of this section of *Elementargeister* (here his own poem was printed first): 'En effet, en lisant en même temps ces deux versions, on voit combien chez l'ancien poëte prédomine la foi antique, tandis que chez le poëte moderne, né au commencement du XIXᵉ siècle, se révèle le scepticisme de son époque; l'on voit combien ce dernier, qui n'est dompté par aucune autorité, donne un libre essor à sa fantaisie, et n'a en chantant aucun autre but que de bien exprimer dans ses vers des sentiments purement humains. Le vieux poëte, au contraire, reste sous le joug de l'autorité cléricale; il a un but didactique, il veut illustrer un dogme religieux, il prêche la vertu de la charité, et le dernier mot de son poëme, c'est de démontrer l'efficacité du repentir pour la rémission de tout péché; le pape lui-même est blâmé pour avoir oublié cette haute vérité chrétienne, et par le bâton desséché qui verdit entre ses mains, il reconnaît, mais trop tard, l'incommensurable profondeur de la miséricorde divine.' (E iv. 621)

entirely surprising. Heine had never claimed to subscribe to a life
in which the senses ruled *over* the spirit. Sensualism meant that
attitude which seeks to harmonize the senses with the spirit, not to
crush it.[59] A life in which the senses held tyrannical sway would
not therefore be so very different from the soulless and material-
istic life of the Philistine.

The demonization of the gods does not exhaust the range of
poetic and symbolical material that Heine found in folklore and
folk literature to bear out his dualistic view of world history and of
human nature. While a long catalogue of further examples could
only be tedious, one last work cannot be neglected and that is
Heine's ballet *Der Doctor Faust*. Heine had long been fascinated
by the Faust theme. It appears in rudimentary form in the
Traumbilder, where in no. 6 the poet sells his soul to the devil, who
appears in the guise of his beloved. In 1820 he also translated
the first scene from Byron's *Manfred*, which depicts the hero, like
Faust, conjuring up spirits. Manfred demands oblivion of them,
not power or any of the worldly things they offer. He is not moved
until one evil spirit appears in the form of a beautiful woman only
to vanish as the enamoured Manfred tries to embrace her.[60] This
association of the devil with womanhood becomes a central feature
of Heine's own version of *Faust*. It is clearly related to the theme
of the demonic and catastrophic attraction of beauty which occurs
repeatedly in Heine's work. It is the obverse side to the Christian
demonization of Venus and lurks over him like some Spiritualist
spectre that he cannot himself exorcize. The Lorelei and the
sphinx who tears the poet to pieces in the preface to the *Buch
der Lieder* of 1839 express the pitiless and destructive power that
passion can exert, while Tannhäuser's sufferings result from a
curious combination of satiety and—if one accepts his appeal to
the Pope at its face value—of helpless enslavement to the goddess
of love herself. Accounts from the early 1820s suggest that Heine
was already toying with the idea of writing his own Faust,[61] and
his brother even claims that he ventured to tell Goethe of this in his
brief and cool meeting with the grand old man in Weimar.[62] Whatever his intentions, he did not at that time produce such a work.
When he comes to discuss *Faust* in *Die romantische Schule* his

---

[59] Cf. E iv. 208 (*Zur Geschichte der Religion und Philosophie*).
[60] E ii. 223–31.   [61] Cf. Houben, *Gespräche*, pp. 74 ff.
[62] Ibid., p. 91.

Interpretation closely fits the pattern that one expects. In his
unquenchable desire for erotic satisfaction Faust symbolizes the
entire German people at the time of the Reformation; a creative
error on Heine's part completes the picture of the Renaissance
man throwing off the shackles of clerical authority, for he identifies Faust with Fust, Gutenberg's creditor. At this point in the
argument Heine's social and political hopes become indissolubly
fused with his interpretation of legend and folk culture:

> Es ist in der That sehr bedeutsam, daß zur Zeit, wo nach der Volks-
> meinung der Faust gelebt hat, eben die Reformation beginnt, und daß
> er selber die Kunst erfunden haben soll, die dem Wissen einen Sieg
> über den Glauben verschafft, nämlich die Buchdruckerei, eine Kunst,
> die uns aber auch die katholische Gemütsruhe geraubt und uns in
> Zweifel und Revolutionen gestürzt — ein anderer als ich würde sagen,
> endlich in die Gewalt des Teufels geliefert hat.

Here the censor cut the text off and deleted some twenty lines.
Elster has restored the original from the Paris German edition of
1833 and from the manuscript:

> Aber nein, das Wissen, die Erkenntnis der Dinge durch die Vernunft,
> die Wissenschaft, gibt uns endlich die Genüsse, um die uns der Glaube,
> das katholische Christentum, so lange geprellt hat; wir erkennen, daß
> die Menschen nicht bloß zu einer himmlischen, sondern auch zu einer
> irdischen Gleichheit berufen sind; die politische Brüderschaft, die uns
> von der Philosophie gepredigt wird, ist uns wohlthätiger als die rein
> geistige Brüderschaft, wozu uns das Christentum verholfen; und das
> Wissen wird Wort, und das Wort wird That, und wir können noch bei
> Lebzeiten auf dieser Erde selig werden; — wenn wir dann noch oben-
> drein der himmlischen Seligkeit, die uns das Christentum so bestimmt
> verspricht, nach dem Tode teilhaftig werden, so soll uns das sehr lieb
> sein. (E v. 260 f.)

And once again Heine commends Goethe's feeling for what is
immediate and yet profound, for his 'unbewußten Tiefsinn' or in
short his genius.

His ballet scenario of 1846[63] is of simple construction. In the
first act Faust summons the spirits, and the devil, assuming the
form of a female, succeeds in tempting him to commit his soul
by showing him the image of an exceedingly beautiful woman, the
duchess. In the second act Faust and Mephistophela arrive at the

---

[63] For dates and biographical details cf. Gerhard Weiß, 'Die Entstehung von
Heines "Doktor Faust"', *Heine-Jahrbuch 1966*, pp. 41–57.

ducal court and the propriety of its chivalric manners is shattered when Faust and the duchess, who is seen from a mole on her neck to be a bride of Satan, dance an openly erotic *pas de deux*. In the third act the couple are reunited at a witches' sabbath. But, prompted by Mephistophela, Faust is overwhelmed by disgust at this too obvious demonstration of crude and deliberately anti-ascetic sensuality. His companion whisks him off to a Greek isle where Helena reigns over a paradise of Greek harmony and beauty. It is the precise opposite of A. W. Schegel's picture of the modern age: 'Nichts erinnert an ein neblichtes Jenseits, an mystische Wollust- und Angstschauer, an überirdische Ekstase eines Geistes, der sich von der Körperlichkeit emanzipiert: hier ist alles reale plastische Seligkeit ohne retrospektive Wehmut, ohne ahnende leere Sehn- sucht.' (E vi. 490.) But the duchess comes to seek revenge on her faithless lover and lays a spell on the island, reminiscent of the evil spell laid on the present age in the 'Berg-Idylle'. The joyous dances continue amid the ruins of the temple; unbeknown to themselves the dancers are but ghosts. In the fifth act Faust is about to be married to a solid middle-class girl, the daughter of the local mayor, but before the couple reach the altar Mephistophela appears to claim her victim, and, in the shape of a serpent, throttles Faust to death.

Mephistophela is, then, the literal embodiment of woman as a devil. Eve and her tempter have become one. In the notes that accompany the scenario Heine justifies this on the basis of the first chapbook printed by Spies in 1587, and indeed the burden of his argument in this essay is to prove how much closer to the original folk sources than Goethe's his own work is. Once more Heine is preoccupied with trying to recapture the original spirit of a folk product. While he admits in familiar terms that Goethe's vocabulary has all the magic of a more ancient and natural lan- guage,[64] he dismisses Faust's ultimate salvation as a 'frivolous farce'. The legend comes to provide the most eloquent substan- tiation of Heine's world view, and in particular of the struggle between the Hellenes and the Nazarenes that has been acted out in

---

[64] 'Er gebot über alle Truhen des deutschen Sprachschatzes, der so reich ist an ausgeprägten Denkworten des Tiefsinns und uralten Naturlauten der Gemütswelt, Zaubersprüche, die, im Leben längst verhallt, gleichsam als Echo in den Reimen des Goetheschen Gedichtes widerklingen und des Lesers Phan- tasie so wunderbar aufregen!' (E vi. 495)

the history of the German people.[65] The ballet ends in tragedy, a tragedy that Heine doggedly insists on adhering to. So in this winter of 1846, little more than a year before the final collapse of his health, Heine depicts what he had believed to be man's most positive drive as leading surely to death, while the reign of beauty remains a short-lived interval restricted to the circumference of a tiny island. Yet without his insatiable urge for the erotic, Faust would never have left the safety of his study and would never have seen Helena—his tragedy is that the very condition for his reaching this ideal place is that he should unleash the forces which ultimately consume him.

In writing his *Faust* and collecting folklore for *Elementargeister* Heine believed he was contributing to the revolutionary cause. Reproducing legends, presenting popular superstitions in a lucid and easily understandable manner—these activities were intended to close the gap between a people and its former possessions, possessions from which it had been alienated by the despotism of the spirit and the intellect. It is on this level that we should understand Heine's almost life-long interest in journalism and his deliberate popularization of what would otherwise have remained the exclusive property of academics. In this sense he continued the tradition of Herder and the second generation of Romantics. Living at a time when greater literacy and a growing middle class were creating a rapidly expanding market for culture in easily assimilable form, Heine welcomed every opportunity that would further the distribution of ideas. Since he believed that the folk material he unearthed could strike deep and hitherto unconscious chords in the hearts of Germans, and that these notes would have revolutionary reverberations throughout the social and political body, he could reasonably consider himself an insurgent even when delving into the most obscure sources. If self-awareness and his own intellect balked his experiments with the folk-songs, he felt no such compunction about his interpretation of genuinely 'ancient poetry'. His words in *Die Götter im Exil* of 1853 speak for themselves:

Ja, was ich sagte, war keine Novität und befand sich längst gedruckt in den ehrwürdigen Folianten und Quartanten der Kompilatoren und Antiquare, in diesen Katakomben der Gelehrsamkeit, wo zuweilen mit einer grauenhaften Symmetrie, die noch weit schrecklicher ist als

[65] Cf. esp. ibid., p. 505.

wüste Willkür, die heterogensten Gedankenknochen aufgeschichtet —
Auch gestehe ich, daß ebenfalls moderne Gelehrte das erwähnte Thema
behandelt; aber sie haben es sozusagen eingesargt in die hölzernen
Mumienkasten ihrer konfusen und abstrakten Wissenschaftssprache,
die das große Publikum nicht entziffern kann und für ägyptische
Hieroglyphen halten dürfte. Aus solchen Grüften und Beinhäusern
habe ich den Gedanken wieder zum wirklichen Leben heraufbe-
schworen durch die Zaubermacht des allgemein verständlichen Wortes, durch die Schwarzkunst eines gesunden, klaren, volkstümlichen
Stiles! (E vi. 78)

And as if to prove the point we find in the manuscript deleted by
hand or hands unknown the following addition:

Solches kühne Ermessen erregte in nicht geringem Grade das Miß-
fallen der sogenannten Zunftgelehrten. Ich hatte aber nicht so Viel
dadurch zu leiden wie durch den Unmuth der heimischen Staatsbehör-
den, den ich mir zuzog, als ich meine Nekromantie auch im Gebiete
politischer oder kirchlicher Doktrinen ausübte. Nicht der gefährlichen
Ideen wegen, welche 'das junge Deutschland' zu Markte brachte,
sondern der populären Form wegen, worin diese Ideen gekleidet waren,
dekretierte man das berühmte Anathem über die böse Brut und
namentlich über ihren Rädelsführer, den Meister der Sprache, in welchem man nicht eigentlich den Denker, sondern nur den Stilisten
verfolgte. Nein, ich gestehe bescheiden, mein Verbrechen war nicht der
Gedanke, sondern die Schreibart, der Stil. (E vi. 560)

c. *Dance*

The ultimate barrier between meaning and immediacy of expression is language itself. Beyond this lie mime, gesture, and that most
fundamental form of all cultural expression, dance. It is hardly
suprising to find running through and through Heine's production
the images of dancing and dancers, a revel that strikes up with the
weird dance of the bridal pair of *Traumbild* 5 and the frenzied
circle of devils that whirl around the poet in the next poem and
which does not cease until the Heine of the *Matratzengruft* rings
down the curtain on the stage of his heart in 'Der Scheidende'.[66]
Don Ramiro comes back from the dead to dance with his beloved,
the gods of Greece and their followers are condemned to the

---

[66] E ii. 109 f. The best account of the dance images that recur throughout
Heine's work is in Barker Fairley's *Heinrich Heine. An Interpretation*, Oxford,
1954, pp. 34–46.

frenetic motions of midnight bacchanalia, the Spaniards who are
to be executed by Vitzliputzli's high priest are compelled to dance
a comic step before they are sacrificed, the slaves in 'Das Sklaven-
schiff' are whipped into rhythm to prevent the spread of a ghastly
epidemic. Everywhere dance is the language of the oppressed, of
people whose plight defies verbal expression and where gesture
alone remains. And if the dance of the slave and of the condemned
is enforced and cruelly ironic, for Mlle Laurence, the poor street
dancer of *Florentinische Nächte*, it is a realm of silent yet unmuted
speech. She, who was delivered from the womb of a woman taken
for dead and already entombed, is an outcast from both society and
her troupe, and the patterns and movements that she dances even
when still asleep are

Worte einer besonderen Sprache, die etwas Besonderes sagen
wollte. . . . War es ein südfranzösischer oder spanischer Nationaltanz?
An dergleichen mahnte wohl der Ungestüm, womit die Tänzerin ihr
Leibchen hin und her schleuderte, und die Wildheit, womit sie manchmal ihr Haupt rückwärts warf in der frevelhaft kühnen Weise jener
Bacchantinnen, die wir auf den Reliefs der antiken Vasen mit Erstau-
nen betrachten. Ihr Tanz hatte dann etwas trunken Willenloses, etwas
finster Unabwendbares, etwas Fatalistisches, sie tanzte dann wie das
Schicksal. Oder waren es Fragmente einer uralten, verschollenen Panto-
mime? Oder war es getanzte Privatgeschichte? (E iv. 358)

But perhaps the most obvious example of this intimate relationship
between oppression and its manifestation in dance is to be found
in the apparent extended joke on Berlin ballet in *Die Harzreise*, and
while the narrator is clearly mocking his listener, his point is borne
out by the unending dance of wretched humanity that follows
throughout Heine's works:

Am allerwenigsten begriff der junge Mensch die diplomatische
Bedeutung des Balletts. Mit Mühe zeigte ich ihm, wie in Hoguets
Füßen mehr Politik sitzt als in Buchholz' Kopf, wie alle seine Tanz-
touren diplomatische Verhandlungen bedeuten, wie jede seiner Bewegungen eine politische Beziehung habe, so z. B., daß er unser Kabinett
meint, wenn er, sehnsüchtig vorgebeugt, mit den Händen weit aus-
greift; daß er den Bundestag meint, wenn er sich hundertmal auf
einem Fuße herumdreht, ohne vom Fleck zu kommen; daß er die kleinen Fürsten im Sinne hat, wenn er wie mit gebundenen Beinen herum-
trippelt; daß er das europäische Gleichgewicht bezeichnet, wenn er wie
ein Trunkener hin- und herschwankt; daß er einen Kongreß andeutet,

wenn er die gebogenen Arme knäuelartig ineinander verschlingt; und endlich, daß er unsern allzugroßen Freund im Osten darstellt, wenn er in allmählicher Entfaltung sich in die Höhe hebt, in dieser Stellung lange ruht und plötzlich in die erschrecklichsten Sprünge ausbricht. . . . Beim Apis! wie groß ist die Zahl der exoterischen und wie klein die Zahl der esoterischen Theaterbesucher![67] Da steht das blöde Volk und gafft und bewundert Sprünge und Wendungen, und studiert Anatomie in den Stellungen der Lemiere, und applaudiert die Entrechats der Röhnisch, und schwatzt von Grazie, Harmonie und Lenden — und keiner merkt, daß er in getanzten Chiffern das Schicksal des deutschen Vaterlandes vor Augen hat. (E iii. 60)

In the early 1840s one of Heine's own folk-tales was transformed by Gautier into a ballet. His story of the Willis, brides who died the night before their wedding and who are condemned to continual and desperate dances at midnight on lonely country roads, provides the basis for *Giselle*.[68] Small wonder that when the director of Her Majesty's Theatre in London, Benjamin Lumley, approached Heine in 1845-6, some three years after the English performance of this ballet, and asked him for some more material Heine was soon forthcoming with *Die Göttin Diana* and then his *Der Doktor Faust*. Heine disliked classical ballet because its conventional movements were exactly the opposite of his idea of dance as expression.[69] It was 'nichts . . . als Himmel und Trikot, nichts als Idealität und Lüge!' (E iv. 357.) These ballets, in so far as one can understand the choreography from the sketched scenarios Heine sent to Lumley,[70] attempt to fuse feeling with movement; each individual situation and emotion requires its particular step. And what could be more appropriate than to render Germany's most profound legend in the language of pure expression—to transcend words and to let the spirit of Hellenism actually perform in flesh and blood on the stage—and then, tragically, let the spirit of Nazarenism wither up this flesh and blood in the visual illusion of theatre?

[67] Cf. p. 58 n. 46 above.

[68] For the Willis see *Florentinische Nächte*, E iv. 365, and *Elementargeister*, E iv. 391.

[69] Cf. Carl Enders, 'Heines Faustdichtungen. Der Tanz als Deutungs- und Gestaltungsmittel seelischer Erlebnisse', *Zeitschrift für deutsche Philologie*, 74 (1955), 364 ff.

[70] According to G. Weiß, op. cit. p. 49, all choreographic notes and scores from the London theatre were probably destroyed in the fire of 1890.

But Heine's hopes were dashed. Lumley found himself unable
to produce the work and although he paid the author handsomely,
the comment he makes in his *Reminiscences* is an ironic reflection
on Heine's ambition. Heine believed that dance was the language
of the oppressed—his ballet was to be performed in front of the
wealthy bourgeoisie of Victorian England:

Preparations were already in progress for the production of this
work. Upon examination it was found, unfortunately, impracticable in
respect of its 'situations' and scenic effects for stage purposes. True, it
was the work of a poet; but of a poet unacquainted with the necessities
of stage representation, especially in England—of a man of powerful
imagination, who presumed that a public would see the effects as he
saw them, and feel with his feelings. In short the execution of the ballet
was an impossibility.[71]

And so a work that should have closed the gap between artifice and
direct experience in fact revealed the chasm between its author and
his audience. Behind Lumley's veiled words is the implication that
the sensuality, the overt sexuality, of the piece was more than the
English could stomach. Heine should have been prepared for this
—had he not himself seen ballet in London?

Am ergötzlichsten zeigte sich mir dieser Kontrast beider Denkweisen
(d. h. der frivolen und der puritanischen), als ich einst in der Großen Oper
neben zwei dicken Manchesternen Damen saß, die diesen Versamm-
lungsort der vornehmen Welt zum ersten Male in ihrem Leben besuch-
ten und den Abscheu ihres Herzens nicht stark genug kundgeben
konnten, als das Ballett begann und die hochgeschürzten schönen
Tänzerinnen ihre üppig-graziösen Bewegungen zeigten, ihre lieben,
langen, lasterhaften Beine ausstreckten und plötzlich bacchantisch den
entgegenhüpfenden Tänzern in die Arme stürzten; die warme Musik,
die Urkleider von fleischfarbigem Trikot, die Naturalsprünge, alles
vereinigte sich, den armen Damen Angstschweiß auszupressen, ihre
Busen erröteten vor Unwillen, shocking! for shame, for shame! ächzten
sie beständig, und sie waren so sehr von Schrecken gelähmt, daß sie
nicht einmal das Perspektiv vom Auge fortnehmen konnten und bis zum
letzten Augenblicke, bis der Vorhang fiel, in dieser Situation sitzen
blieben. (*Englische Fragmente*, E iii. 446.)

---

[71] *Reminiscences of the Opera*, London, 1864, p. 199, cited in: Albert Gottschalk, '*Der Doktor Faust*'. *Eine Bibliographie*, Berlin, 1934, p. 14. This information contradicts Eberhard Galley's view that the reasons for the ballet's not being
performed are unknown, cf. Galley, op. cit., p. 53.

III

REVOLUTION AND UTOPIA

A. 'Minnedienst'

THROUGHOUT Heine's production we have found one basic ideal determining the direction of the poet's thought and sympathies: the ideal of a more organic life, itself a central concept for the entire *Goethezeit*, embracing the aims of Weimar Classicism and Romanticism alike. We have traced this ideal in Heine's work on several levels. There is his fascination with the pre-literate *Anschauungsleben* of peasant cultures; closely related to this is his constant admiration for folk arts and literature, while at the other end of the intellectual scale he looked up enviously at geniuses like Goethe and Napoleon, whose powers of perception were such that they could move beyond abstract reasoning and analysis to a form of supra-conceptual thought. From his love of dance to his sense of wonder at the mind of the genius Heine remains suspicious of the reflective intellect—this is the greatest obstacle to harmony in civilized cultures.

Nowhere is this suspicion expressed more frequently and more consistently than when Heine writes about love, and it is impossible to discuss any of Heine's work for long without encountering this fundamental human experience in some form. Contrary to what one might expect and to the impression one gains from Heine's own scornful references to the introspection of the love poet, Ratcliff's 'magenkrank schwindsüchtelnder Poet', his treatment of the subject is almost always related in some way to his view of society. As I have suggested, from the earliest *Minnelieder* in the manner of Uhland and Fouqué and his admiration of the *Minne-dienst* of chivalric times in the works of the Bonn period[1] to the 'Berg-Idylle' in *Die Harzreise* the experience of happiness in love is equally the experience of a different way of life whether in Granada, the German Middle Ages, or simply the countryside. In

---

[1] In addition to *Almansor* and the close of 'Die Romantik' see also 'Deutschland. Ein Traum', E ii. 159 ff.

the *Buch der Lieder* love alone, seems to provide direction in the
darkness of existence, a feeling beautifully captured in a poem of
Die Heimkehr that reveals the quasi-religious function of love in
the young Heine's work:

> Das Herz ist mir bedrückt, und sehnlich
> Gedenke ich der alten Zeit;
> Die Welt war damals noch so wöhnlich,
> Und ruhig lebten hin die Leut'.
>
> Doch jetzt ist alles wie verschoben,
> Das ist ein Drängen! eine Not!
> Gestorben ist der Herrgott oben,
> Und unten ist der Teufel tot.
>
> Und alles schaut so grämlich trübe,
> So krausverwirrt und morsch und kalt,
> Und wäre nicht das bißchen Liebe,
> So gäb' es nirgends einen Halt.   (E i. 114).

Small wonder then that in those many songs in which Heine becomes painfully aware of his failure to recapture the innocence of
the genuine *Volkslied*, his parody is equally—and more obviously
—directed at the loss of his beloved's innocence. If love alone
promises to give meaning to modern life, it is all the more agoniz-
ing and embittering to experience the discrepancy between the
ideal beloved and her real-life counterpart. To take but one
example, where Uhland's 'Zufriedene' had found serenity and joy
beneath the traditional lime-tree:

> Es mocht' uns nichts mehr fehlen,
> Kein Sehnen konnt' uns quälen,
> Nichts Liebes war uns fern.
> Aus liebem Aug' ein Grüßen,
> Vom lieben Mund ein Küssen
> Gab Eins dem Andern gern.[2]

Heine's lovers, sitting in the same time-honoured place, are more
temperamental:

> Das war ein Schwören und Schwören aufs neu',
> Ein Kichern, ein Kosen, ein Küssen;
> Daß ich gedenk des Schwures sei,
> Hast du in die Hand mich gebissen.

---

[2] Ludwig Uhland, *Gedichte*, ed. E. Schmidt and J. Hartmann, Stuttgart,
1898, i. 22 f.

> O Liebchen mit den Äuglein klar!
> O Liebchen schön und bissig!
> Das Schwören in der Ordnung war,
> Das Beißen war überflüssig. (E i. 85 f.)

In polite society, as Heine knows it, genuine feeling has been replaced by hypocrisy and verbal titillation, a situation brilliantly reflected in the renowned tea-party conversation of *Lyrisches Intermezzo* 50:

> Sie saßen und tranken am Theetisch,
> Und sprachen von Liebe viel.
> Die Herren, die waren ästhetisch,
> Die Damen von zartem Gefühl. (E i. 84 f.)

and satirized at length in Gumpelino's unpoetic raptures in *Die Bäder von Lucca*.[3] In later years love continues to preoccupy Heine in all its ambivalence. But like any ideal it seemed most attractive from afar. Indeed that is its lasting function in Heine's thought: as an ideal mode of existence where the physical and spiritual are perfectly integrated it serves to illuminate the defects of the present and of real experience. The love that seems to come into the grasp of Tannhäuser and Faust soon proves wanting. The soulless passion of Faust's duchess consumes and kills, while Tannhäuser degenerates into an ageing rebel turned Philistine. Perhaps it was Faust's salvation that Mephistophela came to claim him before he had to endure the 'Höllenqual' of respectable and lasting matrimony . . .

By the late 1820s love had become firmly established as Heine's yardstick of contemporary society's worth. In Italy the author finds a land of ruins. The glories of Classical Antiquity can only appear in the traveller's daydreams as he wanders through its mighty amphitheatres, while the Gothic architecture of medieval Christianity is itself ancient and crumbling. Yet amongst these ruins there are still signs of life, of the beauty that once constituted the civilization of the Classical world. He writes of Trent:

> ...wundersam wird einem zu Sinn beim ersten Anblick dieser uralter-tümlichen Häuser mit ihren verblichenen Freskos, mit ihren zerbröckel-ten Heiligenbildern, mit ihren Türmchen, Erkern, Gitterfensterchen und jenen hervorstehenden Giebeln, die estradenartig auf grauen alter-schwachen [*sic*] Pfeilern ruhen, welche selbst einer Stütze bedürften. Solcher Anblick wäre allzu wehmütig, wenn nicht die Natur diese

---

[3] E iii, esp. pp. 324–37.

abgestorbonen Steine mit neuem Leben erfrischte, wenn nicht süße
Weinreben jene gebrechlichen Pfeiler, wie die Jugend das Alter, innig
and zärtlich umrankten, und wenn nicht noch süßere Mädchengesichter
aus jenen trüben Bogenfenstern hervorguckten und über den deutschen
Fremdling lächelten, der, wie ein schlafwandelnder Träumer, durch
die blühenden Ruinen einherschwankt.   (E iii. 241 f.)

If these girls are more concrete evidence of the survival of the life
force beneath the stifling spiritualism of Christianity than the
gods of German folklore, how much more so are Heine's adven-
tures with the beautiful Franscheska that follow. In their playful,
eighteenth-century eroticism they are a deliberately mischievous
example of the role that physical love comes to play in Heine's
ideal, 'jene besseren Götterzeiten, wo es noch keine gotische Lüge
gab, die nur blinde, tappende Gefühle im verborgenen erlaubt und
jedem freien Gefühl ihr heuchlerisches Feigenblättchen vorklebt.'[4]
The reader will remember Heine's vision of a new age at dawn on
the battlefield at Marengo: the very origins of this new race of
men will symbolize freedom, for, Heine prophesies, they will be
conceived 'in freier Wahlumarmung'.[5] The poet, who some twelve
years before had knelt in pious infatuation before the statue of the
Madonna and swore to serve her for the duration of his life, is now
the warrior in the campaign to liberate mankind. But in both cases
the poet's true mistress was the goddess of love.

B. *Saint-Simonism*

> Die Franzosen sind . . . das auserlesene Volk der neuen
> Religion, in ihrer Sprache sind die ersten Evangelien und
> Dogmen verzeichnet, Paris ist das neue Jerusalem, und der
> Rhein ist der Jordan, der das geweihte Land der Freiheit
> trennt von dem Lande der Philister.   (*Englische Fragmente*,
> E iii. 501.)

It was in Paris that Heine's goddess seemed to reign and there he
found a philosophy whose panacea for a sick age corresponded
astoundingly closely to his own—the liberation of the senses from
the tyranny of the spirit. Heine reached his Jerusalem in May
1831, nearly a year after the Revolution. The period of aimlessness
that followed the embittered reception of his Platen polemic in

---

[4] E iii. 318.   [5] Ibid. 281.

Die Bäder von Lucca and his failure to obtain a chair of literature in Munich ended with his resolve to go to Paris, where the world's destiny seemed to be acted out. The Revolution itself had clearly not been sufficient reason for him to leave his homeland.[6] Now the French capital held out a second attraction, and that was Saint-Simonism.[7] This movement was based on the writings of Saint-Simon, who had died in 1825, but the substance of the teaching had been significantly elaborated and popularized in the late 1820s by a group of disciples, the most important of whom were Enfantin and Bazard. Theirs was the doctrine with which we are concerned here.[8]

Heine's debt to the Saint-Simonians is common currency.[9] What is of principal interest in the present context is that Saint-Simonism seemed to present a systematic confirmation of Heine's own views on the historical role of Christianity and the need for a new age of harmony between the senses and the mind.[10] While the philosophy in no way contradicted but rather seemed to coincide with Hegel's interpretation of historical progress, with which

[6] The Heligoland letters in *Ludwig Börne* are not convincing proof of his feelings at the time of the Revolution. They have no parallel in the preserved correspondence with the possible exception of a letter to Varnhagen five months after the Revolution, which Heine sent on completing *Reisebilder* IV (*Br* i. 463 ff.). In this letter Heine mentions a new political work, which he has just begun (pp. 465 f.). Hirth (*Br* iv. 247) supposes this to be the Heligoland Letters. As Butler ('Heine and the Saint-Simonians: The Date of the Letters from Heligoland', *Modern Language Review*, 18 (1923), 68–85) and Sammons (*Heinrich Heine*, pp. 257 ff.) have argued, there are conceptual elements in these letters which must date from later, and there are powerful reasons for thinking that they are the 'mountain' which Heine specially wrote to satisfy Laube's criticism of the Börne essay. If a skeleton already existed—and this cannot be discounted—it was certainly rewritten and deliberately heightened in effect for compositional reasons.

[7] Cf. *Br* i. 475 f., 478.

[8] A good account ¡of the movement and its philosophy is Henri-René d'Allemagne, *Les Saint-Simoniens, 1827–1837*, Paris, 1930, on which the summary below is based.

[9] The standard work on the influence of Saint-Simonism on Heine is E. M. Butler, *The Saint-Simonian Religion in Germany*, Cambridge, 1926. Lichtenberger also devoted a part of his study to the subject, cf. esp. pp. 150 ff., while Margaret A. Clarke's study (cited above) closes with an appendix on Heine and Saint-Simonism. One of the most illuminating accounts is George Iggers, 'Heine and the Saint-Simonians: a Re-examination', *Comparative Literature*, 10 (1958), 289–308. Dolf Sternberger's recent work, op. cit., is a further major contribution to this line of Heine research, and places Heine in a wider religious and philosophical tradition than almost any previous critic.

[10] See Butler, *The Saint-Simonian Religion*, pp. 141 f.

Heine had been familiar since his Berlin days,[11] it also spoke far more specifically of the coming Golden Age and enabled Heine to integrate his ideas on love and erotic expression into a reasonably coherent *Weltanschauung*. Above all it secured the Utopian element in his thought.

Perhaps the most influential account of Saint-Simonism was Bazard's *Exposition de la doctrine saint-simonienne, première et deuxième années*, which the disciple presented from 1828 to 1830. Like Hegel, Bazard believed in the perfectibility of man and saw an analogy to the growth of mankind in the growth of the individual. Society evolves, he claimed, in a series of phases alternating between organic and critical epochs. An organic age is one in which all social activities are governed by a generally accepted ideology or religion. The doctrine considered Greece before Socrates and the Christian Middle Ages to be such ages and here, as in the analysis of the critical epochs, the Saint-Simonian philosophy was remarkably close to the theories of culture propounded by the German Romantics, theories that had provided Heine's first decisive intellectual sustenance. These periods of stability were succeeded by times in which the grip of religion became weaker, social cohesion grew looser, and individuals began to struggle among themselves for domination. One such critical period stretched from Luther to the present. The Saint-Simonians believed that mankind was now moving towards a final epoch, when the alternation of phases would cease, and religion, philosophy, the sciences, and economic institutions would begin to co-operate harmoniously in a new Golden Age. Men would work in association and the age-old exploitation of man by man that had so far characterized all forms of social organization would cease. The state, now universal, would abolish private property and the present minority who control the instruments of production would vanish. The state system would replace the former hierarchy based on inheritance with a scheme that would reward each according to his capacity— in short with a meritocracy. The processes of the state would be co-ordinated in this new organic age in a religion that preached the kingdom of heaven on earth and an end to the anathema on flesh which Christianity and particularly Catholicism had pronounced. The most striking feature of human progress would be the rejection of the Christian dualism of body and soul; the new

[11] See next section of this chapter below.

life would foster the rehabilitation of the flesh and the emancipation of woman. All in all it is difficult to imagine a philosophy
more likely to appeal to Heine.

It might easily be assumed that the vision at Marengo in *Die
Reise von München nach Genua* is the earliest evidence of Saint-
Simonian influence on Heine, for its proclamation of the religion
of freedom and the age of free love when there would be no ecclesiastical overseers sounds much like Père Enfantin himself. It seems
highly unlikely, however, that Heine could have known anything
of the movement by that time.[12] The *Exposition* only began in
1828, while according to Butler the German press devoted no
space to the movement until 1830, after which it admittedly became
a talking-point—two journals to which Heine had himself contributed or was about to contribute, the *Augsburger Allgemeine
Zeitung* and the *Morgenblatt*, both published a very large number
of articles on the topic.[13] The chief organ of the movement was
Le Globe but despite Hirth's implication[14] that it devoted space to
Saint-Simonism from 1828 it was not in fact taken over until
October 1830,[15] and an examination of the journal up to 1829, by
which time we know Heine read it,[16] reveals practically nothing on
the subject. It was still one of the principal mouthpieces for the
French Romantic movement. The Varnhagens, at whose home
Hirth assumes Heine read *Le Globe*, did not display enthusiasm
for Saint-Simonism until 1832, and then in terms which suggest
that Heine could not already have been acquainted with their new
cause.[17] By that time Heine had been in Paris for a year.

[12] It is odd that Sternberger, op. cit., pp. 211, 369, quotes the echo of the
passage in question in *Zur Geschichte* (E iv. 170) as evidence of Enfantin's
influence and of Heine's Saint-Simonian persuasions in the early 1830s but
omits to mention this, its source in Heine's own work.

[13] Cf. Butler, op. cit., pp. 52–9. The chapters in question in *Die Reise von
München*, nos. 29–31, were not published in Nov. 1829 in the *Morgenblatt* with
the rest of the second half but Campe had already started to print *Reisebilder*
III by Oct. of that year. The working manuscript examined by Elster ran on
continuously from chs. 18–37, 18–25, and 26–37 each having their own page
numbers. (iii. 533.) (N.B. the printing error in Elster—ch. XXVII for XXXVII
(cf. p. 547)—note also that ch. 37 in manuscript corresponds to ch. 33 in
present text.) We must therefore conclude that the Saint-Simonian tone of
Heine's words was a coincidence.   [14] *Br* iv. 208.

[15] Cf. d'Allemagne, op. cit., pp. 175 ff.

[16] A letter of April 1829 (to Moser, *Br* i. 387) shows Heine was following the
discussion on French Romanticism in *Le Globe*. His desire to see earlier issues
suggests it was a new journal to him.

[17] Cf. Rahel's letter to Heine, 5 June 1832 in *Heine: Briefwechsel*, ed. Hirth,

The poet chose to see in Saint-Simonism what he wished to see and what he could recognize as his own. The Utopian tone and religious fervour of the movement must have appealed, following so closely on the July Revolution. A new age that would relieve the dissonance of the present era was precisely what he had himself sought throughout the 1820s. More important still, Saint-Simonism condemned Catholicism as one of the prime causes of this dissonance and proclaimed an earthly religion in which the erotic would be recognized as a healthy and necessary function of life. It is a pattern of thought that had emerged in Heine's work as early as in *Almansor* of 1820. Further, if Hegelianism seemed abstract to Heine,[18] this philosophy clothed the skeleton with flesh:

> Das ist kein abstraktes Begriffspoem!
> Das Lied hat Fleisch und Rippen,
> Hat Hand und Fuß; es lacht und küßt
> Mit schöngereimten Lippen.
>
> Hier atmet wahre Poesie!
> Anmut in jeder Wendung!
> Und auf der Stirne trägt das Lied
> Den Stempel der Vollendung. (E ii. 35)

And indeed a large part of his poetic output in the early and mid 1830s consisted of poems that sing of sexual love, cycles with suggestive titles like 'Angelique', 'Diana' and 'Yolante und Marie'. A distinct movement is observable in these works away from the last remnants of Heine's folk-song days in *Neuer Frühling* towards an open celebration of sexuality, a development that is hardly surprising when one thinks of some of the poems in the *Buch der Lieder*, and especially those that he later suppressed such as 'Hast du die Lippen mir wund geküßt' or 'Himmlisch war's, wenn ich bezwang/ Meine sündige Begier'.[19] But it would be wrong to assume that Heine was so blinded by this new religion that he really believed Paris and its 'grisettes' to have reached the new age. While many of these poems are informed by a mood of sexual elation they are also

Munich, 1914–20, ii. 23. Varnhagen himself wrote a eulogistic article on Saint-Simonism for the *Augsburger Allgemeine Zeitung*, which Heine may have been sent and possibly used for an article of his own in *Le Globe* in Feb. 1832; cf. F. H. Eisner, 'Ein Aufsatz Heines in "Le Globe", Februar 1832?', *Weimarer Beiträge*, 5 (1959), 421–5.

[18] See below pp. 89 f.
[19] E ii. 10, 13.

seasoned with a liberal dash of anacreontic humour.[20] Heine was too much an artist and too detached from his experiences not to ironize them—as in the closing verses of his 'Song of Songs':

> Versenken will ich mich, o Herr,
> In deines Liedes Prächten;
> Ich widme seinem Studium
> Den Tag mitsamt den Nächten.
>
> Ja, Tag und Nacht studier' ich dran,
> Will keine Zeit verlieren;
> Die Beine werden mir so dünn —
> Das kommt vom vielen Studieren. (E ii. 35)

When critics, like Karl Gutzkow, accused him of immorality they quite missed this comic element, which makes the poem readable and not, as it were, propaganda for free love. Nor did Gutzkow notice the underlying tone of pessimism with which several of the cycles ended: Heine makes it abundantly clear that Eros does not protect against old age and death. One of his finest poems in *Verschiedene*, or indeed altogether, 'Dieser Liebe toller Fasching', evokes a frequent theme of these songs in its last strophe:

> Morgen kommt der Aschenmittwoch,
> Und ich zeichne deine Stirne
> Mit dem Aschenkreuz und spreche:
> Weib bedenke, daß du Staub bist. (E i. 235)

The seeds of disenchantment had already germinated in Heine before his failing health made his paganism a sad irrelevance. In the meantime Heine found many of his earlier ideas and beliefs confirmed. His own view of the Christian Middle Ages as an epoch of enforced uniformity but also of spiritual security was borne out by the Saint-Simonists, for whom it was an organic age, while the *Zerrissenheit* of the modern age could now be seen as characteristic of the critical age that began with Luther.

But perhaps Heine's greatest debt to the Saint-Simonians was

---

[20] Manfred Windfuhr, 'Heine und der Petrarkismus. Zur Konzeption seiner Liebeslyrik', *Jahrbuch der deutschen Schillergesellschaft*, 10 (1966), is right to mention the anacreontic element in this poetry but underplays it (p.272). The Anacreontics, and particularly Gleim's *Scherzhafte Lieder* with its celebration of a whole parade, a 'Revue', of girls and its tone of teasing eroticism enjoyed for its own sake, are clear precursors of Heine's poems. Nor are his songs of this type limited to the middle period, as I have just suggested.

on the level of vocabulary. The manuscript of his ninth article for
the *Allgemeine Zeitung* in 1832, which was not published except in
the later book version, *Französische Zustände*, observes that 'die
Saint-Simonisten überall in der französischen Geschichte nichts
anderes gesehen, als den Kampf des Spiritualismus und des Sen-
sualismus, welcher letztere, nach langer Unterdrückung sich
wieder in seine Rechte zu setzen suche.'[21] Did not these two Saint-
Simonian terms summarize the whole of European history? And
what more suitable slogan for the campaign to end the hegemony
of the spirit than the Saint-Simonian 'rehabilitation of the flesh'?
The historical analysis is already familiar from the pre-Paris years:

> Die nächste Aufgabe ist: gesund zu werden; denn wir fühlen uns
> noch sehr schwach in den Gliedern. Die heiligen Vampire des Mittel-
> alters haben uns so viel Lebensblut ausgesaugt. Und dann müssen
> der Materie noch große Sühnopfer geschlachtet werden, damit sie die
> alten Beleidigungen verzeihe. Es wäre sogar ratsam, wenn wir Fest-
> spiele anordneten und der Materie noch mehr außerordentliche Ent-
> schädigungsehren erwiesen. Denn das Christentum, unfähig die Materie
> zu vernichten, hat sie überall fletriert, es hat die edelsten Genüsse
> herabgewürdigt, und die Sinne mußten heucheln, und es entstand Lüge
> und Sünde. Wir müssen unseren Weibern neue Hemden und neue
> Gedanken anziehen, und alle unsere Gefühle müssen wir durchräu-
> chern, wie nach einer überstandenen Pest.
> Der nächste Zweck aller unserer neuen Institutionen ist solcher-
> maßen die Rehabilitation der Materie, die Wiedereinsetzung derselben
> in ihre Würde, ihre moralische Anerkennung, ihre religiöse Heiligung,
> ihre Versöhnung mit dem Geiste. Purusa wird wieder vermählt mit
> Prakriti. Durch ihre gewaltsame Trennung, wie in der indischen
> Mythe so sinnreich dargestellt wird, entstand die große Weltzerrissen-
> heit, das Übel.   (E iv. 221 f.)

But despite these debts Heine's thought was essentially Hegelian
in outline. After the passage in *Zur Geschichte* quoted here Heine
correctly argued that the basis for the Saint-Simonian rehabilitation of the flesh was a form of pantheism. The doctrine saw God
manifested in all things spiritual and material.[22] This was probably
the inspiration for Heine's renewed interest in folk literature and
the pantheistic religion that he believed to be its primary source.
His description of the pantheist view of the world that now follows
is a simplified version of the process by which Hegel had seen the

---

[21] E v. 508 f.   [22] *Œuvres de Saint-Simon et d'Enfantin*, xlii. 293 f.

Idee coming to itself through human consciousness in the course of history:

> Im Menschen kommt die Gottheit zum Selbstbewußtsein, und solches Selbstbewußtsein offenbart sie wieder durch den Menschen. Aber dieses geschieht nicht in dem einzelnen und durch den einzelnen Menschen, sondern in und durch die Gesamtheit der Menschen: so daß jeder Mensch nur einen Teil des Gottweltalls auffaßt und darstellt, alle Menschen zusammen aber das ganze Gottweltall in der Idee und in der Realität auffassen und darstellen werden. (E iv. 222 f.)

And he goes on to state specifically that God is the motive force of history, from which he concludes that men are themselves the incarnation of God. In the first version of an almost identical passage in *Die romantische Schule* this fusion of the two schools of thought is openly stated: 'Aber Gott ist nicht bloß in der Substanz enthalten, wie die Alten ihn begriffen, sondern Gott ist in dem "Prozeß" wie Hegel sich ausgedrückt und wie er auch von den Saint-Simonisten gedacht wird.' (E v. 540.) To regard God as 'the true hero of world history'[23] was no serious distortion of Saint-Simonism. But Heine's purpose in reinforcing the Saint-Simonian view of the historical process with Hegelian metaphysics was to show the absolute inevitability of revolution. If mankind in its totality was the incarnation of God then men had divine rights and those rights would be claimed in Germany as they had been in France, for the Germans, so the argument runs, were not merely materialists but pantheists. The Saint-Simonians may have been proscribed in France (on 22 January 1832):[24] in Germany, Heine is virtually saying, the Saint-Simonian ideals are predestined to succeed.

The idea of revolution, however, with its implications of violence, bloodshed, and anarchy was alien to Saint-Simonism. Heine's entire argument led to a conclusion that the Saint-Simonians could not accept. Their ideas may have been 'revolutionary' in the broadest sense but they certainly did not advocate the violent overthrow of the *status quo*. Indeed, they stood for the strictest law and order, albeit a different law and order from that which existed. It is here that we find the roots of Heine's disenchantment with the movement. He had dedicated the first edition of *De l'Allemagne* (which contained *Zur Geschichte*) to Enfantin.

---

[23] E iv. 223.   [24] Cf. Butler, op. cit., p. 21.

Enfantin's reaction to the work is instructive.[25] He points out that Heine's Spinozan pantheism neglects the structure of society itself and the importance of a ruling hierarchy. He even proceeds to bless Metternich's Austria as a place of order and authority amid the turmoil of revolutionary ideas. He praises its very defence of feudal rights, criticizes Heine's frivolity towards positive religions, and rejects Heine's advocacy of revolution.[26] The dedication did not appear in subsequent editions. Heine's enthusiasm, his probable assumption that similarity of views meant their identity, had blinded him to the real nature of the movement. Behind the 'meritocratic' ideals that had attracted Heine lay a strictly authoritarian and hierarchical scheme. Its new organic age may have placed the erotic at a premium; it also sought a stability similar to that of the last organic age, the Middle Ages. Nor did Heine understand, or choose to understand, the practical and economic aspirations of the movement. When he spoke of Saint-Simonism in his initial exuberation it was as of a religion. The political aspects seemed to him to be just a 'part' of the doctrine which, he implied, one was not compelled to embrace.[27] Indeed, he wrote in the preface to his *Tableaux de voyage* (1834) that despite his earlier attacks on the clergy:

Notre vieux cri de guerre contre le sacerdoce a été également remplacé par une meilleure devise. Il ne s'agit plus de détruire violemment la vieille église, mais bien d'en édifier une nouvelle, et bien loin de vouloir anéantir la prêtrise, c'est nous-mêmes qui voulons aujourd'hui nous faire prêtres. (E iii. 507 f.)[28]

In short, his involvement was emotional. He greeted the doctrine with religious fervour and did not care to scrutinize it with a critical eye. A suggestive example of how Heine deliberately neglected the practical side of Saint-Simonism is provided by his quip in *Französische Zustände* that the Saint-Simonians considered themselves immune to the cholera epidemic since their numbers had not yet reached their proper total. An article in *Le Globe* had argued that if one's morale was high the danger was negligible—but within the context of sound proposals for improving the hygiene and the water-supplies of Paris.[29] This Heine omitted to mention.

---

[25] Cf. Iggers, op. cit., pp. 303 ff., and Sternberger, op. cit., pp. 113 ff.
[26] *Œuvres*, x. 108–36.
[27] Cf. *Br* ii. 22 (to Varnhagen von Ense, May 1832).
[28] Cf. *Br* i. 478 (1 April 1831).   [29] Cf. Butler, op. cit., p. 98.

One of Saint-Simon's most acute insights was to assert 'that the development of economic relationships is the determining factor in history' and to understand 'the historical process as a continuous conflict between economic *classes*, between those who, at any given period, are the possessors of the main economic resources of the community, and those who lack this advantage and come to depend upon the former for their subsistence'.[30] The Saint-Simonians believed that industrialization could at last mean a relative degree of well-being for all but insisted that it could only be achieved within the State. The new industrialists would be proven experts and would thus form part of the administrative layer, while State control would be tightened by the abolition of inherited wealth and the centralization of banking.[31] Indeed the Saint-Simonians anticipated on many counts the present development of industrial societies into centrally organized economic units based on a welfare service for all and a broad élite of highly qualified and similarly rewarded professional workers. Even the changing sexual *mores* and the increasing integration of women into the wage-earning world that characterize the consumer society would seem to fulfil Saint-Simonian demands. Heine was happy to adopt the economic optimism of the movement, and indeed he used it to underpin his ideal of the new age. In a letter to Laube (10 July 1833) he makes the penetrating observation that industrialization was decisive for the material happiness of a people and not the external political organization, thus disagreeing with the Republicans, and in effect with the Saint-Simonians themselves:

Sie stehen höher als alle die Anderen, die nur das Aeußerliche der Revoluzion, und nicht die tieferen Fragen derselben verstehen. Diese Fragen betreffen weder Formen noch Personen, weder die Einführung einer Republik, noch die Beschränkung einer Monarchie, sondern sie betreffen das materielle Wohlseyn des Volkes. Die bisherige spiritualistische Religion war heilsam und nothwendig, solange der größte Teil der Menschen im Elend lebten und sich mit der himmlischen Seeligkeit vertrösten mußten. Seit aber, durch die Fortschritte der Industrie und Oekonomie, es möglich geworden die Menschen aus ihrem materiellen Elende herauszuziehen und auf Erden zu beseligen, seitdem — Sie verstehen mich. Und die Leute werden uns schon verstehen, wenn wir ihnen sagen, daß sie in der Folge alle Tage Rindfleisch statt Kartoffel essen sollen und weniger arbeiten und mehr tanzen werden. — Verlassen Sie sich darauf, die Menschen sind keine Esel. (*Br* ii. 40)

---

[30] Berlin, op. cit., p. 90.   [31] Cf. d'Allemagne, op. cit., pp. 80 ff.

But unlike Marx, who pursued Saint-Simon's economic analysis of history, Heine left the matter as a self-evident truth. Exactly how, in concrete terms, industry would develop and the people would begin to share the wealth that was the prerequisite of their new joyous attitude towards life Heine did not consider. He abhorred the inhumanity of industrialism as he witnessed it in practice and when he saw former Saint-Simonians investing in the growing capitalist system and making fortunes from the rapidly expanding railway network he was scandalized: '— on va vite avec les chemins de fer. Ces ci-devant apôtres qui ont rêvé l'âge d'or pour toute l'humanité, se sont contentés de propager l'âge de l'argent, le règne de ce dieu-argent, qui est le père et la mère de tous et de toutes . . .' (1855 preface to De l'Allemagne, E iv. 569.) Heine's love affair with the Saint-Simonians was finally over[32].

c. The Left Hegelian

The similarity of Heine's thought in the early 1830s to that of the Saint-Simonians is striking, and cannot be denied. But this similarity should not deceive us into assuming that the Saint-Simonians exercised *the* seminal influence on his mature philosophy. As we have seen, Heine learnt relatively little that was entirely new to him from the movement. Bazard and Enfantin provided a welcome corroboration of much of what he already held to be true. Alien elements he ignored. More decisive and of longer standing was the influence of Hegel. And it was as a Hegelian of the Left that Heine himself significantly contributed to the development of German Socialism.[33]

As early as 1819 Heine had been involved in politics. When Metternich forced through the Karlsbad Decrees in that year fresh fuel was added to the feeling among liberals and students that the so-called 'War of Liberation' had in fact betrayed German liberty. Heine himself experienced this betrayal when the torch-

---

[32] Apart from this attack Heine was remarkably reluctant to voice criticism of the Saint-Simonians, which suggests the strength of his original affection—see Butler, op. cit., pp. 109 ff. and Sternberger, pp. 108 ff.

[33] Cf. Reeves, 'Heine and the young Marx', op. cit. Sternberger takes the opposite view, arguing that Heine's interest in Hegel only became positive when he had met Marx, cf. ch. 11, esp. pp. 272 ff. Yet he concedes the possibility that Marx may have been influenced by Heine before (p. 271).

light procession to the Kreuzberg in the autumn of 1819 led, at
the instigation of the government, to an interrogation, to which he
was called as a witness. Especially for the Rhinelanders, who had
benefited from the civil liberties introduced under French rule,
Napoleon symbolized the French Revolution and its positive
achievements. His defeat left a vacuum and a lack of direction.
Metternich now tried to crush the upsurge of vague and chiefly
emotional patriotism that offered another outlet for youthful
enthusiasm. Heine reflected the sense of frustration that must have
been shared by many of the idealistic students in 'Deutschland.
Ein Traum'. His dream is of an earlier, more honest and ascetic
age in the tradition of the 'chivalric' literature that extends from
Götz von Berlichingen to works by Fouqué and Uhland. But

> Schau' ich jetzt von meinem Berge
> In das deutsche Land hinab:
> Seh' ich nur ein Völklein Zwerge,
> Kriechend auf der Riesen Grab.
>
> Such' ich jetzt den goldnen Frieden,
> Den das deutsche Blut ersiegt,
> Seh' ich nur die Kette schmieden,
> Die den deutschen Nacken biegt. (E ii. 159 f.)

Then in 1821 Napoleon died in exile on St. Helena. The last of
the giants was dead. A virtual flood of memoirs and books on his
last days soon began to appear. Between 1822 and 1826 his physi-
cians, companions in exile, and even the captain of the *Bellerophon*
all published.[34] Soon Sir Walter Scott's forthcoming biography
was announced. The fervour of the poet of 'Die Grenadiere' was
aroused again. *Die Nordsee* III, which celebrated Napoleon as an
archetypal genius and hailed Ségur's account of the Moscow
campaign as a major epic was written in 1826. In *Ideen. Das Buch
Le Grand*, which immediately followed, childhood memories of
Napoleon's entry into Düsseldorf raised the general to the level
of a god—this was Jesus entering Jerusalem:

Aber wie ward mir erst, als ich ihn selber sah, mit hochbegnadigten,
eignen Augen ihn selber, hosianna! den Kaiser.

Es war eben in der Allee des Hofgartens zu Düsseldorf. Als ich
mich durch das gaffende Volk drängte, dachte ich an die Thaten und
Schlachten, die mir Monsieur Le Grand vorgetrommelt hatte, mein

[34] For details see E iii. 111 f. Maitland's book on Napoleon's reception on the
Bellerophon was published in German by Heine's own publisher, Campe, in 1826.

Herz schlug den Generalmarsch — und dennoch dachte ich zu gleicher
Zeit an die Polizeiverordnung, daß man bei fünf Thaler Strafe nicht mitten durch die Allee reiten dürfe. Und der Kaiser mit seinem Gefolge ritt
mitten durch die Allee, die schauernden Bäume beugten sich vorwärts,
wo er vorbeikam, die Sonnenstrahlen zitterten furchtsam neugierig
durch das grüne Laub, und am blauen Himmel oben schwamm sichtbar ein goldner Stern. Der Kaiser trug seine scheinlose grüne Uniform
und das kleine welthistorische Hütchen. Er ritt ein weißes Rößlein, und
das ging so ruhig stolz, so sicher, so ausgezeichnet — wär' ich damals
Kronprinz von Preußen gewesen, ich hätte dieses Rößlein beneidet.

(E iii. 158 f.)

But if the Emperor was now dead and a heroic era had come to
a tragic close, Heine was left with the conviction that history was
still capable of moving out of its present stagnation. He believed
that Napoleon's example could charge men with enthusiasm
actively to pursue his revolutionary aims and themselves make
history as he had done. The age had been given its task.[35]

From his days in Bonn under A. W. Schlegel, Heine had been
acquainted with the idea that the purpose of man was revealed in
history and that all his efforts were directed towards an ultimate,
albeit supra-temporal, age of fulfilment and perfection. This was
the Romantic version of German historicism that Herder had been
instrumental in creating. Systematic historicism culminated in the
philosophy of Hegel, and by the time Heine wrote his eulogies
of Napoleon as a monumental historical figure and prototype of
human spiritual capacity he was steeped in the atmosphere of
Hegelian thought.

Hegel had come to Berlin in 1818 and was not long in becoming
a decisive influence on the intellectual life of the Prussian capital.[36]
His *Grundlinien der Philosophie des Rechts* was published in the
same year as Heine took up his studies in Berlin and we know that
Heine attended Hegel's lectures.[37] In the summer term of 1821
Heine could have heard the series on the philosophy of religion,
that winter the series on the philosophy of Right, and, perhaps most
significant of all, in the winter term of 1822 Hegel's first series
on the 'Philosophie der Weltgeschichte'.[38] The poet became a per-

---

[35] E iii. 120, 275 f., 280 f.
[36] Cf. Franz Wiedmann, *Georg Wilhelm Friedrich Hegel in Selbstzeugnissen
und Bilddokumenten*, Hamburg, 1965, pp. 70, 119 ff.   [37] Cf. vii. 526.
[38] Cf. Kuno Fischer, *Hegels Leben, Werke und Lehre*, Heidelberg, 1963
(reprint of 1911 edn.), Part I, p. 147.

sonal acquaintance of Hegel and, if we can believe his own words, one of the philosopher's favourites.[39] In August 1822 Eduard Gans, a student contemporary of Heine's and later professor of criminal law and editor of Hegel's works, recommended Heine as a member of the 'Verein für Kultur und Wissenschaft der Juden'. Heine was later to describe Gans as 'einer der rührigsten Apostel der Hegelschen Philosophie', who fervently encouraged 'die Entwickelung des deutschen Freiheitssinnes, er entfesselte die gebundensten Gedanken und riß der Lüge die Larve ab'.[40] It was in the Verein that Heine also met Moses Moser, who became one of his closest friends in the 1820s. Moser, like Gans, was an enthusiastic follower of Hegelian philosophy.[41] In the autumn of 1822 in Über Polen Heine already called Hegel the most profound of German philosophers, claiming that the interest displayed by Polish students for Hegel 'zeigt, daß sie den Geist unserer Zeit begriffen haben, deren Stempel und Tendenz die Wissenschaft ist'.[42]

In Geständnisse, however, written on his deathbed, Heine was to condemn what he now saw as the dangerous atheism of Hegelianism and claimed that Hegel's abstract systematization had never appealed to him. He speaks of a book on Hegel which he had composed with considerable difficulty as a supplement to Zur Geschichte but then destroyed when he found that it no longer corresponded to his own sentiments.[43] This book would have filled the curious gap in Heine's account in which Hegel is pronounced the consummator of the German philosophical revolution without any attempt being made to describe his philosophy.[44] Again both in his letters[45] and early work we frequently find parodies of Hegelian abstraction. We need only think of his mock dissertation on

---

[39] Cf. Briefe über Deutschland, E vi. 535; Geständnisse, E vi. 47.
[40] E vi. 118 f. Gans was a decisive influence on Marx. It was his lectures that prompted Marx to begin his exhaustive study of Hegel; see Isaiah Berlin, op. cit., pp. 68 f.
[41] See for example Br i. 77 f.   [42] E vii. 205.
[43] E vi. 48.
[44] But it is possible that this story is pure fiction, designed to emphasize his change of heart on his deathbed. Heine makes it clear in Kahldorf über den Adel (E vii. 281 f.) that he regarded Hegel as an eclectic thinker, assembling earlier thought rather than contributing innovations himself. In that case Zur Geschichte as it stands would contain the fundamental ingredients of Hegelian philosophy, in Heine's view at least.
[45] Br i. 78, 90 f. Compare ibid., p. 155.

Ideen with its thoroughly Hegelian list of contents in *Das Buch Le Grand*[46] or his encounter with the lizard in *Die Stadt Lucca* to understand that, like Goethe, Heine was instinctively repelled by analytical thought and cold logic.[47] This dislike of systematic reasoning in favour of thought by association, 'das Aneinanderreihen' of 'ganz unverschuldete Einfälle', as the lizard sarcastically terms it, is a fundamental characteristic of Heine's work. He had proclaimed it as the structural principle of his prose writings as early as 1822 in *Briefe aus Berlin* as if in conscious opposition to the methods of his teachers—'Assoziation der Ideen soll immer vorwalten.'[48] But Heine's obvious desire to leave his hands untied in order to obtain humorous effects does not absolve the poet of the need for ideas, and while it is clearly difficult to derive an organized philosophy from Heine's often disparate and sporadic remarks, his thought revolves constantly around certain fundamental concepts and ideals. One such ideal is the life and literature of simplicity. We can follow how this and related themes are fitted into a simplified version of Hegel's thought, for what Heine may not have grasped in Hegel's own 'Spinnweb der Dialektik'[49] undoubtedly formed constant topics for discussion outside the lecture-hall among his friends. It is only natural that Hegel's ideas should have been reinterpreted and reformulated in more concrete and popular terms. In tracing the evolution of Heine's thought into the mid 1830s and how it came to centre on ideas of revolution and the Utopia to come, we watch the birth of Left Hegelianism. By examining the nature of the revolution and the age that Heine hoped would follow it we understand more clearly the dilemma that underlies Heine's self-analysis as the dreaming poet on the one hand and the warrior for freedom on the other.

Of central significance in Hegel's system was not simply that he interpreted world history in the light of a philosophy but that for him the history of the world and the history of philosophy were essentially identical.[50] It is in history that the Absolute Spirit, the divine entity that lies behind all human activity, gradually comes

---

[46] E iii. 173.
[47] Ibid. 381 ff. See also the poem 'Zu fragmentarisch ist Welt und Leben', E i. 121.
[48] E vii. 561.
[49] E vi. 51.
[50] Cf. Karl Löwith, *Die Hegelsche Linke*, Stuttgart, 1962, p. 7.

to itself, reaching a final stage of self-realization or of concrete reality on earth in men's awareness of it:

Alles was im Himmel und auf Erden geschieht — ewig geschieht — das Leben Gottes und alles was zeitlich gethan wird, strebt nur darnach hin, daß der Geist sich erkenne, sich sich selber gegenständlich mache, sich finde, für sich selber werde, sich mit sich zusammenschließe.[51]

The paradox in this process, as Hegel himself saw,[52] is that it would seem logically impermissible for the Absolute to attain historical reality, for the eternal to become temporal, the unalterable to appear in the very flux of time. Hegel himself believed that this contradiction was resolved in the process whereby the Absolute spirit *an sich*, a potential force, became aware of itself, made itself an object for its own contemplation or in short became *für sich*. It was this paradox that allowed Hegel to make the famous statement in his introduction to the philosophy of Right that: 'Was vernünftig ist, das ist wirklich; Und was wirklich ist, das ist vernünftig.'[53] If history is the process in which the Spirit becomes concrete then all that happens in history is meaningful. It is governed by reason, by *Vernunft*, and is moving towards its final goal. This observation is, claimed Hegel, the theodicy that Leibniz had sought. It is the justification for the evil and apparently accidental that occurs in the world. Furthermore, he was able to deny that his philosophy involved metaphysics, which had, of course, been suspect since Kant's *Critique of Pure Reason*, and to assert:

. . . daß die Philosophie, weil sie das *Ergründen des Vernünftigen* ist, eben damit das Erfassen des *Gegenwärtigen* und *Wirklichen*, nicht das Aufstellen eines *Jenseitigen* ist, das Gott weiß wo seyn sollte, — oder von dem man in der That wohl zu sagen weiß, wo es ist, nämlich in dem Irrthum eines einseitigen, leeren Raisonnirens.[55]

Today it is apparent that Hegel had transposed metaphysical speculation into his all-embracing analysis of history. The metaphysical lay not in the material that he examined but in his interpretation of this material. Thus the door was opened to Utopian theories that claimed to be neither Utopian nor theoretical but the Truth that was waiting to be confirmed historically. Heine,

---

[51] *Sämtliche Werke*, ed. H. Glockner (henceforth referred to as Glockner), Stuttgart, 1927 ff., xvii. 52.
[52] Ibid., pp. 35 ff. [53] Ibid. vii. 33. [54] Ibid., pp. 32 f.

we shall see, was ouch a Utopian and yet sufficiently sceptical to subject his vision to constant criticism.

The younger generation, growing up in the stagnation of the Restoration, were virtually invited by Hegel's own words to translate his interpretation of the world into a programme for action. For, if reality was reasonable and what was reasonable reality, the Left Hegelians could argue that Hegel was referring not to any reality but to true reality and that the task of the individual was to rid this true reality of what was anachronistic.[55] Had not the master closed his lectures on the history of philosophy with words that were a direct challenge to them to act?

Auf sein [des Einen Geistes] Drängen — wenn der Maulwurf[56] im Innern fortwühlt — haben wir zu hören, und ihm Wirklichkeit zu verschaffen; — sie [die Geister] sind ein schlechthin nothwendiger Fortgang, der nichts als die Natur des Geistes selbst ausspricht, und in uns Allen lebt. Ich wünsche, daß diese Geschichte der Philosophie eine Aufforderung für Sie erhalten möge, den Geist der Zeit, der in uns natürlich ist, zu ergreifen, und aus seiner Natürlichkeit, d. h. Verschlossenheit, Leblosigkeit hervor an den Tag zu ziehen, und — jeder an seinem Orte — mit Bewußtseyn an den Tag zu bringen.[57]

But this was not the only possible reaction to the challenge of history. Hegel also saw that an awareness of constant change and the repeated fall of the mighty and glorious could awake a sense of deep sorrow and encourage a withdrawal from all activity into self-centred isolation.[58] Yet it was also apparent that the final goal of world history could only be achieved through action, through men's passions.[59] This suggested to those who saw in Hegel's analysis an implied value-judgement that the traditional place of the philosopher in the realm of contemplation had profoundly

---

[55] Cf. Karl Löwith, *Von Hegel zu Nietzsche* (2nd edn.), Stuttgart, 1950, p. 83. See also Berlin, op. cit., pp. 63 ff.

[56] Cf. Hamlet of his father's ghost, I. v: 'Well said, old mole! canst work i' the earth so fast? / A worthy pioneer.'

[57] Glockner, xix. 691. Hegel completed the series on the following dates: 22 Mar. 1817, 14 Mar. 1818, 12 Aug. 1819, 23 Mar. 1821, 30 Mar. 1824, 28 Mar. 1828, 20 Mar. 1830. Unfortunately from the Hegel editions available we cannot know the exact text of Hegel's lectures in any given year. K. L. Michelet's edition, on which Glockner based his text, uses Hegel's own lecture notes from Jena with his later additions, conflated with students' notes, from the years 1823/4, 1825/6, 1829/30. Cf. Glockner, xvii. 2 f.

[58] Cf. *Vorlesungen über die Philosophie der Geschichte*, Glockner, xi. 48 f.

[59] Ibid., p. 52.

altered. He was no longer involved in *theoria* but in action, *praxis*, which was after all the manifestation of Truth. Hegel himself neglected to draw this radical conclusion but his followers on the Left were characterized above all else by this approach:

> Der Ausgangspunkt der 'letzten Philosophen' ist das praktische Bedürfnis der sozialen und politischen, überhaupt der zeitgeschichtlichen Verhältnisse. Sie denken nicht an das Immerseiende und Sichgleichbleibende, sondern an die wechselnden Erfordernisse der Zeit. Der Geist wird ihnen zum 'Zeitgeist'.[60]

In short the previously unquestioned detachment of the thinker is now regarded in a negative light and termed indifference.

We can now examine how these central elements in Left Hegelianism, which has been regarded as starting in the late 1830s well after the philosopher's death,[61] already begin to appear in Heine's work and thought from the mid 1820s. The fundamental yardstick by which Left Hegelians measured the worth of a man's ideas and activities was by their relevance to the demands of the present, by their *Zeitgemäßheit*. Heine was to apply this yardstick to none other than to the monarch of the literary world, Goethe. In the autumn of 1824, a few months after he had left Berlin for Göttingen to complete his studies, Heine made a pilgrimage to Weimar to visit the grand old man who was so highly revered in the salon of his friends, the Varnhagens. Yet in *Die Harzreise* there is a conspicuous absence of comment on the Weimar visit. The travel account ends as the narrator leaves the mountains and for some months nothing is said in his correspondence. When he finally comes to describe the meeting some nine months later in letters to Christiani and Moser he speaks of a natural antipathy that he sensed in Goethe's presence, and his depiction of the temperamental difference between the two poets that he thought responsible for this antipathy is couched in similar terms to those used by Hegel. While Goethe is less the quietist observer of the historical process than the detached epicurean artist, Heine sees himself prevented from such aesthetic indifference by his natural enthusiasm for the *Idee*.[62]

---

[60] Löwith, *Die Hegelsche Linke*, pp. 9 f.

[61] Cf. David McLellan, *The Young Hegelians and Karl Marx*, London, 1969, pp. 6 ff. Despite his reference to Heine's view that thought precedes action as lightning does thunder (p. 8) and to Heine's likening of modern German philosophy to the French Revolution (p. 148), McLellan seems to present Heine not as a Hegelian but as a Saint-Simonian (pp. 35, 46).

[62] *Br* i. 216 f. (to Moser, 1 July 1825). See also ibid., p. 210.

In a series of subsequent passages, beginning with his review of
Menzel's history of German literature of 1828,[63] Heine evolves
his theory of the *Kunstperiode* and its replacement by the new age
of committed literature.[64] He claims that in the heyday of Goethe's
classicism and the Schlegels' campaign for objectivity in art the
indifference of literature to the political issues of the day itself
exerted 'einen quietisierenden Einfluß auf die deutsche Jugend'
and 'einer politischen Regeneration unseres Vaterlandes entgegen-
wirkte'.[65] On the other hand he recognizes with the July Revolution the end of the old regime on whose soil alone objective and
purely detached art could flourish. In a very Hegelian[66] manner he
argues that the movement of history itself has condemned the age
of Goethe:

> Meine alte Prophezeiung von dem Ende der Kunstperiode, die bei
> der Wiege Goethes anfing und bei seinem Sarge aufhören wird, scheint
> ihrer Erfüllung nahe zu sein. Die jetzige Kunst muß zu Grunde gehen,
> weil ihr Prinzip noch im abgelebten, alten Regime, in der heiligen
> römischen Reichsvergangenheit wurzelt. Deshalb, wie alle welken
> Überreste dieser Vergangenheit, steht sie im unerquicklichsten Wider-
> spruch mit der Gegenwart. Dieser Widerspruch und nicht die Zeit-
> bewegung selbst ist der Kunst so schädlich; im Gegenteil, diese
> Zeitbewegung müßte ihr sogar gedeihlich werden, wie einst in Athen
> und Florenz, wo eben in den wildesten Kriegs- und Parteistürmen die
> Kunst ihre herrlichsten Blüten entfaltete. Freilich, jene griechischen und
> florentinischen Künstler führten kein egoistisch isoliertes Kunstleben,
> die müßig dichtende Seele hermetisch verschlossen gegen die großen
> Schmerzen und Freuden der Zeit; im Gegenteil, ihre Werke waren nur
> das träumende Spiegelbild ihrer Zeit, und sie selbst waren ganze
> Männer, deren Persönlichkeit ebenso gewaltig wie ihre bildende Kraft;
> . . . sie trennten nicht ihre Kunst von der Politik des Tages, sie
> arbeiteten nicht mit kümmerlicher Privatbegeisterung, die sich leicht
> in jeden beliebigen Stoff hineinlügt. (*Französische Maler*, E iv. 72 f.)[67]

[63] E vii. 255 f.
[64] In the section of the *Ästhetik* on the lyric Hegel had spoken of a new
Kunstepoche in Germany, which had been inspired by Klopstock. It was an
entirely positive development, an expression above all of patriotic feeling
(Glockner, xiv. 475). Heine's concept seems to have no connection with this.
[65] E v. 255 (*Die romantische Schule*, 1833–6).
[66] Hegelian, that is, in method. Ironically Hegel held Goethe in the highest
esteem (Glockner, xiv. 478). This is an example of how Heine pushes Hegel's
thought in a new direction, a Left Hegelian direction.
[67] See also Glockner, xiv. 272 f.

What Heine here calls the indifference of the *Kunstperiode* to the times, he had called in his letters of six years before Goethe's indifference to the *Idee*.[68] This is a fundamental Hegelian term, which Heine again alters in meaning to favour his own philosophy of action. In his *Logik* the master had employed it to signify the perfect fusion of abstraction and reality, 'die Kongruenz des Begriffs und der Realität',[69] or in other words the concrete embodiment of the spirit, towards which world history is moving. Heine sees the *Idee* as a basic driving force in the affairs of men, of which the individual can become aware and by which he is compelled to act. In the lectures on the philosophy of history, which Heine attended, Hegel called the world's ultimate purpose the realization of the 'Idee der Freiheit.'[70] By freedom he meant the state in which the Spirit becomes aware of itself.[71] Heine does not care to define his concept of *Freiheit*: it is an emotive word in which is subsumed all that he held to be good and desirable in society. And it was easy for Heine to identify this *Idee* with the liberal 'ideas' that remained alive after the French Revolution—namely the desire for a new progressive state such as Napoleon seemed to have wanted, views which were otherwise undefined except in negative terms, i.e. that the power of the nobility, Church, and absolute monarchy would be broken and that by virtue of this destruction of the *status quo* equality, fraternity, and liberty would automatically reign. As one critic has said, what most attracted Heine in the *Idee* was its dramatic quality.[72] While its direction was determined for the poet by political ideals foreign to Hegel himself, it retained traces of its metaphysical and historical character in the demonic power with which it could bear an artist along irrespective of his desires or well-being:

Die Leute glauben, unser Thun und Schaffen sei eitel Wahl, aus dem Vorrat der neuen Ideen griffen wir eine heraus, für die wir sprechen und wirken, streiten und leiden wollten, wie etwa sonst ein Philolog sich seinen Klassiker auswählte, mit dessen Kommentierung er sich sein ganzes Leben hindurch beschäftigte — nein, wir ergreifen keine Idee, sondern die Idee ergreift uns und knechtet uns und peitscht uns

[68] See above, p. 93 n. 62.
[69] Glockner, v. 238.
[70] Ibid. xi. 47.
[71] Ibid. pp. 44 f.
[72] Cf. Ewald Boucke's exhaustive account, 'Heine im Dienste der "Idee"', *Euphorion*, 16 (1909), 116–31, 434–60.

in die Arena hinein, daß wir, wie gezwungene Gladiatoren, für sie
kämpfen. So ist es mit jedem echten Tribunat oder Apostolat.

('Vorrede' to *Salon* I, E iv. 14)[73]

Such an artist thus fills the role that Hegel awarded to the monumental figures of history who in passionate devotion to their own
tasks unconsciously help to further the Spirit in its course towards
final realization. His lectures on the history of philosophy had
presented 'die Reihe der edlen Geister, die Galerie der Heroen
der denkenden Vernunft':[74] in the philosophy of history he turned
to the men of action:

Solche Individuen hatten in diesen ihren Zwecken nicht das Bewußtseyn der Idee überhaupt; sondern sie waren praktische und politische
Menschen. Aber zugleich waren sie denkende, die die Einsicht hatten
von dem, was Noth und was *an der Zeit* ist. Das ist eben die Wahrheit
ihrer Zeit und ihrer Welt, so zu sagen die nächste Gattung, die im
Innern bereits vorhanden war. Ihre Sache war es, dies Allgemeine, die
notwendige, nächste Stufe ihrer Welt zu wissen, diese sich zum
Zwecke zu machen und ihre Energie in dieselbe zu legen. Die welt-
historischen Menschen, die Heroen einer Zeit, sind darum als die Ein-
sichtigen anzuerkennen; ihre Handlungen, ihre Reden sind das Beste
der Zeit.[75]

But these men were not happy. Their lives were absorbed by their
passion and they died young like 'Alexander, sie werden wie Cäsar
ermordet, wie Napoleon nach St. Helena transportirt'.[76] It is
clearly in this spirit that Heine wrote his *Nordsee* essay and the
insight he had gained into the nature of Goethe's genius from
reading the *Morphologie*[77] was easily transposed to the most recent
of world historical figures in Hegel's account. Indeed in a letter of
1827 Heine directly calls Napoleon Bonaparte 'der Mann der Idee,
der ideegewordene Mensch'.[78] Small wonder he could assume
messianic proportions in *Ideen. Das Buch Le Grand*: rarely does
one find a clearer example of how the Left Hegelians secularized
the notion of God in his new role as the motive force of history.

For Heine Napoleon incorporated the spirit of the Revolution.
In Hegel's view revolution was a necessary part of the historical
process for it was in the destruction of the old that the seeds of
the new lay. He likened the human spirit to a phoenix, which, in

---

[73] See also E vii. 375 (1847).
[74] Glockner, xvii. 27.
[75] Ibid. xi. 60.
[76] Ibid., pp. 61.
[77] See above ch. 1, pp. 29 ff.
[78] *Br* i. 310.

burning itself alive, was reborn from its own ashes.[79] Thus history progressed in a series of collisions between the *status quo* and new elements already emerging from within the fabric of the now anachronistic social framework.[80] Clearly the most obvious example of such a clash between the progress of the *Idee* and a stagnating regime was the French Revolution, and Hegel hailed it as such at the close of his lectures on world history.[81] From Heine's earliest days in Berlin the Revolution begins to appear in his work and correspondence. A letter of April 1822 shows that at this stage his interest was a purely liberal one—he associates the Revolution with the tradition of German humanism: he tells Sethe that one of his loves is 'eine olla Potrida von: Familie, Wahrheit, französische Revoluzion, Menschenrechte, Lessing, Herder, Schiller &c., &c., &c.'[82] For his *Briefe aus Berlin* the young reporter attended a Royal wedding. Nevertheless his report still managed to introduce the unmentionable theme of the Revolution by allowing a comic figure, the Kammermusicus, to burst into a burlesque Jacobin rage at the sight of a barber 'in seinem neuen altdeutschen Rock':

> Kirschbraun wurde jetzt das Gesicht des Kammermusici, und er fletschte mit den Zähnen: 'O Sankt Marat! so ein Lump will den Freiheitshelden spielen. O Danton, Callot d'Herbois, Robespierre —' Vergebens trällerte ich das Liedchen:

> > Eine feste Burg, o lieber Gott,
> > Ist Spandau u. s. w. (E vii. 186)

The voices cheering 'Lafayette' in the mines of *Die Harzreise* are a further veiled reference to the Revolution, as we have seen, while in *Ideen. Das Buch Le Grand* the theme dominates the entire work. But it was not until the July Revolution of 1830 that Heine came to see revolution as the universal remedy, the solution to the evils

[79] Glockner, xi. 112.
[80] Ibid. xi. 59.
[81] Ibid. xi. 556 ff. But in Germany, it must be noted, Hegel saw no justification for revolution thanks to the Reformation and the establishment of Protestantism. The Prussian state was itself an advanced stage in the progress of the Spirit (ibid., pp. 554 f.). Admittedly the precise content of Hegel's lectures in the 1822–3 series cannot be ascertained from available editions. Eduard Gans and then Karl Hegel conflated Hegel's own manuscripts with students' notes. We know that Hegel concentrated chiefly on China and India as concrete illustrations of his theory, but later European history was presented in schematic form to illuminate the progress of the *Idee*. Cf. Glockner, xi. 15 and esp. 17.
[82] *Br* i. 37.

of Church and aristocracy against which he had fulminated so
long. Especially revealing is the ninth article of *Englische Fragmente*.[83] This article is devoted to a eulogy of revolution, which is
seen in the Hegelian manner as the way in which society must
advance:

> Ich spreche von der französischen Revolution, jener Weltepoche, wo
> die Lehre der Freiheit und Gleichheit so siegreich emporstieg aus jener
> allgemeinen Erkenntnisquelle, die wir Vernunft nennen, und die als
> eine unaufhörliche Offenbarung, welche sich in jedem Menschenhaupte
> wiederholt und ein Wissen begründet, noch weit vorzüglicher sein muß
> als jene überlieferte Offenbarung, die sich nur in wenigen Auserlesenen
> bekundet und von der großen Menge nur geglaubt werden kann. Diese
> letztgenannte Offenbarungsart, die selbst aristokratischer Natur ist,
> vermochte nie die Privilegienherrschaft, das bevorrechtete Kasten-
> wesen, so sicher zu bekämpfen, wie es die Vernunft, die demokratischer
> Natur ist, jetzt bekämpft. Die Revolutionsgeschichte ist die Kriegs-
> geschichte dieses Kampfes, woran wir alle mehr oder minder teilgenom-
> men; es ist der Todeskampf mit dem Ägyptentum.   (E iii. 498)

In his introduction to *Kahldorf über den Adel* of 1831 Heine
went on to speak of the remarkable parallel between the French
Revolution in the political and social spheres and the German
philosophical Revolution of the same period. While the Germans
were dreaming their transcendental dreams and philosophizing,
the French acted—but the course their action took followed a
strikingly similar course to that taken by the thoughts of the
German philosophers. This idea, later elaborated in *Zur Geschichte*
to form the central argument and framework of the entire account
of religion and philosophy in Germany, practically provided the
Young Hegelians with their justification and marching orders
before the master had died:

> Seltsam ist es, daß das praktische Treiben unserer Nachbaren
> jenseits des Rheins dennoch eine eigne Wahlverwandt schaft hatte
> mit unserem philosophischen Träumen im geruhsamen Deutschland.
> Man vergleiche nur die Geschichte der französischen Revolution mit
> der Geschichte der deutschen Philosophie, und man sollte glauben:
> die Franzosen, denen so viel wirkliche Geschäfte oblagen, wobei sie

---

[83] This was written after the July Revolution although the date on the *Schluß-
wort* deliberately implies that everything else was written before. Heine confessed
his ruse to Varnhagen (*Br* i. 464). But at least it provides evidence of Heine's
sentiments within a few months of the Revolution. Caution is required when
evaluating biographically the ecstatic praise of revolution in the Heligoland
Letters of *Ludwig Börne*—see above, p. 77 n. 6.

durchaus wach bleiben mußten, hätten uns Deutsche ersucht, unterdessen für sie zu schlafen und zu träumen, und unsre deutsche Philosophie sei nichts anders als der Traum der französischen Revolution. So hatten wir den Bruch mit dem Bestehenden und der Überlieferung im Reiche des Gedankens, ebenso wie die Franzosen im Gebiete der Gesellschaft, um die Kritik der reinen Vernunft sammelten sich unsere philosophischen Jakobiner, die nichts gelten ließen, als was jener Kritik standhielt, Kant war unser Robespierre — Nachher kam Fichte mit seinem Ich, der Napoleon der Philosophie, die höchste Liebe und der höchste Egoismus, die Alleinherrschaft des Gedankens, der souveräne Wille, der ein schnelles Universalreich improvisierte, das ebenso schnell wieder verschwand, der despotische, schauerlich einsame Idealismus —

and there followed the counter-revolution against Reason and the *Idee* led by Schelling with the Romantics in his train:

bis Hegel, der Orleans der Philosophie, ein neues Regiment begründete oder vielmehr ordnete, ein eklektisches Regiment, worin er freilich selber wenig bedeutet, dem er aber an die Spitze gestellt ist und worin er den alten Kantischen Jakobinern, den Fichtischen Bonapartisten, den Schellingschen Pairs und seinen eignen Kreaturen eine feste, verfassungsmäßige Stellung anweist. (E vii. 281 f.)

Kant had already been described as the theoretical fulfilment of the French Revolution by Hegel himself at the end of his lectures on the philosophy of history.[84] Heine, in his turn, declared that with Hegel the German philosophical Revolution was completed. It had needed the July Revolution in Paris to consolidate Heine as a Left Hegelian—his ideas did not crystallize until the full revolutionary pattern seemed to have emerged in reality. Instead of continuing to mock the obscurity of Hegel's ideas he now felt it was his task to illuminate and to present in popular form the master's 'eclectic regiment': 'Ich glaube, es ist nicht Talentlosigkeit, was die meisten deutschen Gelehrten davon abhält, über Religion und Philosophie sich populär auszusprechen. Ich glaube, es ist Scheu vor den Resultaten ihres eigenen Denkens, die sie nicht wagen, dem Volke mitzuteilen. Ich, ich habe nicht diese Scheu, denn ich bin kein Gelehrter, ich selber bin Volk.'[85] Here may lie the origin of the Young Hegelian distinction between the esoteric and the exoteric Hegel.[86]

[84] Glockner, xi. 553 f. Cf. above, p. 97 n. 82.
[85] E iv. 164.
[86] For 'esoteric' and 'exoteric' see above pp. 58 and 71.

In *Zur Geschichte* Heine cleverly links this revolution in the realm of thought with what we have seen he regarded as the source of revolution in the German people itself—its pantheist religion. He thus fuses his ideal of harmonious life, which he derived from Schlegel and Herder, with his Left Hegelian thought, for he selects as the precursor of Kant a thinker whose identification of the physical world with the godhead comes close to the unreflective religion of the ancient German pantheists. Since for Spinoza, he claims, matter and spirit are one, the presumptuous reign of the mind alone is over and the flesh will regain its rightful place, working in unison with all man's other faculties.[87] With Spinoza the circle has begun to close. The lost age of harmony can return, the time is ripe for the revolution that will end 'die große Weltzerrissenheit'.[88] And in the words with which Heine introduces Kant he clearly formulates the central tenet of the Left Hegelians that theory precedes and determines practice, that conceptual thinking and action cannot be separated:

Der Gedanke will That, das Wort will Fleisch werden. Und wunderbar! der Mensch, wie der Gott der Bibel, braucht nur seinen Gedanken auszusprechen, und es gestaltet sich die Welt, es wird Licht oder es wird Finsternis, die Wasser sondern sich von dem Festland, oder gar wilde Bestien kommen zum Vorschein. Die Welt ist die Signatur des Wortes.   (E iv. 248)

Heine's essay ends in a prophetic vision, a vision of the Apocalypse that will shake Germany and even Europe to its very foundations when at last the philosophers and their frenzied followers take to the sword and destroy root and branch the rotten edifice of Christian society. The end of the world and the subsequent millennium, which had been central elements in Christian folklore itself for nearly 2,000 years, here emerges in pagan Nordic guise. But this upheaval is no less inevitable than the Second Coming:

Der Gedanke geht der That voraus wie der Blitz dem Donner. Der deutsche Donner ist freilich auch ein Deutscher und ist nicht sehr gelenkig und kommt etwas langsam herangerollt; aber kommen wird er, und wenn ihr es einst krachen hört, wie es noch niemals in der Weltgeschichte gekracht hat, so wißt: der deutsche Donner hat endlich sein Ziel erreicht.   (E iv. 294)

---

[87] E iv. 215 ff.   [88] Ibid., pp. 222 ff.

And for Heine the goal of history was, of course, a paradise of joy
on earth, an unashamedly sensualist version of Hegel's reconciliation of Spirit and Matter. Men were to be restored to their own
divinity, there was to be music and dancing, nectar and ambrosia,
love-making, 'cakes and ale' for everyone.[89] Heine is writing in an
ancient chiliastic tradition but at the time his words seemed
startling and new. *Zur Geschichte* was a seminal work and should
be regarded as an early and major Young Hegelian document.[90]

D. *Utopia*

Und Schönes blühte, wo die Schönheit herrschte,
Kunst, Wissenschaft, Ruhmsucht und Frauendienst . . .
(*Almansor*, 1820, E ii. 290)

. . . ein Schloß . . . ,
Voller Lust und Waffenglanz;
Blanke Ritter, Fraun und Knappen . . .
('Berg-Idylle', 1824, E iii. 47)

Nektar und Ambrosia, Purpurmäntel, kostbare Wohlge-
rüche, Wollust und Pracht, lachenden Nymphentanz, Musik
und Komödien . . .   (*Zur Geschichte*, 1834, E iv. 223)

. . . un chaud royaume de lumière et de plaisir . . .
(*De l'Allemagne*, 1835, E iv. 618)

Wir wollen hier auf Erden schon
Das Himmelreich errichten . . .

Es wächst hienieden Brot genug
Für alle Menschenkinder,
Auch Rosen und Myrten, Schönheit und Lust, . . .
(*Deutschland*, 1844, E ii. 432)

Der Venusberg: . . . an arabische Feenmärchen erinnernd . . .
exotische Blumen . . . antike Basreliefs . . . magisches Licht . . .
zauberische Üppigkeit . . . das süßeste *dolce far niente* . . .
(*Die Göttin Diana*, 1846–54, E vi. 108 f.)

---

[89] E iv. 223 f.   [90] Cf. Reeves, op. cit., 54 ff. and 66 ff.

Eine Insel im Archipel . . . weiße Bildwerke . . . fabelhafte
Pflanzen . . . blühende Menschen . . . Jungfrauen in leicht-
geschürzter Nymphentracht, ihre Häupter geschmückt mit
Rosen oder Myrten . . . Freudendienst . . . griechische Heiter-
keit, ambrosischer Götterfrieden, klassische Ruhe.
(*Der Doktor Faust*, 1847, E vi. 489 f.)

The philosophies that Heine embraced may have changed but
the vision they served to justify remained constant. Greece,
Arabia, the age of chivalry, flowers, ambrosia, music and dance,
the ingredients are interchangeable in these scenes of hedonist
delight. They may appear in a historical tragedy or in a history of
philosophy, in a political satire or in a ballet—they are equally
nebulous and equally evocative. The ideal to which Heine's
arguments and his dancers lead us alike is Utopian, if by Utopian
we mean not a detailed scheme of the perfect state but a new and
different world to be striven for, somewhere as unlike the present
as one can imagine, literally a 'non-place'. If politics is 'the art of
the possible' then Heine's goal is hardly political at all.

When Heine became familiar with the machinations of the political activists in Paris, a realm that had been remote to him even
in Berlin or Munich, he too began to realize the non-political
nature of his ideals. He mentions this on a number of occasions in
his correspondence and particularly to his friend, Heinrich Laube,
who was one of the few with any deep understanding of the poet
in his later years:

In den politischen Fragen können Sie so viel Concessionen machen,
als Sie nur immer wollen, denn die politischen Staatsformen und
Regierungen sind nur Mittel; Monarchie oder Republik, demokratische
oder aristokratische Instituzionen sind gleichgültige Dinge, solange der
Kampf um erste Lebensprinzipien, um die Idee des Lebens selbst,
noch nicht entschieden ist.   (*Br* ii. 103)[91]

For the Republicans and the Communists, on the other hand,
the organization of the state was of qualitative importance. This
also explains what appears to be a glaring anomaly in Heine's
thought, namely that in the same years in which he consistently
advocates revolution he also adheres to the principle of monarchy.

---

[91] Cf. also *Br* ii. 40 (quoted above, p. 85) and *Br* ii. 158. Compare E v. 509 f.
(MS. of *Französische Zustände*, Article ix).

He clearly believed that the kings were victims of the aristocracy and that it was possible for the monarch to execute the wishes of the people directly. This is stated specifically in *Die Stadt Lucca*, where he speaks of the emancipation of kings from the aristocratic parasites and from the robes and sceptre that seem to separate them from the people. Despite Heine's claims to the contrary[92] it is likely that he wrote this after the Revolution, in the knowledge that it had produced the first 'citizen king', Louis-Philippe. Thus he could safely state that such an ideal was 'etwas Ausführbares', as the Italian insurgents had believed when they attempted to depose the King of Sardinia:

> Sie wollten jene Ideen realisieren, die von den weisesten Menschen dieser Erde als wahr befunden worden, und wofür die besten geblutet. Sie wollten Gleichheit der Rechte aller Menschen auf dieser Erde, keinen bevorrechteten Stand, keinen bevorrechteten Glauben, und keinen König des Adels, keinen König der Pfaffen, nur einen König des Volks. (E iii. 568)

Beneath this curious mixture of revolution and that oldest of all European political theories, Plato's philosopher-king, lie the remains of Heine's admiration for Napoleon. Here was a leader who had both risen from the people and seemed to be the embodiment of the 1789 Revolution. This emerges clearly at the close of *Französische Maler*, where he goes over to a frontal attack against the 'Jacobins', calling Napoleon and Louis-Philippe two miraculous emissaries, dispatched by God, to save royalty.[93] Both in his admiration of Napoleon and in his dogged faith in the monarchy Heine agreed with Hegel. Monarchism played a significant role in the *Rechtsphilosophie*, lectures that were delivered while Heine was a student in Berlin. For Hegel the World Spirit would finally find concrete expression in the State, and the embodiment of the State was its monarch.[94] Hegel thus provided a new if indirect justification of the divine right of kings. Heine imagined that revolution could liberate the kings for their proper task. Again we have evidence of Heine's special position as a Hegelian of the Left.

---

[92] E iii. 417, 420. The work ends with a 'spätere Nachschrift (November 1830)'. There is no reason to suppose that this alone was written later. Only chs. 1 and 2 had appeared before 1831. See also E v. 149 ff.

[93] E iv. 89 (1833).

[94] Glockner, vii. 382 f.

Heine expected Louis-Philippe literally to work wonders. As he wrote in *Französische Zustände* nearly two years later:

Ludwig Philipp mußte an die Spitze der europäischen Freiheit treten, die Interessen derselben mit seinen eigenen verschmelzen, sich selbst und die Freiheit identifizieren, und wie einer seiner Vorgänger ein kühnes 'L'Etat c'est moi!' aussprach, so mußte er mit noch größerem Selbstbewußtsein ausrufen: 'La liberté c'est moi!'   (E v. 85)

But, the passage continues, 'Er hat es nicht gethan'. It should not surprise us to find that in *Französische Zustände* Heine's views of the 'citizen-king' swing from disappointed criticism in the first of the articles to reconciliation at the close, nor that he could blandly use arguments from Republican and Legitimist sources to attack Louis-Philippe while censuring the Republicans with the arguments of the Philippists,[95] a fluctuation that earned Heine the ire of Börne and the charge that he was a chameleon and turncoat— 'Tournez la feuille. M. Heine a tourné.'[96] Nor do we need to seek the answer to his changeability in the theory that he was in the secret pay of Metternich, as one critic has claimed.[97] As a Utopian Heine expected something of the king that was beyond political feasibility.

But nowhere does the specific quality of Heine's Utopianism appear more clearly than in his disapproval of the English political system. He visited England in 1827, and it was here that his conception of the Republicans and their cause was largely formed before he had encountered them in France at all.

A central theme of *Englische Fragmente* is the difference between the German's dreamy idealism and the Englishman's unimaginative pragmatism. This is already treated in the conversation between the 'yellow man' and the narrator, the 'junge Enthusiast', as their boat steams upstream through the Port of London towards the City and the Tower ('Gespräch auf der Themse'). The English-man's parting remark that there is as little freedom and equality between the stars in the heavens as there is on earth is presented as a tenable view: the scene seeks to bring out the contrast between the Utopian and the cynic rather than to plead for one or the other. It may be compared with the poem 'Gespräch auf der Paderborner

---

[95] See Margaret A. Clarke's detailed documentation, op. cit.
[96] In *Le Réformateur*, May 1835, cited Clarke, p. 48.
[97] The drift of Clarke's entire book, culminating in this groundless charge, p. 230.

Heide' of 1821. In the later chapter, 'Die Befreiung', which was probably written after the July Revolution, the pragmatic evolution of political rights in England is roundly condemned. Heine argues that since freedom is a right to which a man is entitled by virtue of his birth and not a privilege to be won, the Englishman's rights are of little intrinsic value; they are mere concessions granted by the ruling class to maintain its supremacy in the face of pressure. The proposed Reform Bill was merely a patch on the threadbare fabric, which would soon tear more gravely still. Instead, the poet proclaims 'ein dreifarbiges Evangelium . . . wonach nicht bloß die Form des Staates, sondern das ganze gesellschaftliche Leben nicht geflickt, sondern neu umgestaltet, neu begründet, ja neu geboren werden sollte.'[98] Here we have the crux of the matter. Social life, the quality of living, has to change and change radically: it has to be reborn. Clearly Heine believed that revolution could achieve this total transformation.

For Heine there could be no concessions to the past in his new world. Equally there could be no concessions to ugliness. Whether he dreamt of Greek serenity or of Herder's age of song, poetry and life were to be one. Here he remained true to his Romantic origins. The most concrete element in his Utopia would thus have been the disappearance of the Philistine, for decades the butt of the Romantics' scorn and the symbol of all that was hostile to the life of the imagination, to originality, enthusiasm, and genius. Indeed the very structure of Die Harzreise and Die Reise von München is based on the narrator's journey away from the Philistinism of polite society to the immediacy of simple folk. From the early years the Philistine is the opposite of his ideal of organic harmonious living. The Philistine sees life as teleological: everything has to be justified by its usefulness.[99] When confronted with the beauty of nature, he succeeds only in destroying its magic—as in the famous scene on the Brocken.[100] Above all the Philistine is

---

[98] E iii. 496 ff. Cited passage p. 498. Heine was surprised, when in the following year, 1832, the Reform Act was passed. Suddenly Englishmen became interesting to him, as he puts it. He now favourably compares the Englishman's unyielding adherence to facts and to *his* freedom with the German's adherence to ideas while accepting imprisonment in all docility. Cf. *Französische Zustände*, E v. 125 ff. One detects no influence from this lesson on *Zur Geschichte*, however.

[99] Cf. esp. *Die Harzreise*, E iii. 43 and the satirical poem 'Zur Teleologie', E ii. 75 ff.

[100] E iii. 56.

anti-poetic. Poetry is reduced to *Bildung* that has to be accumulated for personal prestige. It is learnt mechanically according to the metrical patterns that Gumpelino tries to impress on his manservant: 'Poesie? Ich kenne alle Schauspielerinnen Deutschlands, und die Dichter weiß ich auswendig. Und gar Natur! Ich bin zweihundert Meilen gereist, Tag und Nacht durch, um in Schottland einen einzigen Berg zu sehen . . .' (E iii. 303.)

And from the Philistine of the 1820s grew the Puritan and the Nazarene of the 1830s and 1840s. It was easy to associate the Englishmen whom Heine met bustling about their business in the dirty, smoky streets of London with the Puritans who put an end to the colour and licence of the Stuarts two centuries before. To link the Republicans in Paris, and especially the kill-joy Börne, with the Puritans was another obvious step. Only a few years later it was the Communists in whom Heine discovered the same desire for grey uniformity, the same suspicion of pleasure, and the same antipathy to the whims and frivolity of poetic genius. In 1839, the year in which Heine made his final reckoning with Börne, he published a poem which gives eloquent expression to the deepest feelings behind his Utopianism. Above all Heine dreamt of escape, escape from the world's banality. 'Anno 1829' was probably written in Bremen just before he left for France and for what he thought was the promise of a new Jerusalem:

> Daß ich bequem verbluten kann,
> Gebt mir ein edles, weites Feld!
> O, laßt mich nicht ersticken hier
> In dieser engen Krämerwelt.
>
> Sie essen gut, sie trinken gut,
> Erfreun sich ihres Maulwurfglücks,
> Und ihre Großmut ist so groß
> Als wie das Loch der Armenbüchs.
>
> Zigarren tragen sie im Maul
> Und in der Hosentasch' die Händ';
> Auch die Verdauungskraft ist gut, —
> Wer sie nur selbst verdauen könnt'!
>
> Sie handeln mit den Spezerei'n
> Der ganzen Welt, doch in der Luft,
> Trotz allen Würzen, riecht man stets
> Den faulen Schellfischseelenduft.

O, daß ich große Laster säh',
Verbrechen, blutig, kolossal, —
Nur diese satte Tugend nicht,
Und zahlungsfähige Moral!

Ihr Wolken droben, nehmt mich mit,
Gleichviel nach welchem fernen Ort!
Nach Lappland oder Afrika,
Und sei's nach Pommern — fort! nur fort!

O, nehmt mich mit — Sie hören nicht —
Die Wolken droben sind so klug!
Vorüberreisend dieser Stadt
Ängstlich beschleun'gen sie den Flug.

(E i. 271 f.)

IV

PESSIMISM AND ART

A. *Human history—progress or futility?*

THE importance of history in Heine's thought can hardly be exaggerated. The evolution of his ideas which I have outlined in the preceding pages is essentially an evolution within the bounds of historicism. In the early years he embraced the cultural critique of the Romantics, which was itself derived from Herder, and his experiments with the folk-song and later his undeterred enthusiasm for folklore and legend should be seen in the light of this philosophy. The transition to a political interpretation of Hegel's thought was almost a natural development from such beginnings, while the Saint-Simonian theory of history and avowed intention to bring about the Golden Age also belong to the tradition. The surprising continuity of Heine's ideals is, then, the result of his adherence to the historical philosophy. It is a philosophy which sees in human history the key to the understanding of mankind. It claims that history follows a meaningful and recognizable pattern of progression and rests its argument on the metaphysical assumption that God has either preordained this pattern or constitutes the pattern itself.

But this is not the only possible view of history, and it did not go unchallenged even in Heine's time. Thus it is extremely interesting that among his unpublished papers Strodtmann found a short essay which discusses three different approaches to the question of human progress. Strodtmann gave it the title 'Verschiedenartige Geschichtsauffassung', and Elster dates it to the early 1830s. Two of the interpretations are familiar to us. One compounds Hegel's view that history is created by a succession of monumental figures with Saint-Simonian evolutionary Utopianism. In his account Heine adopts Saint-Simon's and Bazard's statement that the Golden Age lies before us and not behind and fits this Utopianism into a German context by referring to the ideals of the *Humanitätsschule*. One is reminded of his 'olla Potrida' of 'Lessing,

Herder, Schiller, &c., &c., &c.' which he mentions in an early
letter.¹ It is a view,

> ... die mehr mit der Idee einer Vorsehung verwandt ist, . . .
> wonach alle irdischen Dinge einer schönen Vervollkommenheit entgegenreifen und
> die großen Helden und Heldenzeiten nur Staffeln sind zu einem höheren
> gottähnlichen Zustande des Menschengeschlechtes, dessen sittliche und
> politische Kämpfe endlich den heiligsten Frieden, die reinste Ver-
> brüderung und die ewigste Glückseligkeit zur Folge haben. Das goldne
> Zeitalter, heißt es, liege nicht hinter uns, sondern vor uns, wir seien
> nicht aus dem Paradiese vertrieben mit einem flammenden Schwerte,
> sondern wir müßten es erobern durch ein flammendes Herz, durch die
> Liebe; die Frucht der Erkenntnis gebe uns nicht den Tod, sondern das
> ewige Leben. — 'Zivilisation' war lange Zeit der Wahlspruch bei den
> Jüngern solcher Ansicht. In Deutschland huldigte ihr vornehmlich die
> Humanitätsschule. Wie bestimmt die sogenannte philosophische Schule
> dahin zielt, ist männiglich bekannt. Sie war den Untersuchungen
> politischer Fragen ganz besonders förderlich, und als höchste Blüte
> dieser Ansicht predigt man eine idealische Staatsform, die, ganz basiert
> auf Vernunftgründen, die Menschheit in letzter Instanz veredeln und
> beglücken soll. (E vii. 295)

This Utopianism differs from Heine's own in one respect only:
it does not envisage revolution. For this reason he rejects it. In its
place he puts forward a view of history which does not relegate the
present to a mere function of the future. He argues that life is not
a teleological process. The good life is every man's right, and it can
only be realized through the overthrow of an unjust *status quo*:

> ... die Schwärmerei der Zukunftsbeglücker soll uns nicht verleiten,
> die Interessen der Gegenwart und das zunächst zu verfechtende
> Menschenrecht, das Recht zu leben, aufs Spiel zu setzen. — *Le pain est le
> droit du peuple*, sagte Saint-Just, und das ist das größte Wort, das in der
> ganzen Revolution gesprochen worden. (E vii. 296)

Revolution alone will ensure that men's material welfare will be
cared for immediately, not rosy dreams about what may happen in
the future. The present is too important to be squandered.

How can we accommodate this view with Heine's own Utopian
visions? After all the real difference between his position and that
of the Saint-Simonians or for that matter of the humanists lay not
in the proclamation of a golden Age but in the means to the end—

---

¹ See above, p. 97.

revolution or evolution [2] It was he who saw man as 'gottähnlich' and who adjusted Saint-Just's words to 'Le pain est le droit divin de l'homme'.[3] 'Verschiedenartige Geschichtsauffassung' suggests that Heine was aware of the unrealistic quality of his ideals and that he was attempting to resolve this shortcoming by insisting on the practical nature of revolutionary action. We may thus compare it to 'Briefe über Deutschland' of 1844, where he claims that the Utopian vision of a new hedonist age in *Zur Geschichte* of ten years before is a political programme, the programme of the Communists. Certainly we can surmise that it was written later than Elster suggests, at least after the break with Enfantin or even at the time when Heine co-operated with Marx. More significant than any polemic against the Saint-Simonians is, however, Heine's patent attempt to elucidate his own position. He is in fact engaged in a polemic against himself.

This is equally true of the first interpretation with which he deals in the short essay. Here history signifies not progress but mere movement: it is an unending cycle of birth, life, and death which can only cause its observer to abandon political action. Those who accept this view:

... sehen in allen irdischen Dingen nur einen trostlosen Kreislauf; im Leben der Völker wie im Leben der Individuen, in diesem, wie in der organischen Natur überhaupt, sehen sie ein Wachsen, Blühen, Welken und Sterben: Frühling, Sommer, Herbst und Winter. 'Es ist nichts Neues unter der Sonne!' ist ihr Wahlspruch; ... Sie zucken die Achsel über unsere Zivilisation, die doch endlich wieder der Barbarei weichen werde; sie schütteln den Kopf über unsere Freiheitskämpfe, die nur dem Aufkommen neuer Tyrannen förderlich seien; sie lächeln über alle Bestrebungen eines politischen Enthusiasmus, der die Welt besser und glücklicher machen will, und der doch am Ende erkühle und nichts gefruchtet. (E vii. 294)

Heine imputes this negative approach to Goethe and the poets of the *Kunstperiode* on the one hand and to the 'historische Schule' on the other, the name by which the school of historical jurisprudence founded by Carl Savigny and K. F. Eichhorn is known. I shall return to the case against Goethe later. Savigny and Leopold Ranke, the historian, whom Heine censures next, were exponents of historicism in their field. Equally they were pillars

---

[2] A distinction which I believe Sternberger, op. cit., underestimates.
[3] See also E iv. 223.

of the Prussian establishment: both were Berlin professors, while
Ranke was to be made State Historian in 1841, Savigny Minister
of Justice in 1842. For Savigny the task of the legislator was essentially descriptive, giving formal expression to customs and pro-
cedures that had been the organic creation of society.[4] For Heine
(as incidentally for Hegel)[5] this conservative approach implied an
indifference to the present. None the less, and surprisingly perhaps, the vision of history as a dreary and unending cycle, which
he here associates with the Historical School, was in fact one of his
own deepest fears and is an almost constant foil to his Utopianism.
When, at the close of the essay, he demands that 'der elegische
Indifferentismus der Historiker und Poeten soll unsere Energie
nicht lähmen', he is struggling with a latent paralysis within himself. It may have been physical paralysis which, coinciding with
the fiasco of 1848, finally shattered his hopes of a new age, his
faith in revolution, and his Hellenistic lust for life, but this was only
the cruel confirmation of what he had suspected and dreaded since
his earliest works.

B. *The art of ambivalence*—Ideen. Das Buch Le Grand

In almost every work from which I have drawn material to show
Heine as a Utopian thinker and early Left Hegelian these ideas and
hopes are later modified or eventually dispelled. History emerges
as a destructive force even in *Almansor*. I have shown that Almansor's heaven on earth in the arms of his beloved anticipates Heine's
later ideals but it would be to distort the play if one suggested
that it were a mere vehicle for ideas Heine wished to promote.
Unendearing though its lyrical excesses and melodramatic tone
may be, Heine intended it as a serious tragedy. When Hassan's
troops are routed and Almansor dies, the fall of Granada is made
complete and irreversible. When he wrote this play (or for that
matter the fate tragedy *Ratcliff* with its background derived from
Scott)[6] he was undoubtedly moved by the idea that it was the

---

[4] Cf. S. Avineri, 'Hegel and Nationalism', in *Hegel's Political Philosophy*, ed.
W. Kaufmann, New York, 1970, p. 124.

[5] Cf. ibid., pp. 125 ff.

[6] Cf. H. Mutzenbecher, op. cit., pp. 40 f. Besides the obvious debts to the
contemporary cult of the Spanish and Moorish e.g. in Fouqué (cf. *Br* i. 81.)
and Byron (cf. Ochsenbein, op. cit., pp. 211 ff.), and to the interest in the
Orient stimulated by Goethe's *Divan* and Schlegel's and Bopp's studies of
Sanskrit, Heine probably owed the theme of historical change to Scott.

destiny of the most perfect ages and of the noblest men to perish. His tragedies were published in 1823, and he accompanied the copy he sent to his brother-in-law with these words:

Sie lesen in diesem Buche, wie Menschen untergehn und Geschlechter, und wie dennoch dieser Untergang von einer höheren Nothwendigkeit bedingt und von der Vorsehung zu großen Zwecken beabsichtigt wird. Der ächte Dichter giebt nicht die Geschichte seiner eigenen Zeit, sondern aller Zeiten, und darum ist ein ächtes Gedicht auch immer der Spiegel jeder Gegenwarth. (*Br* i. 74)

These Hegelian arguments, which Heine must have heard in the lectures of the same winter, justify the destruction of human achievement in the flux of time as the process by which the Spirit advances. But Hegel himself stated that the sight of the mighty who are doomed to die and of civilizations which flower only to wither and fall could equally induce in the observer a feeling of the most profound despair and lead him to retreat into his own selfish little world.[7] Thus the same knowledge of the same events can result in two antithetical attitudes—quietism and passionate enthusiasm. In *Die Nordsee* III the balance tips in favour of enthusiasm, but as is evident from my account of this essay Heine is at pains to present conflicting viewpoints in action, and states specifically that his own divided opinion is a living example of the

---

[7] Wenn wir dieses Schauspiel der Leidenschaften betrachten, und die Folgen ihrer Gewaltthätigkeit, des Unverstandes erblicken, der sich nicht nur zu ihnen, sondern selbst auch, und sogar vornehmlich zu dem, was gute Absichten, rechtliche Zwecke sind, gesellt, wenn wir daraus das Uebel, das Böse, den Untergang der blühendsten Reiche, die der Menschengeist hervorgebracht hat, sehen; so können wir nur mit Trauer über diese Vergänglichkeit überhaupt erfüllt werden, und indem dieses Untergehen nicht nur ein Werk der Natur, sondern des Willens der Menschen ist, mit einer moralischen Betrübniß, mit einer Empörung des guten Geistes, wenn ein solcher in uns ist, über solches Schauspiel enden. Man kann jene Erfolge ohne rednerische Uebertreibung, blos mit richtiger Zusammenstellung des Unglücks, den [*sic*] das Herrlichste an Völkern und Staatengestaltungen, wie an Privattugenden erlitten hat, zu dem furchtbarsten Gemälde erheben, und ebenso damit die Empfindung zur tiefsten, rathlosesten Trauer steigern, welcher kein versöhnendes Resultat das Gegengewicht hält, und gegen die wir uns etwa nur dadurch befestigen, oder dadurch aus ihr heraustreten, indem wir denken: es ist nun einmal so gewesen; es ist ein Schicksal; es ist nichts daran zu ändern; und dann, daß wir aus der Langenweile, welche uns jene Reflexion der Trauer machen könnte, zurück in unser Lebensgefühl, in die Gegenwart unserer Zwecke und Interessen, kurz in die Selbstsucht zurücktreten, welche am ruhigen Ufer steht, und von da aus sicher des fernen Anblicks der verworrenen Trümmermasse genießt. (Glockner, xi. 48 f.)

dissonance which characterizes the modern age. He lets his reader observe the very workings of his mind. Until now I have concentrated on the trend in Heine's thought towards political optimism and faith in revolution, which emerges after this essay. But it was not a trend which went uncontested.

Within the economy of *Das Buch Le Grand* Heine's childhood memory of Napoleon entering Düsseldorf, or in short Napoleon's apotheosis, is deliberately contrasted with the scene where an older and now more worldly-wise narrator meets the pathetic remnants of the French army struggling back from the Russian front. Le Grand, the former symbol of revolution, dies before his eyes in the place that had formerly resounded to his rousing marches. The drum which had awoken the enthusiastic dreams of the boy is now silenced by the man, so that 'sie sollte keinem Feinde der Freiheit zu einem servilen Zapfenstreich dienen'.[8] These tragic events are themselves enveloped in the tragicomic framework provided by a web of partly ironic, partly sentimental tales of unhappy love. The narrator and his beloved vanish behind a series of Oriental and Petrarchan[9] masks, the Graf der Ganges and Laura, the Sultan and Sultana of Delhi, the poet himself at different stages in his life, little Veronica and the mysterious 'Madame', to whom the narrative is addressed. In its complex game of hide-and-seek with the reader, its disruption of the threads of action, its relativization of the serious with the absurd, the deeply felt with the sickly sentimental, this work is a miniature *Tristram Shandy*. We know that Heine had been reading Sterne since at least 1823.[10] This English novel must count as one of the most extraordinary *tours de force* in the history of humorous literature. From its masterly use of deflation and non-action to its verbal and even direct pictorial slapstick it is a clown performance. But above all it is a performance. This is what must have fascinated Heine, for he tells us in the last chapter of his work that all this reflects the deviousness of a man's mind and the game he plays with his own misery: 'Bis auf den letzten Augenblick spielen wir Komödie mit uns selber. Wir maskieren sogar unser Elend, und während wir an einer

---

[8] E iii. 166.

[9] Cf. Windfuhr, 'Heine und der Petrarkismus', p. 277.

[10] Cf. *Br* i. 109. See for Heine and Sterne John C. Ransmeier, 'Heines "Reisebilder" und Laurence Sterne', *Archiv für das Studium der neueren Sprache und Literatur*, 118 (1907), 289–317, and Stefan Vacano, *Heine und Sterne*, Diss., Berne, 1907.

Brustwunde sterben, klagen wir über Zahnweh.' (E iii. 194.) No
matter how we twist and turn, pretend or perform, life is suffering:
'... ich habe dieses Elend mit mir zur Welt gebracht. Es lag schon
mit mir in der Wiege, und wenn meine Mutter mich wiegte, so
wiegte sie es mit, und wenn sie mich in den Schlaf sang, so schlief
es mit mir ein, und es erwachte, sobald ich wieder die Augen
aufschlug.' (E iii. 194.) To intensify this sense of futility in
human affairs Heine had already woven into the work a parody of
Hegelian systematization in the form of a mock treatise on *Ideen*,
including a suitable list of contents, which bears no relevance to
what follows.[11] Indeed, the very use of Sterne's comic techniques and
constant shifts of perspective may be seen as a deliberate reaction
against the claims to absolute validity made by Hegel. Napoleon's
fall appears symptomatic of the senselessness with which the world
proceeds and we are reminded of a little poem that had already
appeared in *Die Heimkehr*:

> Zu fragmentarisch ist Welt und Leben —
> Ich will mich zum deutschen Professor begeben.
> Der weiß das Leben zusammenzusetzen,
> Und er macht ein verständlich System daraus;
> Mit seinen Nachtmützen und Schlafrockfetzen
> Stopft er die Lücken des Weltenbaus.   (E i. 121)

So that nothing should remain hidden the narrator then shows
himself at work as a satirist, for whom the fools and foibles of this
world are daily sustenance. The reader is given a mouth-watering
menu of buffoons of all shapes, sizes, and flavours, served in the
most bizarre of manners. But as in any good treatise the author has
already informed his reader why he now presents the tragic spectacle of the world as something ludicrous:

> *Du sublime au ridicule il n'y a qu'un pas, Madame!* Aber das Leben ist
> im Grunde so fatal ernsthaft, daß es nicht zu ertragen wäre ohne
> solche Verbindung des Pathetischen mit dem Komischen. Das wissen
> unsere Poeten. Die grauenhaftesten Bilder des menschlichen Wahn-
> sinns zeigt uns Aristophanes nur im lachenden Spiegel des Witzes, den
> großen Denkerschmerz, der seine eigne Nichtigkeit begreift, wagt
> Goethe nur in den Knittelversen eines Puppenspiels auszusprechen,
> und die tödlichste Klage über den Jammer der Welt legt Shakespeare

---

[11] E iii. 173.

in den Mund eines Narren, während er dessen Schellenkappe ängstlich schüttelt.[12]

Sie haben's alle dem großen Urpoeten abgesehen, der in seiner tausendaktigen Welttragödie den Humor aufs höchste zu treiben weiß, wie wir es täglich sehen:—nach dem Abgang der Helden kommen die Clowns und Graziosos mit ihren Narrenkolben und Pritschen, nach den blutigen Revolutionsszenen und Kaiseraktionen kommen wieder herangewatschelt die dicken Bourbonen mit ihren alten abgestandenen Späßchen und zartlegitimen Bonmots, und graziöse hüpft herbei die alte Noblesse mit ihrem verhungerten Lächeln, und hintendrein wallen die frommen Kapuzen mit Lichtern, Kreuzen und Kirchenfahnen . . .

(E iii. 166)

The farce is complete when we see the Lord God sitting before the familiar metaphor of the world's stage, growing bored at the gesticulations of its actors and deciding which to dismiss.

I have analysed this work at some length (though it is worthy of a far closer interpretation)[13] since it demonstrates two vital points. In the first place, it shows the danger of extracting ideas from Heine's work without looking also to their context. The Utopian Heine, whom I have so far treated in isolation, is constantly accompanied by the sceptic—indeed his optimism and his pessimism are interdependent and part of the same psychological phenomenon. In the second place, *Das Buch Le Grand* illuminates the difference between a treatise, pamphlet, or philosophical proposition, and a work of art. The work of art, because of its detachment, is not committed to setting out or defending a single argument or worldview. It is privileged to be able to display conflicting standpoints without passing judgement. In the final analysis *Das Buch Le Grand* is a portrait of the artist himself in whom these dissonances and tensions lead their chaotic dance. If one claims unity of structure as a necessary criterion of art this does not have to lie in external shape, although in this particular case Heine was plainly anxious to provide such shape by incapsulating the political and satirical elements within the 'love tragedy'. It can equally well lie in the discord and the polarities which constitute the psyche of the narrator himself. This work is a running report on the flux of memories, loves, hates, and fears of the artist. According to the

[12] See also Heine's letter to Friederike Robert, Oct. 1825 (*Br* i. 233), which he clearly used for this passage.
[13] Such as Jeffrey Sammons has undertaken in his study of Heine, op. cit., pp. 116–49.

fiction that the work establishes, Madame or the reader is granted a live glimpse into this remarkable complex of conflicting emotions and thoughts.

When Heine first wrote to his friends about *Almansor* he was proud to speak of its confessional nature, for it seemed to contain all that he had to give: 'In dieses Stück habe ich mein eignes Selbst hineingeworfen, mitsammt meinen Paradoxen, meiner Weisheit, meiner Liebe, meinem Hasse und meiner ganzen Verrücktheit.' (*Br* i. 15.) But he was not slow to realize that it was precisely this which made it a bad play. He had failed to create independent, convincing characters.[14] It was Sterne who helped him find his way back to his own essential talent. In *Die romantische Schule* Heine was to portray this novelist as the ward of the tragic muse and yet the darling of the goddess of laughter. The passage characterizes beautifully this juxtaposition of wit and despair which we also find in Heine and which made him an artist rather than a political theorist:

Er war das Schoßkind der bleichen tragischen Göttin. Einst, in einem Anfall von grausamer Zärtlichkeit, küßte diese ihm das junge Herz so gewaltig, so liebesstark, so inbrünstig saugend, daß das Herz zu bluten begann und plötzlich alle Schmerzen dieser Welt verstand und von unendlichem Mitleid erfüllt wurde. Armes, junges Dichterherz! Aber die jüngere Tochter Mnemosynes, die rosige Göttin des Scherzes, hüpfte schnell hinzu und nahm den leidenden Knaben in ihre Arme und suchte ihn zu erheitern mit Lachen und Singen und gab ihm als Spielzeug die komische Larve und die närrischen Glöckchen und küßte begütigend seine Lippen und küßte ihm darauf all ihren Leichtsinn, all ihre trotzige Lust, all ihre witzige Neckerei.

Und seitdem gerieten Sternes Herz und Sternes Lippen in einen sonderbaren Widerspruch: wenn sein Herz manchmal ganz tragisch bewegt ist und er seine tiefsten blutenden Herzensgefühle aussprechen will, dann, zu seiner eignen Verwunderung, flattern von seinen Lippen die lachend ergötzlichsten Worte. (E v. 331 f.)

A few pages later we read some lines that could serve as a motto to Heine's art, the art of ambivalence:

Der Verfasser des 'Tristram Shandy' zeigt uns die verborgensten Tiefen der Seele: er öffnet eine Luke der Seele, erlaubt uns einen Blick in ihre Abgründe, Paradiese und Schmutzwinkel und läßt gleich die Gardine davor wieder fallen. Wir haben von vorn in das seltsame

---

[14] *Br* i. 23 f.

Theater hineingeschaut, Beleuchtung und Perspektive hat ihre Wirkung nicht verfehlt, und indem wir das Unendliche geschaut zu haben meinen, ist unser Gefühl unendlich geworden, poetisch. (E v. 338 f.)

My analysis of *Das Buch Le Grand* suggests that it is the contest between Heine's vision of Utopia and his ultimate sense of the tragic and futile in human endeavour which is the essence of his art. This contest provides more than 'subject-matter'—it is the very form of the work. In a world where reader would not flag nor writer tire my earlier account of the Utopian would now be supplemented by a detailed examination of the sceptic and a work-by-work interpretation to illuminate this intimate relationship between the artist's mental turmoil and the structure of his production. Clearly that is beyond the scope of a study of this nature. Since a poet's formative years are always amongst the most instructive for the critic I shall restrict myself to certain of the *Reisebilder* and related works of the 1830s, each of which supplies further evidence of Heine's pessimist traits while employing artistic techniques which were to be of significance in later works.

c. *The poem cycle*—Die Nordsee *I and II*

The evolution of Heine's art in the 1820s is largely the story of how he came to terms with his particular talent for self-scrutiny, a self-scrutiny which becomes of increasing interest and significance as Heine's highly receptive mind absorbed more and more of the thought and aspirations of his age. I have already discussed his debt to teachers such as A. W. Schlegel and Hegel at length. Sterne was an exciting discovery for Heine since he confirmed that there were kindred spirits of a similar mental complexity to his own, who refused to accept the discipline of systematic thought. Further he provided a method of writing which raised reflection and humour to the very content of a work. But even in his frustrating experiments with the *Kunstlied* Heine was able to make significant advances in technique. The song may have appeared as mere artifice even before he wrote the majority of his own *Lieder*, but this did not deter him from continuing the experiment, and his reasons for doing this were not mere hypocrisy or dishonesty. As we have seen, in Müller's own poems he found a method for expressing his disenchantment, the *Stimmungsbrechung*. Müller's *Die schöne Müllerin* is not even a pretence at *naïveté*, for in the prologue and epilogue it openly shows us the sophisticated and cultured aping the simple journeyman. Heine's own songs, which were written in full awareness of this state of affairs, and which often seem to be self-destructive in their irony, are the direct expression of a divided mind. We are given lyrical insight into the feelings of a poet who longs for simplicity but is too honest to claim he has found it. Now, the cycle as a whole can record this crisis still more effectively. Both the Romantics and Goethe had used the cycle form, but no one produced a more coherent unit than Müller.[15] Moreover, it was only shortly before Heine first read *Die schöne Müllerin* that he had studied under Schlegel, who showed great interest in the cycle as a poetic form and had already drawn attention to Petrarch's songs as 'ein wahrer und vollständiger lyrischer Roman'.[16] From this time on it became Heine's standard practice to publish his poems in cycles. It was not that they were written in their present order;[17] one needs only to look at the revisions he undertook in new editions to see that he was prepared to omit poems and adjust the sequence. But the cycle, which could reflect the growth, deterioration, and finally disappearance of love, could also express the process of disillusionment with the song form itself and hence the reference to the poems or the 'Büchlein' at the close of a cycle.

The most remarkable example of a cycle used to portray the process in which scepticism gradually overwhelms and destroys the poet's optimistic vision is the two sets of North Sea poems. The striking contrast between the artificial *Minnelied* setting of 'Krönung' which opens the work and the simple but effective memory of childhood aroused by the sight and sound of the sea in 'Abenddämmerung' introduces the fundamental theme—the power of nature to liberate the poetic imagination from convention and artificiality. With pleasure he told Moser: 'Ich bin also doch

---

[15] Cf. Helen Meredith Mustard, *The Lyric Cycle in German Literature*, New York, 1946 (for Müller, esp. pp. 80 ff.)

[16] A. W. Schlegel, *Vorlesungen über schöne Litteratur und Kunst*, ed. J. Minor, (Deutsche Literaturdenkmale 19), Heilbronn, 1884, p. 204. Although Heine did not attend this lecture series (see above, p. 12), Schlegel certainly introduced his pupil to the sonnet (cf. E i. 56–62), and as he regarded Petrarch as one of the finest exponents of this form it seems likely that they would have discussed Petrarch's 'novel', too. In the lectures the examination of Petrarch had led to a consideration of the sonnet as a genre. Windfuhr, op. cit., does not mention this but argues that from Heine's adherence to the theme of disappointed love down to images and set phrases, he wrote in the Petrarchist tradition.

[17] Cf. Mustard, op. cit., p. 100. Urs Belart's *Gehalt und Aufbau von Heinrich Heines Gedichtsammlungen*, Berne, 1925, is too forced and 'tidy' to persuade.

nicht auf eine bloß lyrisch maliziöse zweystrophige Manier be-
schränkt',[18] while an announcement for the work probably written by
Heine[19] as good as says that the old struggle with the *Lied* is over,
for these poems take the reader 'in ein neues Reich der Reflexion
und zu einer neuen Art der Auffassung und Gestaltung, die den
Übergang zu einer neuen Periode dieses reichen Dichterlebens
bilden wird.' Heine was hardly the first to seek simplicity in nature,
any more than contrary to popular belief he was the first German poet
of the sea.[20] But it was precisely his 'reflections' which became his
stumbling-block. In 'Abenddämmerung' the genuine and direct
correspondence between the poet's own mood and the flux of the
ocean appears to have ended the ironic play with outworn lyrical
material so completely that one critic has used the poem to illustrate
the essential creative process of the lyric.[21] But as the cycle progresses the visions evoked by the water grow wilder on the one hand
and more disturbing on the other. 'Sonnenuntergang' introduces
gods of the elements, the sun and moon, as a couple separated by evil
gossip. Analogy brings the poet to speak of the fate of the Olympian
gods, whom immortality has condemned to eternal wanderings:

> Und die armen Götter, oben am Himmel
> Wandeln sie, qualvoll,

[18] *Br* i. 244.

[19] Text in *Heinrich Heine. Werke und Briefe*, ed. Hans Kaufmann, Berlin,
1961–4, x. 178 f. For authorship see F. H. Eisner, 'Echtes, Unechtes und Zweifelhaftes in Heines Werken. Ergebnisse der Heine-Philologie seit 1924', *Heine-
Jahrbuch 1962*, p. 51.

[20] There has been some dispute both about Heine's models and whether he is
the first German sea poet. The latter has often been assumed following Jules
Legras's statement, op. cit., p. 97, that he was preceded only by Goethe's 'lignes
banales' in 'Meeresstille' (1796). Did he not notice that the sequence from
Heine's own 'Meeresstille' to 'Reinigung' echoes Goethe's sequence from
'Meeresstille' to 'Glückliche Fahrt'? This in itself would throw doubt on the
pioneering originality of Heine's work. But in his review of Legras (*Euphorion*,
5 (1898), 149 ff.) Oscar Walzel already pointed out that pride of place with regard
to subject-matter, free verse form, and the use of sun/moon imagery and mythology must go to Friedrich von Stolberg's sea poems of 1779 (pp. 154 f.).
This adds weight to an interpretation which finds in these poems a further
struggle with established literary material similar to that in the preceding cycle.
The use of free verse, neologisms, and compounds suggests more than Tieck
and Robert as Heine's models (cf. Elster, 'Das Vorbild der freien Rhythmen
Heinrich Heines', *Euphorion*, 25 (1924), 63–86). It is more likely that these, his
confessed models, stimulated a technical interest at least in the free verse of
Klopstock and Goethe.

[21] Cf. J. Murat, 'A propos d'un poème de Heine. Notes sur la création poétique',
Bulletin de la Faculté des Lettres de Strasbourg, 35 (1956), 151–9.

Trostlos unendliche Bahnen,
Und kömmen nicht sterben,
Und schleppen mit sich
Ihr strahlendes Elend.

Ich, aber, der Mensch,
Der niedrig gepflanzte, der Tod-beglückte,
Ich klage nicht länger. (E i. 166)

Rootlessness, a life condemned to aimless and futile wanderings, these are constituent elements in Heine's pessimism. For the moment the absurdity and humour of the visions that follow dispel the depression. The mysterious Byronic figure who strides swathed in a cloak across the beach in 'Die Nacht am Strande' proves to be less demonic when he reaches his beloved's cottage and orders tea and rum as if at a beach café. Similarly 'Poseidon' offers some light relief in the realm of the gods. A climax is reached, however, in 'Seegespenst', where the poetic vision becomes so hallucinatory that the poet tries to dive into the sea to fetch his long-lost beloved, whom he believes he sees below in an ancient sunken city. But perhaps the most extreme of all the visions is that of the closing poem 'Frieden'. The poet sees Christ walking on the waters and behind him is a town where calm, beauty, and harmony reign. The poetic imagination reaches new heights. But in the first edition this Utopia was followed by a brilliant and merciless satire of a burgher of the town as it was in reality, a sycophantic civil servant, who was quite capable of using such pious fantasies to obtain a rise in salary—'Gelobt sey Jesu Christ!'[22]

Heine removed this section from the *Buch der Lieder* version, probably because he feared arousing too much hostility.[23] The second cycle, despite its elated opening, intensifies the theme of futility and the feeling of senselessness adumbrated in the first. The greeting to the ocean is that of the Greeks reaching the Bosporus on their retreat from Asia, and the cycle that follows plots the journey of the poet's own 'Rückzugherz', a journey which ironically ends not at the ocean-side but in retreat from it in the port. The ship is shaken by a tempest. The survivor of the shipwreck lives only to despair of love and life, life which is mere senseless repetition:

Vor mir woget die Wasserwüste,
Hinter mir liegt nur Kummer und Elend,

[22] E i. 531.
[23] As we can deduce from his letter to Moser, 28 July 1826 (*Br* i. 285).

Und über mich hin ziehen die Wolken,
Die formlos grauen Töchter der Luft,
Die aus dem Meer, in Nebeleimern,
Das Wasser schöpfen,
Und es mühsam schleppen und schleppen,
Und es wieder verschütten ins Meer,
Ein trübes, langweil'ges Geschäft,
Und nutzlos, wie mein eignes Leben. (E i. 182)

Rejected by the Oceanides, the poet next sees the wretched gods of the Greeks dragging pathetically across the heavens until the moon is obscured and they, now subject to the laws of empirical reality, have to vanish. Alone, the poet calls out to the ocean to answer life's riddle, but the futility of the very question is already emphasized when he absurdly characterizes the world's thinkers by their particular mode of national headgear:

'O löst mir das Rätsel des Lebens,
Das qualvoll uralte Rätsel,
Worüber schon manche Häupter gegrübelt,
Häupter in Hieroglyphenmützen,
Häupter in Turban und schwarzem Barett,
Perückenhäupter und tausend andre
Arme, schwitzende Menschenhäupter —
Sagt mir, was bedeutet der Mensch?
Woher ist er kommen? Wo geht er hin?
Wer wohnt dort oben auf goldenen Sternen?

Es murmeln die Wogen ihr ew'ges Gemurmel,
Es wehet der Wind, es fliehen die Wolken,
Es blinken die Sterne gleichgültig und kalt,
Und ein Narr wartet auf Antwort. (E i. 190)

This is the low point of the cycle. The mood begins to lift with the parrot-like cry of 'Der Phönix': 'sie liebt ihn! sie liebt ihn!' and finally the poet reaches his haven, the Ratskeller in Bremen. As he drinks weighty problems grow lighter and soon world history, Hegel and Gans, Goethe's Oriental beauties, and the twelve apostles begin to revolve in the wild dance of his befuddled brain. And as he staggers up into brilliant sunshine he sees that:

Die glühende Sonne dort oben
Ist nur eine rote, betrunkene Nase,

Die Nase des Weltgeists;
Und um die rote Weltgeistnase
Dreht sich die ganze betrunkene Welt.   (E i. 193)

D. *The* Reisebild—*from Bacharach to Genoa*

Art which concentrates on mental realities rather than creating
character and action needs some external framework to carry it.
The cycle, by organizing disparate lyrical moments into a whole,
provides a pattern which is particularly effective if, like Heine, the
poet seeks to present not progress but a futile, circular process. In
the second North Sea cycle this pattern is reinforced with the
voyage back to Bremen, and undoubtedly the journey motif is
Heine's favourite artistic technique. Its attraction is obvious since
it removes the need for a 'story' and can directly reflect the peregrinations of the mind he wishes to depict. Even *Briefe aus Berlin*
of 1822 as a journalistic travel-report gave the narrator a free hand
to record the impressions he thought important or amusing in an
order purely determined by the 'association of ideas'.[24] More
grandiose in plan at least was his projected novel *Der Rabbi von
Bacherach*.[25] Inspired by the activities of the Jewish Verein in
Berlin, there is reason to believe that the novel was intended to
trace the wanderings of a Jewish couple across the changing face
of Europe in the fifteenth century.[26] Fleeing from Germany, which
was still medieval in character, they would probably have reached
the Italy of the Renaissance. The novel would thus have provided
a cross-section of Jewry, and raised the still-live problems of the
ghetto as opposed to integration and of emancipation as opposed to
orthodoxy. Above all it would have symbolized the age-old suffering
of the Jews in exile by adopting a new version of the legendary
Wandering Jew. But the novel did not get beyond three chapters,
of which one or one and a half were tacked on fifteen years later in
1840 for publication as a fragment,[27] following the plundering of
the Jewish quarter in Damascus at Passover time. The Jews were
accused of having murdered a Capuchin monk and used his blood

[24] See E vii. 561.
[25] Heine changed the spelling of the actual town from Bacharach to Bacherach.
[26] Cf. Erich Loewenthal, 'Heines Fragment "Der Rabbi von Bacherach" ',
Der Morgen. Zeitschrift der Juden in Deutschland (4 July 1936), 173 f.
[27] Cf. Franz Finke, 'Zur Datierung des "Rabbi von Bacherach" ', *Heine-
Jahrbuch 1965*, pp. 26–32. An examination of the manuscript in the Heine
Archives, Düsseldorf, bears out Finke's findings.

for their feast[28]—a remarkable parallel to the opening incident in
Heine's own novel, where Bacharach Jews are falsely charged with
the slaughter of a Christian baby. We are left with the initial
Passover scene ending in the flight of Rabbi Abraham and his wife,
Sara, to safety from an imminent blood-bath. We see them reach
Frankfurt and witness some colourful scenes in the medieval city,
the walled ghetto, and the synagogue. All that remains of the
confrontation with Renaissance humanism is the figure of Isaac
Abarbanel, an outspoken Hellene, who verges on caricature. The
portrayal of medieval Jewry ends in some brilliantly cruel thumb-
nail sketches during the service at the synagogue.

There has been considerable debate why the novel remained
a fragment. The traditional view stresses the importance of Heine's loss of interest following his conversion in 1825.[29] Sammons
has pointed to inherent weaknesses in the narrative scheme.[30] But
still more important was probably Heine's inability to create
characters who could carry the psychological realism, the close
observation of mood and inner realities which Heine achieves in
so much of his finest work. There is a striking contrast between
the fruitless effort entailed by the novel and the apparent ease with
which he 'wrote up' his *Harzreise*.[31] The difference between the
works is patent. In *Die Harzreise* the journey enabled a first-
person narrator to range freely over nature and Philistine, dream
and reality, to break into lyric, to reflect or to satirize at will. It is
in short a 'sentimental journey' in the Sterne tradition.[32] *Der Rabbi
von Bacherach* provided Heine with neither this freedom nor the
scope. He managed to incorporate a dream sequence into the

[28] Cf. E vi. 166 f.
[29] An argument recently restated by Sternberger, op. cit., pp. 150–80.
[30] Sammons, 'Heine's "Rabbi von Bacherach" ' (cited above) and *Heinrich
Heine*, pp. 302–13. See also Lion Feuchtwanger, *Heinrich Heines Fragment 'Der
Rabbi von Bacherach'*, Diss., Munich, 1907; Erich Loewenthal, ' "Der Rabbi von
Bacherach" ', *Heine-Jahrbuch 1964*, pp. 3–16 (reprint of 1937 article); Dorothy
Lasher-Schlitt, 'Heine's Unresolved Conflict and "Der Rabbi von Bacherach" ',
The Germanic Review, 27 (1952), 173–87. Feuchtwanger proposes the curious
argument that the novel was written in its entirety, most of the manuscript
burnt in the fire at his mother's home, and then rounded off again. One wonders
in that case why Heine only took two chapters to Paris and why he did not
rewrite the entire fragment in the light of his later scepticism. Finke has shown
that even most of the second chapter has to be ascribed to 1840.
[31] See *Br* i. 183 ff., 188, 191, 201.
[32] Cf. Manfred Link's useful account *Der Reisebericht als literarische Kunstform
von Goethe bis Heine*, Diss., Cologne, 1963.

voyage on the Rhine, when Sara dreams of her childhood and the legends she heard, but any lengthy depiction of her inner life was clearly obstructed by the third-person characterization. In his *Reisebild*,[33] on the other hand, the journey registers both the poet's encounters and experiences and his mental responses to them. The pattern is provided by the terrain through which the narrator travels. Leaving the sterile academicism of Göttingen below, he climbs into the mountains to his 'Berg-Idylle' and its ironic echo on the Brocken. One might have expected the mood to drop as the narrator approached the plains on the other side but the work ends on a merry but abrupt note beside the tumbling Ilse, before the narrator reaches the confinement of town life again.[34] The reality of Heine's cold reception in Weimar is not allowed to obtrude and *Die Harzreise* remains his gayest work.[35]

In the more elaborate *Reise von München nach Genua* a very similar pattern is followed but here the descent from the mountains is pursued the entire way down to sea-level. The opening chapters confront us with the Philistines of Berlin and a lively satire of a capital without history but with pretensions.[36] Fleeing this the narrator seeks spring across the Alps in Italy. The theme of political liberation for the Tyrol and the motif of the beautiful young girls who still contrive to live and love amid the ruins of Classical and Renaissance Italy and beneath the repressive rule of Catholicism are fused in the glorious vision of the new age on the battlefield at Marengo. This is the high point of the work and thus corresponds thematically and structurally to the 'Berg-Idylle', even, as it turns out, in its degree of fantasy. For no sooner has the

---

[33] See above, pp. 21 ff.

[34] See the manuscript fragments in Elster, 2nd edn., iii. 379–84 and 461 f., in which the journey continues to Ilsenburg. Some of the earlier anti-Philistine satire is repeated and the narrative then tails off. See also the letters on the interview with Goethe, *Br* i. 210, 216 f.

[35] Jost Hermand has claimed that *Die Harzreise* should be seen as a conscious reaction against the deep disappointment Heine experienced on meeting Goethe. It is, he argues ingeniously, in 'Werthers Harzreise', *Von Mainz bis Weimar, 1793–1919. Studien zur deutschen Literatur*, Stuttgart, 1969, pp. 129–51, a careful parody of *Werther* and far from being a fragment it ends on a happy note in comic contrast to the suicide of Goethe's love-sick hero, a reading that the text certainly seems to bear out—'Mädchen, erschrick nicht! ich hab' mich nicht totgeschossen'.

[36] The leitmotiv repetition of comic phrases, 'Es ist heut eine scheene Witterung' etc., the banter with the reader, and the apparently naive autobiographical touch, with e.g. references to his brother Maximilian, all reflect the influence of Sterne's *Sentimental Journey*.

narrator left Marengo and set out downhill than the journey comes
to a rapid and disturbing end. We have been prepared for this,
when, between the satire of nobility and clergy, of servility and
mortification on the one hand and the celebration of a rosy future
on the other, we catch glimpses of a darker side of life. Even as he
starts his journey, 'Tirily! Tirily! ich lebe!', his reflective sentimentality seems strangely ambiguous in its enjoyment of pain and
with its melancholic reminder that the greatest men, finest trees,
or noblest eagle all suffer and will die.[37] Again, some chapters
later, Heine detects unexpected depths beneath the burlesque
surface of the Italian *opera buffa*. It is 'jene wundersame Gattung,
die dem Humor den freiesten Spielraum gewährt, und worin er
sich all seiner springenden Lust, seiner tollen Empfindelei, seiner
lachenden Wehmut und seiner lebenssüchtigen Todesbegeisterung
überlassen kann'.[38] In Genoa the narrator visits the gallery of the
Durazzo Palace. Comparing Rubens and Cornelius he feels the
former's joyful paintings reflect the 'tanzende Kirmesmusik'[39]
which must have surrounded the painter as he worked. Cornelius,
however, must have painted on Good Fridays since his works are
filled with melancholy and pain. This is the polarity established
earlier between the vine and the cross round which it has entwined
itself,[40] between the pagan and the Christian, mirrored in art. But
then Heine abruptly upsets this contrast. He sees beneath the
jolly faces of Rubens's figures the seeds of death. Their very
exuberance spells their imminent end. The last chapter emphasizes
that death will finally destroy all, as the narrator comes to realize
that nothing more remains of the beautiful women whose portraits hang in the palace than these mere strips of canvas:

Melancholisch überkriecht uns der Gedanke: daß von den Originalen
jener Bilder, von all jenen Schönen, die so lieblich, so kokett, so witzig,
so schalkhaft und so schwärmerisch waren, von all jenen Maiköpfchen
mit Aprillaunen, von jenem ganzen Frauenfrühling nichts übriggeblie-
ben ist als diese bunten Schatten, die ein Maler, der gleich ihnen längst

[37] E iii. 225 f.
[38] Ibid. 250.
[39] Though he may have been thinking of Rubens's painting of the Flemish
kermis, the Durazzo Palace at this time contained only two Rubens portraits and
a picture of Silenus and bacchantes—cf. Karl Hessel, *Heinrich Heines Verhältnis
zur bildenden Kunst*, Marburg, 1931, p. 86.
[40] E iii. 240. Cf. Link, op. cit., p. 153.

vermodert ist, auf ein morsch Stückchen Leinwand gepinselt hat, das ebenfalls mit der Zeit in Staub zerfällt und verweht. So geht alles Leben, das Schöne ebenso wie das Häßliche, spurlos vorüber, der Tod, der dürre Pedant, verschont die Rose ebensowenig wie die Distel, er vergißt auch nicht das einsame Hälmchen in der fernsten Wildnis, er zerstört gründlich und unaufhörlich, überall sehen wir, wie er Pflanzen und Tiere, die Menschen und ihre Werke, zu Staub zerstampft, und selbst jene ägyptischen Pyramiden, die seiner Zerstörungswut zu trotzen scheinen, sie sind nur Trophäen seiner Macht, Denkmäler der Vergänglichkeit, uralte Königsgräber.   (E iii. 286)

Subtly the love episodes and the earlier motifs of spring and beautiful women are woven together with the melancholy and thus placed in an altogether different perspective. Nor is this remarkably Baroque reflection his most terrifying vision. Life appears as an unending cycle which devours the individual—it is a poetic and evocative picture of the interpretation of history which he was to attack so vehemently in 'Verschiedenartige Geschichtsauffassung':

Aber noch schlimmer als dieses Gefühl eines ewigen Sterbens, einer öden gähnenden Vernichtung, ergreift uns der Gedanke, daß wir nicht einmal als Originale dahinsterben, sondern als Kopien von längst verschollenen Menschen, die geistig und körperlich uns gleich waren, und daß nach uns wieder Menschen geboren werden, die wieder ganz aussehen und fühlen und denken werden, wie wir, und die der Tod ebenfalls wieder vernichten wird — ein trostlos ewiges Wiederholungsspiel, wobei die zeugende Erde beständig hervorbringen und mehr hervorbringen muß, als der Tod zu zerstören vermag, so daß sie, in solcher Not, mehr für die Erhaltung der Gattungen als für die Originalität der Individuen sorgen kann.   (E iii. 286 f.)

The work closes as the narrator claims to recognize his own 'maliziös sentimentalen Lippen' in one portrait by Giorgione and the features of his dead beloved, Maria, in another. *Die Reise von München* is perhaps Heine's finest 'travel picture', since it succeeds in fusing the journey motif so perfectly with the rise and fall of the poet's mood. The physical situation of Genoa by the sea and on a steep slope corresponds exactly with the precipitous drop in his spiritual barometer after his lofty experience up in the hills.

c. *The Itinerant—Don Quixote, the Wandering Jew, the Flying Dutchman*

It is that settled, ceaseless gloom
The fabled Hebrew wanderer bore;

That will not look beyond the tomb,
But cannot hope for rest before.

(Byron, *Childe Harold*, Canto 1)

Formally *Die Stadt Lucca* is more diffuse than *Die Reise von München* since it does not adhere to any single structural principle. The body of the work is devoted to one of Heine's longest and poetically most evocative attacks on Christianity, occasioned by an ecclesiastical procession he chances to witness on his return to Lucca. The journey motif serves to introduce the discussion that follows but is restricted to this function. Even before Heine lets the actors in the macabre ceremony pass by, he has made its symbolical significance clear to us: ' "es ist das Leben selbst, das sein Vermählungfest mit dem Tode feiert und Schönheit und Jugend dazu eingeladen hat." Ja, es war so ein lebendes Totenfest …' (E iii. 390.) But this is no simple polemic relying on the powers of the poet to conjure up the scene in its grotesque incongruity: beneath the habits of these priests of death the narrator recognizes his own sickness, a sickness by which the entire world has been infected: 'O! es ist keine Übertreibung, wenn der Poet in seinem Schmerze ausruft: das Leben ist eine Krankheit, die ganze Welt ein Lazarett!'[41]

These thoughts can, of course, still be accommodated within the historical scheme which sees in Christianity the religion that destroyed the harmony of Greek culture, and the following chapter begins with the renowned vision of a Christ figure who bursts into the gods' banquet on Mount Olympus, hurls his cross over their table and drives them off as evil spirits. Nevertheless, in the conversations which now take place between the narrator and his two female companions in Lucca, Franscheska and Mathilde, Christianity remains less a subject for polemic than a topic for discussion, and Heine constructs around it a network of antitheses. The narrator's mistress, Franscheska, is a devout believer, 'eine katholische Einheit', and yet in her frivolity and eroticism she is the living denial of this religion as it has been presented to us. Mathilde, an Anglo-Irish noblewoman, is physically just as attractive but is a sceptic in religious matters. Yet ethically she considers herself a Christian. The narrator moves between the two, now defending religion, now condemning the Jews, who first

[41] E iii. 393.

brought the evil of a positive faith into the world. If these chapters
lack the concision of 'Gespräch auf der Paderborner Heide' or
'Gespräch auf der Themse' in *Englische Fragmente* and are therefore
less memorable, they surpass them in subtlety. The intention is
less to plead for one particular case than to reveal the seemingly
irresolvable conflict between different men's natures and viewpoints. The work thus anticipates the theme of *Ludwig Börne*.

Heine now switches to a round attack on state religion and to
his demand that kings should be liberated from the poisonous in-
trigue of the aristocrats. A clear polemical line at last seems to be
emerging, as he claims that history will nonchalantly crush priest
and nobleman alike beneath its advancing feet. But he immediately
reflects that the progress of history does little to alleviate the agony
of those that suffer at the hands of the nobility and clergy before
the new age has been realized. These men are the martyrs of the
present. And what if these martyrs have themselves lost their
faith and are victims of scepticism?

Es gibt nichts Entsetzlicheres als jene Stunden, wo ein Marcus Brutus
zu zweifeln begann an der Wirklichkeit der Tugend, für die er alles
geopfert! Und ach! jener war ein Römer und lebte in der Blütezeit der
Stoa; wir aber sind modern weicheren Stoffes, und dazu sehen wir
noch das Gedeihen einer Philosophie, die aller Begeisterung nur eine
relative Bedeutung zuspricht und sie somit in sich selbst vernichtet oder
sie allenfalls zu einer selbstbewußten Donquichotterie neutralisiert![42]

We have to wait until the next chapter to discover the identity
of this apparently obvious philosophy but in the meantime, in
a curious shift of viewpoint, the narrator now firmly adopts the
image of Don Quixote to describe the enthusiast, whom he had
seemed to be defending. Stating that the ventures of this absurd
knight-errant can stand for the ways of life itself, he even claims that
the sceptics and the apathetic many are in fact the Sancho Panzas
of this world, led on despite themselves to seek the rewards their
mad master has promised. And so they are committed to accompanying him on his wild exploits. To bring this highly self-
conscious and ironic passage to a climax Heine now likens his
work itself to Don Quixote's route and its reader to Sancho Panza,
who has to drag along behind the peregrinations of the mad poet.
It is patent that this Sternesque narrative is not intended to present

---

[42] This and following passages quoted are from E iii. 421 ff.

a single line of argument: rather Heine wishes to record the tortuous path of his own reasonings, hopes, and fears.

This continues in the next chapter where he illustrates the progress of his youthful enthusiasm by reference to his changing view of Don Quixote over the years. The child had seen him simply as a hero misunderstood and cruelly persecuted by the world. He had been equally blind to the irony in all human affairs and to the irony of Cervantes's novel. Yet, as he compares his love of Don Quixote with the enthusiasm of his youth for the heroic figures of history, a list which casually ends with 'Jesus von Jerusalem' and 'Robespierre und Saint-Just von Paris', he confesses his still unrepentant idealism:

In meiner Brust aber blüht noch jene flammende Liebe, die sich sehnsüchtig über die Erde emporhebt, abenteuerlich herumschwärmt in den weiten, gähnenden Räumen des Himmels, dort zurückgestoßen wird von den kalten Sternen, und wieder heimsinkt zur kleinen Erde, und mit Seufzen und Jauchzen gestehen muß, daß es doch in der ganzen Schöpfung nichts Schöneres und Besseres gibt als das Herz der Menschen.

Ultimately it is a mental process of this kind which the entire *Reisebilder* is concerned to display. Youth, he continues, is always more idealistic and disinterested than its elders, who have given up rebelling against what they cannot change. The excuse which he puts in their mouths is of interest: it is a brief attack on the arguments of the Right Hegelians who, it will be remembered, concluded that the identity of the world with the Spirit in its historical process of self-realization automatically justified the present state of affairs:

... sie erkriechen mit klebrichter Beharrlichkeit die Höhe des Bürgermeistertums oder der Präsidentschaft ihres Klubs und zucken die Achsel über die Heroenbilder, die der Sturm hinabwarf von der Säule des Ruhms, und dabei erzählen sie vielleicht: daß sie selbst in ihrer Jugend ebenfalls mit dem Kopf gegen die Wand gerannt seien, daß sie sich aber nachher mit der Wand wieder versöhnt hätten, denn die Wand sei das Absolute, das Gesetzte, das an und für sich Seiende, das, weil es ist, auch vernünftig ist, weshalb auch derjenige unvernünftig ist, welcher einen allerhöchst vernünftigen, unwidersprechbar seienden, festgesetzten Absolutismus nicht ertragen will.

This must be the unnamed philosophy to which Heine referred in the earlier passage on Brutus. But still worse is the Historical

School, which he was to pillory later in 'Verschiedenartige Geschichtsauffassung': it does not even deserve to be called philosophy. Its exponents are:

... jene Verworfenen, die bei der Verteidigung des Despotismus sich nicht einmal auf vernünftige Vernunftsgründe einlassen, sondern ihn geschichtskundig als ein Gewohnheitsrecht verfechten, woran sich die Menschen im Laufe der Zeit allmählich gewöhnt hätten, und das also rechtsgültig und gesetzkräftig unumstößlich sei.

Today, he adds, he can still see himself as a Don Quixote but one whose *idée fixe* is revolution, whose Amadis is Rousseau, and who sees the world's giants as mere windmills and its castles as taverns. But his enemies are no less ubiquitous for that, and in his dreams he cries out that Dulcinea is the most beautiful woman in the world and calls upon the barber in disguise[43] to drive home his lance.

What are we to make of the patent ambiguity which attaches to this figure, an ambiguity directly expressed in Sancho Panza, who unwittingly serves to parody Don Quixote's every endeavour? The 'Spätere Nachschrift', which purports in contrast to what went before to have been written after the July Revolution, seems to curtail this ambivalence. The Revolution has now occurred, the *Marseillaise* is being played in the streets and the narrator summons his readers to arms in a whirl of ecstasy. But are we, who have followed the labyrinth of his previous reflections, persuaded that this optimistic mood will last? If the advent of revolution proves that the author's wildest hopes were justified and not a mere chimera, why does he retain the Don Quixote image? It seems that Heine still seeks less to set out a straightforward argument than to depict his own changing state of mind, the relative merit of his most cherished ideals, and the troublesome range of opinion that even reasonable human beings can hold. After all, the opening episode with the lizard has already warned us to regard all human thought as potential humbug and to consider the idea of human progress towards a kingdom of heaven on earth to be as meaningful as the hieroglyphs on the ancient animal's tail.[44]

---

[43] It was a forgivable error which led Heine to identify the Knight of the White Moon with the barber whose bowl Don Quixote had previously mistaken for a helmet. The knight was in fact Bachelor Carrasco but the use of the barber brings out the contrast between reality and Don Quixote's delusion more strikingly. (See *Don Quixote*, Part I, ch. 21, Part II, chs. 64 and 65.)

[44] E iii. 381 ff.

Perhaps it is hindsight which prompts this interpretation of *Die Stadt Lucca*, and ambivalence is openly intended only in the earlier *Reisebilder*. Whatever the case, in 1837 Heine wrote an introduction to an edition of *Don Quixote* and this allowed him to look back over the years that had passed since the July Revolution and his last *Reisebild*. He begins by reprinting the first of the Don Quixote chapters from *Die Stadt Lucca*. He now observes that although he had loved Cervantes's novel as a child, it had not satisfied the yearnings of his youthful years, and that as a young man he had laughed at the antics of the wretched knight. This marks a cooler attitude than *Die Stadt Lucca* suggested, so it is all the more remarkable that the poet claims to have noticed the figures of the knight and his squire riding beside him as he crossed the border into France in 1831, then to gallop off ahead towards Paris. The meaning of the incident is soon elucidated. In 1837 he could see that it was possible to be not simply a Don Quixote who mistook the present for the past but a Don Quixote who thought the future was already about to arrive 'und bei solchem Ankampf gegen die schweren Interessen des Tages nur einen sehr mageren Klepper, eine sehr morsche Rüstung und einen ebenso gebrechlichen Körper besitzt!'[45] The Revolution had not heralded the new age; his Utopian hopes had been misplaced. And yet he refuses to give in like other youthful idealists and insists on closing the passage by still declaring Dulcinea the most beautiful woman in the world as he awaits the barber's *coup de grâce*. To confuse the issue further he goes on to argue that, while Cervantes's conscious intention was to ridicule the absurd epics of chivalry, unconsciously he had written the world's greatest satire against human enthusiasm as such. And so once more the argument for and against Utopianism is made to hinge on the idea of fervour and the desire for action as opposed to detached resignation and quietism, the two views which Hegel knew could result from observing the same process of human history.

Heine did not come back to Don Quixote merely because a piece of occasional writing gave him the opportunity. Throughout his creative life he found it helpful to express himself in terms of symbolical figures with all the poetic suggestiveness and conceptual ambiguity which symbols involve. Clearly Cervantes's two characters captured perfectly Heine's own peculiar mixture of

visionary enthusiasm and sceptical reserve. In *Die Stadt Lucca* he
claims significantly that *Don Quixote* was the first book he ever
read[46] and one only needs to think of the early poem 'Gespräch
auf der Paderborner Heide' with its incisive exchange between a
'Phantast' and a realist to see how soon his inner dissonance found
adequate expression in the Don Quixote–Sancho Panza relationship. Again, one of his most interesting early letters uses the figure
of Don Quixote to describe a luckless visit to his beloved's house
one dreary winter's night in Hamburg, a situation far removed
from the romantic Spanish setting one expects, and Heine knows
how to turn the contrast between his fond dreams and crass reality
to effective satirical account.[47] Nevertheless, it is not only the
element of self-questioning and self-irony which is common to the
recurrent figures in his work. Rather they are all wanderers, condemned to unceasing, aimless itinerancy. There is a distinct
similarity in their function to that of the journey motif and the
cycle, for they are all of more than structural significance and
directly express the theme of human and historical futility.

It would be easy to play down Heine's Jewishness and to point
out that he was a product of Enlightenment education and brought
up in a non-orthodox home outside the ghetto. Nevertheless, he
undoubtedly inherited a distinctly Jewish feeling of social in-
security and homelessness, a feeling which was all the more acute
because he was not an orthodox believer. A letter to Moses Moser, a
fellow Jew, member of the Verein, and pupil of Hegel, is particularly revealing in the context. Heine writes from Norderney that
he wishes he could simply wash off his Jewishness. He then moves
on to his life beside the North Sea and returns by association of
ideas to the legend of the Wandering Jew. He rapidly sketches
children gathering round their mother one winter's evening to hear
the terrifying tale: 'das Posthorn tönt — Schacherjuden fahren
nach Leipzig zur Messe. — Wir, die wir die Helden des Mährchens
sind, wir wissen es selbst nicht. Den weißen Bart, dessen Saum die
Zeit wieder verjüngend geschwärzt hat, kann kein Barbier abrasie-
ren.'[48] Certainly Heine's membership of the Verein, much like
his initial passion for Saint-Simonism as a Church, suggests a
desire to belong to a spiritual community. His sense of alienation
was further reinforced within his family and especially its circle

[46] E iii. 422.   [47] Cf. *Br* i. 28 f. (to Straube, spring 1821).
[48] *Br* i. 285 (July 1826).

of acquaintances in Hamburg by his realization that in their terms
he was a misfit. Not only was he Salomon's poor nephew, he was
also an unsuccessful businessman and a poet into the bargain.

Moreover, when Heine began writing, the Byronic vogue was
sweeping Germany.[49] Like his contemporaries Heine was fascinated by the Byronic hero, the Cain figure who is driven by some
mysterious inner agony into misanthropy and a life of wandering.
One should, however, distinguish between his attraction to the
general mood of alienation and rootlessness which pervades Byron's
early work and his specific attempt to imitate the Byronic hero in
an early experiment like *Ratcliff*.[50] The latter was a passing phase
in the young poet's search for appropriate modes of expression.
The former continued to preoccupy Heine for most of his life. It
was part of his own experience, an experience which enabled
Byron to captivate a whole generation old enough to remember the
ideals of the French Revolution and to have witnessed Napoleon's
defeat and the subsequent Restoration. The poems 'Farewell' and
'To Inez', and the extract from the narrative text of *Childe Harold*,
which Heine translated, take up the theme of exile and the hero's
incurable misery:

> Es ist die düstre Glut, die stets getragen
> In tiefer Brust der ew'ge Wandersmann,
> Der nirgendwo sich kann ein Grab erjagen,
> Und doch im Grab nur Ruhe finden kann.

> Welch Elend kann sich selbst entfliehn? Vergebens
> Durchjag' ich rastlos jedes fernste Land,
> Und stets verfolget mich der Tod des Lebens,
> Der Teufel, der 'Gedanke' wird genannt.   (E ii. 234)

In *Die Nordsee* III Heine had mentioned in passing the legend
of another itinerant, the Flying Dutchman. This figure reappears
in Heine's fragmentary novel *Aus den Memoiren des Herren von
Schnabelewopski*, published in the *Salon* of 1834. The narrator
speaks of a play about this legendary sea-captain, which he saw
in Amsterdam. In the context of the novel the incident serves
a frivolous purpose since the visit to the theatre enables the hero to
make contact with 'eine holländische Messaline', as she is termed,
and by the time he can return the performance is almost over.

---

[49] Cf. Ochsenbein, op. cit., pp. 4 ff., for the history of Byron's reception in
Germany.   [50] Cf. Ochsenbein, op. cit., pp. 211 ff.

Again, Heine has introduced a moment of humour to relieve tragic tension. The Flying Dutchman and his ship have been condemned by the devil to sail endlessly across the oceans until the Day of Judgement. The only possibility of release from this fate is for him to discover a woman who will be loyal to him to the point of death. Every seven years he is allowed to go on shore, and on one occasion he meets a girl who falls in love with him. She has been warned of the Flying Dutchman and his portrait hangs in their house so that he can be recognized. When he enters the house he is forced to mock his own person to avoid suspicion and here, as if in a mirror reflection of the *Rahmengeschichte*, laughter makes the Dutchman's fate seem all the more bitter:

Auch jener ist betroffen bei dem Anblick des Porträts. Als man ihm bedeutet, wen es vorstelle, weiß er jedoch jeden Argwohn von sich fern zu halten; er lacht über den Aberglauben, er spöttelt selber über den fliegenden Holländer, den ewigen Juden des Ozeans; jedoch unwillkürlich in einen wehmütigen Ton übergehend, schildert er, wie Mynheer auf der unermeßlichen Wasserwüste die unerhörtesten Leiden erdulden müsse, wie sein Leib nichts anders sei als ein Sarg von Fleisch, worin seine Seele sich langweilt, wie das Leben ihn von sich stößt und auch der Tod ihn abweist: gleich einer leeren Tonne, die sich die Wellen einander zuwerfen und sich spottend einander zurückwerfen, so werde der arme Holländer zwischen Tod und Leben hin- und hergeschleudert, keins von beiden wolle ihn behalten; sein Schmerz sei tief wie das Meer, worauf er herumschwimmt, sein Schiff sei ohne Anker und sein Herz ohne Hoffnung. (E iv. 117)

From the hero's pseudo-Polish name, which would seem to echo Reuter's Schelmuffsky, to the opening chapters which recall *Candide*, it immediately appears likely that the novel was intended as a *Schelmenroman*.[51] The Flying Dutchman's fate would thus have reflected the wanderings and thoughts of the hero, which are a disturbing mixture as it is of high jinks, satire, and despair. When Schnabelewopski returns to Hamburg one winter, for example, he finds that the populace he had mocked for its buffoonery is now nothing but a series of grotesque numbers without identity, while the swans which had adorned the river so attractively in warmer months are trapped in the ice with their wings broken. Recognizing his own fate in theirs he looks up into

---

[51] And indeed Manfred Windfuhr has argued the point in detail: cf. 'Heines Fragment eines Schelmenromans. "Aus den Memoiren des Herren von Schnabelewopski" ', *Heine-Jahrbuch 1967*, pp. 21–39.

the darkening sky: '— wohl begriff ich jetzt, daß die Sterne keine liebende, mitfühlende Wesen sind, sondern nur glänzende Täuschungen der Nacht, ewige Trugbilder in einem erträumten Himmel, goldne Lügen im dunkelblauen Nichts . . .'[52] The novel ends with the description of how Schnabelewopski's Jewish friend, Simson, suffers a tragicomic death. An ardent deist, little Simson has had a fierce argument with a fellow-student and atheist, which led to a duel and Simson's defeat. He is convalescing in bed but gets so excited when he is read the story of his namesake's capture by the Philistines that he tugs at the posts of the bed, the bandage slips and he dies. If little Simson is not directly the Wandering Jew, his fate is certainly a reflection of the age-old persecution endured by his people. Beneath its often cruel humour the novel is concerned to capture a sense of futility and emptiness and is closely reminiscent in its antithetical mood and structure of *Das Buch Le Grand*. *Schnabelewopski* appeared in 1834 and immediately precedes *Zur Geschichte* in the *Salon*. Ultimately Heine's collections of works, such as the *Reisebilder* and the *Salon*, themselves serve a function similar to that of the cycle, which is to relate the apparently incongruous in a world of contradictions.

In *Elementargeister* Heine tells an anecdote about a learned friend, Heinrich Kitzler, who would write the most thorough treatise on a subject (and appropriately in the context on Christianity) only to throw the finished product on the fire. When challenged, Kitzler confesses that, as he writes, the opposite view to his own gradually becomes ever more apparent to him until in the end he has no choice but to destroy the entire work.[53] This man left nothing for posterity. Heine did not often write treatises but when he did, as in *Zur Geschichte*, the end of the essay was liable to give the lie to the substance of its argument. Who could expect the positive assessment of the historical process and of revolution earlier in the essay to culminate in the terrifying apocalypse which Heine finally prophesies? This chaos which is let loose by the forces of repressed nature is hardly 'un chaud royaume de lumière et de plaisir'. Nevertheless, it would be quite mistaken to reject Heine as a muddled thinker. We have seen that within the bounds of his Utopianism there is an almost astounding degree of consistency, while on the other hand the patterns of his scepticism are similarly constant. In contrast to the philosophers and

<hr />

[52] E iv. 106 f.   [53] E iv. 417 ff.

the political theoreticians he was able and could allow himself to feel and think from both standpoints—which is less extraordinary when one remembers that his optimism and his pessimism alike stem from essentially the same historical analysis and are responses to the same age of historical upheaval. One approach welcomes the change for the better, the other sees it as a symptom of human transiency. But this radical divergence of attitude did not lead Heine to remain silent like Heinrich Kitzler: rather it was his inspiration, for instead of resolving the tension his work sought to portray it. The artist stands above the revolutionary and the sceptic. In the *Reisebilder* this art took the form of the sentimental journey. In 1848 Heine's own journeyings came to a definitive halt but the heroes of *Romanzero* remain wanderers and above all the martyrs of a pitiless reality. It is no longer the artist's psyche which reflects the world: it is the artist's fate which symbolizes the cruel irony of life. But before Heine reached the final disillusionment of his mattress grave, his vision of art and the artist had fluctuated between two extremes, the harnessing of art to politics and the proclamation of art's supreme independence. These fluctuations reflect the complex history of Heine's political commitment between the Revolutions of 1830 and 1848.

V

POETRY AND POLITICS

A. *In the shadow of Goethe*

IN Heine's formative years the monarch of German literature
was Goethe and like many of his contemporaries Heine both
loved and hated this man, who, it seemed, was the living embodiment of genius and could never be emulated. If Goethe had
once known inner conflict and had abhorred the established society
of his day, the struggle was long since past—at least as far as the
outside observer could judge. From his scientific studies to his
political and social standing in Weimar he seemed to be the epitome of the man who had come to terms with the world. This
world was that of the Restoration. In the early days of Schlegel's
lectures and then of the Varnhagens' salon Heine seems to have
admired Goethe's genius without reflecting unduly on the political
implications of his position. As we have seen, Goethe seemed to
possess those qualities of detachment and of intuitive vision which
Heine felt so agonizingly that he lacked himself. The young poet
longed for Goethe's lucidity and artistic control. Moreover, Goethe
seemed to stand above the sense of alienation and the destructive
self-observation which Heine, like Byron, experienced so deeply.
And yet even in *Briefe aus Berlin* he remarked sarcastically:

Ich will nicht ungerecht seyn und hier unerwähnt lassen die Vereh-
rung, die man hier dem Namen G ö t h e zollt, der deutsche Dichter,
von dem man hier am meisten spricht. Aber Hand aufs Herz, mag das
feine, weltkluge Betragen unseres Göthe nicht das meiste dazu beigetra-
gen haben, daß seine äußere Stellung so glänzend ist und daß er in so
hohem Maße die Affekzion unserer Großen genießt? Fern sey es von
mir, den alten Herrn eines kleinlichen Charakters zu zeihen. G ö t h e
ist ein großer Mann in einem seidnen Rock. (E vii. 577)[1]

[1] See Hermand, op. cit., p. 135. Ulrich Maché, 'Der junge Heine und
Goethe', *Heine-Jahrbuch 1965*, pp. 42–7, has argued that at this stage Heine
had read much less Goethe than he claimed. He did not even read *Werther* till
at least 1824. His attitude towards Goethe must thus have been determined by
a primarily theoretical interest inspired by Schlegel and a natural repugnance
to Goethe's position in the 'Establishment'.

The years in Hegelian circles in Berlin helped to develop the ambivalence of Heine's attitude towards Goethe. The cold recep tion in Weimar in the autumn of 1824 was a blow to his pride. A student contemporary reported that Heine 'fühlte sich eben in seinem Dichterstolz gekränkt und hatte mehr erwartet'.[2] By the following year Heine was able to present Goethe in his correspondence as an aged hedonist whose detachment left him unmoved by the problems of his age.[3] Applying the Left Hegelian criterion of *Zeitgemäßheit*, Heine now came to see in Goethe the 'Indifferentist', the exponent of quietism as opposed to his own enthusiasm for the *Idee*, for progress and revolution. Furthermore, as Jost Hermand has persuasively argued, *Die Harzreise* itself may be a parody that Heine could not make too blatant for fear of offending his influential friends, the Varnhagens, and the circle around them.[4] In 1826 the pendulum swung back towards Goethe as the archetypal intelligence, though as I have shown, Napoleon, the genius of history, already begins to supplant the poet by the close of *Die Nordsee*. Soon afterwards Heine sharpened his criticism of Goethe and began to evolve his theory that the Goethean *Kunstperiode* had come to a close. Heine was not alone in his critical attitude: indeed he first formulated it fully in his review of Menzel's *Deutsche Litteratur* of 1828.[5] Menzel himself and Ludwig Börne were vehement in their attacks, and their so-called criticism of Goethe is often nothing less than invective,[6] but Heine's position vacillated. True, he shared their picture of Weimar Classicism, a picture which today seems astounding in its one-sidedness. But his treatment of Goethe was always more complex than theirs.

Like the others Heine took Goethe's classicism at its face value

---

[2] Cited, Hermand, op. cit., p. 134.   [3] See above, p. 93.

[4] Hermand, op. cit., pp. 137 ff.   [5] E vii. 255 f.

[6] Börne wrote, for example, 'Aber Goethe ist auch kein Dichter: die Muse war ihm nie vermählt, sie war seine Dirne, die sich ihm hingab für Geld und Putz, und Bastarde sind die Kinder seines Geistes.' (Review of *Goethes Brief-wechsel mit einem Kinde*, 1835, in *Sämtliche Werke*, ii. 864.) Börne further charged Goethe with treating his fellow beings as cold-bloodedly as specimens for anatomical dissection, with sexual immorality, and with a desire to kill all living feelings. The burden of Menzel's attack was that Goethe did not belong to the age of political engagement, that he was a false idol, a modern 'golden calf', and above all that he was merely talented and entirely lacked the personal integrity of a 'character', accusations that were to be fateful in Heine's own career. See *Die deutsche Litteratur*, Stuttgart, 1828, Part II, pp. 205 ff., 209 ff., and 2nd edn., Stuttgart, 1836, Part III, pp. 322 ff.—the latter sharpens the historical argument.

to mean that his art was visual, plastic, and therefore the reflection
of the external, objective world and not of personal emotion.
Initially, as we have seen,[7] this seemed to Heine to be a highly
praiseworthy characteristic and even as late as *Die Reise von
München* he cannot conceal his admiration for Goethe's skill in
reproducing the world of reality rather than interpreting it sub-
jectively.[8] But in the letters of 1825 to Moser and Christiani[9]
Goethe's absence of apparent emotion is exclusively associated
with an absence of interest in the demands of the age, and this view
was firmly established from the Menzel review on. Goethe's ideal
of *Bildung* and of devotion to practical, socially significant tasks—
in short of political commitment in the simple sense that one
strives to be a useful citizen—this is ignored. To the younger
generation nurtured on the French Revolution and the grandiose
world-view of Hegel the establishment of a personal ethic as the
basis for one's life together with one's fellow beings was not even
worthy of consideration as a form of political activity.[10] Typical of
this superficial judgement is a letter Heine wrote to Varnhagen in
1830. Heine is paradoxically intent only on looking at Goethe as
a model of style. His sole criterion of political involvement is
enthusiasm for the French Revolution:

Ich lese jetzt den vierten Band von Goethes und Schillers Briefwechsel, und wie gewöhnlich mache ich Stylbeobachtungen. Da finde ich
wieder, daß Sie nur mit dem frühesten Goethe, mit dem Werther-
Goethe, Aehnlichkeit im Styl haben; Ihnen fehlt ganz die spätere
Kunstbehaglichkeit des großen Zeitablehnungsgenies, der sich selbst
letzter Zweck ist. Er beherrscht seinen Stoff, Sie bezwingen ihn.
Abründung, Helldunkel, Perspektive der Zwischensätze, mechanisches
Untermalen der Gedanken, dergleichen kann man von Goethe lernen —
nur nicht Männlichkeit. Es ist noch immer meine fixe Idee, daß mit der
Endschaft der Kunstperiode auch das Goethenthum zu Ende geht; nur
unsere ästhetisirende, philosophirende Kunstsinnzeit war dem Aufkommen Goethes günstig; eine Zeit der Begeisterung und der That kann
ihn nicht brauchen. Aus jenem vierten Briefsammlungstheil sah ich
klar, wie ingrimmig er die Revoluzion haßte, er hat in dieser Hinsicht
ungünstig auf Schiller eingewirkt, den er vielleicht am Ende zum
Mitaristokraten gemacht hätte. (*Br* i. 426)

---

[7] Cf. above, p. 12 and pp. 29 ff.   [8] E iii. 265.   [9] Cf. *Br* i. 210 f., 216 f.
[10] One can date this reaction against Goethe's mature ideals back to the
Romantics' disappointment when the last volume of *Wilhelm Meisters Lehrjahre*
appeared in 1796.

Furthermore the distinction between art as semblance and life as a sphere of moral and physical necessity, which Schiller in fact evolved in the greatest detail, is reduced to the assumption that Schiller and Goethe were indifferent to the realities of life (though usually the charge was made against Goethe alone):

> Der Schiller-Göthesche Xenienkampf war doch nur ein Kartoffel-krieg, es war die Kunstperiode, es galt den Schein des Lebens, die Kunst, nicht das Leben selbst—jetzt gilt es die höchsten Interessen des Lebens selbst, die Revoluzion tritt in die Literatur, und der Krieg wird ernster. (*Br* i. 420)

While in *Französische Maler* Heine argues that this attitude belongs to the past and is therefore doomed,[11] *Die romantische Schule* devotes a lengthy passage to Goethe's views on art. Heine begins by deploring his demand to be the sole ruler and arbiter in the literary world, a desire which could only encourage mediocrity. He then speaks of the challenge thrown down to Goethe by the lovers of Schiller's works. As was common at the time Schiller is portrayed as the poet of freedom and more specifically of the French Revolution; he is identified with his own Marquis Posa.[12] Without himself putting forward the argument Heine also repeats the usual view of the time that Schiller and his characters were morally sound while Goethe and especially his Philine were immoral and profane. The Goetheans' reply to this charge, as Heine formulates it, is significant, for in its one-sided appreciation of art as independent of all moral and didactic purpose it propounds one of the earliest theories of art for art's sake. The Goetheans asserted, Heine says, that:

> ... in der Kunst gäbe es keine Zwecke, wie in dem Weltbau selbst, wo nur der Mensch die Begriffe 'Zweck und Mittel' hineingegrübelt; die Kunst, wie die Welt, sei ihrer selbst willen da, und wie die Welt ewig dieselbe bleibt, wenn auch in ihrer Beurteilung die Absichten der Menschen unaufhörlich wechseln, so müsse auch die Kunst von den zeitlichen Ansichten der Menschen unabhängig bleiben; die Kunst müsse daher besonders unabhängig bleiben von der Moral, welche auf der Erde immer wechselt, so oft eine neue Religion emporsteigt und die alte Religion verdrängt. (E v. 250)

The justification for uncommitted art presented here rests in part on the view that there is no such thing as genuine human change

---

[11] E iv. 72 f. See above, pp. 93 f.   [12] E v. 252.

and that art should not therefore involve itself in the ephemeral issues of the day. Heine had the same point in mind when he stated in 'Verschiedenartige Geschichtsauffassung' that Goethe and the poets associated with him considered history to be movement without progress. But art, Heine continues, cannot sever itself from the world, and he now takes up the arguments of the anti-Goethe camp in his own name again:

> Indem die Goetheaner von solcher Ansicht ausgehen, betrachten sie die Kunst als eine unabhängige zweite Welt, die sie so hoch stellen, daß alles Treiben der Menschen, ihre Religion und ihre Moral, wechselnd und wandelbar unter ihr hin sich bewegt. Ich kann aber dieser Ansicht nicht unbedingt huldigen; die Goetheaner ließen sich dadurch verleiten, die Kunst selbst als das Höchste zu proklamieren und von den Ansprüchen jener ersten wirklichen Welt, welcher doch der Vorrang gebührt, sich abzuwenden. (E v. 251 f.)

The essential difference between Schiller and Goethe, Heine claims, is that Schiller committed himself to changing the world, whereas Goethe was only concerned with the individual, art, and nature.[13] Above all it was Goethe's pantheism which led him to see the world as immutable, for this showed him all phenomena as equally worthy of attention or, as Heine puts it, of indifference. Other modern pantheists such as the Saint-Simonians have, however, realized that God is to be seen in historical movement and that he manifests himself more in some phenomena than in others. This brings us to the crux of the Left Hegelian criticism of Goethe, and it will be recalled that in the original passage of 1833 Hegel was here mentioned by name:

> Gott ist in der Bewegung, in der Handlung, in der Zeit, sein heiliger Odem weht durch die Blätter der Geschichte, letztere ist das eigentliche Buch Gottes; und das fühlte und ahnte Friedrich Schiller, und er ward ein 'rückwärtsgekehrter Prophet', und er schrieb den 'Abfall der Niederlande', den 'Dreißigjährigen Krieg' und die 'Jungfrau von Orleans' und den 'Tell'. (E v. 253)

Heine admits that Goethe had also sung of enthusiasm—but as an *Artist*, an aesthete, for whom human endeavour and passion are mere material waiting to be shaped. Goethe's works are beautiful,

---

[13] Certainly a surprising point considering that Schiller was the chief exponent of the aesthetic theory which is imputed to Goethe in this extreme and distorted form.

certainly, but they are as cold as the marble from which they are hewn and will remain as barren.

Alongside this attack on the *Kunstperiode* emerges a new ideal of engaged art.[14] In *Französische Maler* we have seen Heine praise poets like Dante, who were both artists and deeply involved in the issues of their time.[15] Schiller clearly was another imposing example but still more important was Jean Paul. Menzel had picked out this writer as a model of ethical integrity and passionate engagement, in short as a 'character',[16] who could be contrasted with Goethe's chameleon-like 'talent'. In his review of Menzel's book Heine was quick to join in this praise,[17] and indeed it was probably an earlier interest in Jean Paul which led him to Sterne.[18] In the last section of *Die romantische Schule* Heine proclaims Jean Paul as the forerunner of *Junges Deutschland* and like them as a writer who loved both the good and the beautiful, an artist who was yet so involved in his age that his involvement was his religion:

> Sein Herz und seine Schriften waren eins und dasselbe. Diese Eigenschaft, diese Ganzheit finden wir auch bei den Schriftstellern des heutigen Jungen Deutschlands, die ebenfalls keinen Unterschied machen wollen zwischen Leben und Schreiben, die nimmermehr die Politik trennen von Wissenschaft, Kunst und Religion, und die zu gleicher Zeit Künstler, Tribune und Apostel sind.   (E v. 328)

The terms in which Heine goes on to characterize these writers and particularly his friend, Heinrich Laube, clearly reveal that by this time (1835–6) his Left Hegelian ideal of the engaged artist had taken on the religious quality of the Saint-Simonian priest and leader:[19]

> Ja, ich wiederhole das Wort Apostel, denn ich weiß kein bezeichnenderes Wort. Ein neuer Glaube beseelt sie mit einer Leidenschaft, von welcher die Schriftsteller der früheren Periode keine Ahnung hatten. Es ist dieses der Glaube an den Fortschritt, ein Glaube der aus dem Wissen entsprang. Wir haben die Lande gemessen, die Naturkräfte gewogen, die Mittel der Industrie berechnet, und siehe, wir haben ausgefunden: daß diese Erde groß genug ist; daß sie jedem hinlänglichen Raum bietet, die Hütte seines Glückes darauf zu bauen; daß diese Erde uns alle anständig ernähren kann, wenn wir alle arbeiten und nicht einer auf

---

[14] The central topic in Kurz's detailed study of Heine's concept of the artist.
[15] See above, p. 94, and E iv.72 f.
[16] Menzel, op. cit. (1st edn.), Part II, p. 240.   [17] E vii. 253.
[18] Cf. Friedrich Marcus, op. cit.   [19] Cf. d'Allemagne, op. cit., pp. 80 ff.

Kosten des anderen leben will; und daß wir nicht nötig haben, die größere und ärmere Klasse an den Himmel zu verweisen. (E v. 328)

But perhaps Heine's most radical formulation of the new poet came in the year of his association with another of the new Socialist philosophies, that of Marx. A fragment,[20] which Heine probably intended as a preface to *Neue Gedichte* of 1844, reveals a similar hostility towards Utopian writing to that which informed 'Verschiedenartige Geschichtsauffassung'. It demands an unrelenting devotion to immediate practical tasks, to achieving concrete and drastic change. In 1844, the year of his association with Marx and of *Deutschland. Ein Wintermärchen*, his satire becomes sharper than ever before with the possible exception of the lambasting to which the wretched Graf von Platen had been subjected. The fragment captures precisely this hardening of tone, which Marx may have helped to encourage with his own aversion to any Socialism that smacked of the nebulous or fantastic, and in view of the scanty evidence available to document the Marx–Heine relationship it takes on an interest out of proportion to its size. Like philosophy for the Young Hegelians, poetry is to leave the realm of the imagination and become an active force in *praxis*. Heine's new 'productive lyric' has the task of altering the world—at once:

Unsre lyrike Poesie tritt in eine neue Phase. Die somnambule Periode des Liedes, der stillen Gemüthsblume, hat ein Ende. 'Andre Zeiten, andre Vögel, andre Vögel, andre Lieder.' Fur die Zeit der träumenden Pharaonen paßten die sonnigen Traumdeuterseelen, die frommen keuschen Josephsnaturen — die mit Recht unsere Liebe und Achtung genossen. Der heutige Tag aber verlangt Profeten von minder sanften Stoffe. — Es handelt sich jetzt nicht mehr um Zukunftsträume, sondern um die harte Frohn der Wirklichkeit. Statt wie früher idyllisch unsere Lammer zu weiden müssen wir jetzt Lehm treten und Ziegel brennen, an den Festungswerken von Pissem und Rhamses wird eifrig gebaut und auf den lästigen Arbeiter schlagen die Amtsknechte mit ziemlich dicken Stöcken — für solche Culturinteressen, wie Laube sagen würde, bedarf es eines produktiven Lyrik, einer die nicht lange

[20] The MS. (Sammlung Strauß 160–1) is at the Heine Archives in Düsseldorf and is reproduced with the kind permission of the Director. The paper, a double sheet with the top of one page torn off, is typical of the kind he used in the late 1830s and the 1840s—cf. letters to Renduel, 11 Mar. 1841 (*Br* ii. 383 f.), Venedey, 31 Dec. 1842 (*Br* ii. 448 f.), Betty Heine (22 June 1847 (ibid. iii. 118)), or parts of *Ludwig Börne* (Slg. Strauß 113–14). The MS. is heavily covered with deletions which I shall not indicate. Syntactical and orthographical errors in manuscript.

leyert und den Mizti etwas derbe ansingt und sehr praktische Wunder
verrichtet, z. B .Wasser in Blut verwandelt, Frösche hervorzaubert, auch
Ungeziefer u. s. w. — Laßt uns die Stimmführer der Vergangenh mit
allen möglichen Spereyen [*presumably intended* 'Spezereyen'] des Lobes
einbalsamiren und diesen verjährten Mumien die kostbarsten Mausoleen
erbauen! Aber werft [*fragment breaks off*].[21]

The poetic counterpart to this passage is 'Doktrin':

> Schlage die Trommel und fürchte dich nicht,
> Und küsse die Marketenderin!
> Das ist die ganze Wissenschaft,
> Das ist der Bücher tiefster Sinn.
>
> Trommle die Leute aus dem Schlaf,
> Trommle Reveille mit Jugendkraft,
> Marschiere trommelnd immer voran,
> Das ist die ganze Wissenschaft.
>
> Das ist die Hegelsche Philosophie,
> Das ist der Bücher tiefster Sinn!
> Ich hab' sie begriffen, weil ich gescheit,
> Und weil ich ein guter Tambour bin.   (E i. 301)

Significantly its images derive from *Das Buch Le Grand*. The
revolutionary drumbeats of Le Grand are here finally asserted to be
identical with the profundities of Hegelian philosophy. This poem
thus marks the zenith of Heine's attempt to throw light on the
obscurity of German philosophy. Poetry's task is to translate
thought into reality, and the deliberately naïve tone of the poem is
not ironic: only through simplicity will poetry succeed in awaking
the dormant people. Heine's life-long admiration of the artless and
his experiments with the Romantic song find fulfilment here.

And so as Heine's concept of the engaged artist develops and is
modified with time we are presented with a miniature history of his
association with the left-wing political philosophies of his day. But
we have already seen that Heine also had the most profound
doubts about the ideals which inspired these links, doubts which
hinged on his interpretation of history. At the heart of his concept
of the engaged artist and of the concomitant attack on Goethe lay
the assumption that progress was possible in human affairs. And yet
Heine himself was repeatedly overwhelmed by a sense of historical

[21] The sources of Heine's images are Gen. 40, 41, Exod. 1, 5, 7, 8.

futility and the circular view of history he claimed to find in Goethe was also his own. It is hardly surprising, then, that Heine never went so far as Menzel and Börne in their abuse of the grand old man: indeed Heine never abandoned his admiration for Goethe, and his attempt to protect him even in the midst of an attack makes curious reading.

In the Menzel review Heine is careful to add that for all Goethe's indifference he must be considered Schiller's equal, that his works themselves are not under fire, and that the real villains are Goethe's imitators. He feels shocked by Menzel's ruthless strictures and states that even if Menzel were right he should be as polite to his victim as Charles I's executioners when they kneeled down and asked the monarch's forgiveness before carrying out their task.[22] This, as we shall see, was to be an important analogy. In *Zur Geschichte* Goethe's pantheism is also discussed, but in a favourable light. Spinoza, it will be remembered,[23] was the herald of the new philosophical epoch in Germany, which was characterized by the desire to fuse spirit and matter. But this, he later states, was precisely Goethe's achievement in the literary sphere, for 'der große Heide' not only loved the visual and the plastic as a latter-day Greek—he was no less moved by modern feeling and sentimentality. He was deeply influenced by Christianity despite himself. Thus Heine feels he is justified in calling him the Spinoza of poetry.[24] It is not hard to recognize in this analysis the lingering influence of A. W. Schlegel, and it reasserts his earlier view of Goethe as the undivided poet who stood above the *Entzweiung*, to use Schlegel's term, of the modern Christian age. This passage also contains Heine's eulogy of Goethe's songs: in their fusion of language and thought he sees them as the living embodiment of Spinoza's mathematical formulae.[25] Even in *Die romantische Schule* Heine is far from content to end his presentation of Goethe on a critical note and he rapidly adds that his previous words explain why there was so much ill will towards Goethe in the last days of his life. He then refers to the reservations he had felt about Menzel's attack on the poet and repeats his words on the politeness shown by Charles I's executioners. He next refutes the claim that Schiller is greater than Goethe by pointing to Goethe's mastery of realist detail and proceeds to his appreciation of *Faust*

---

[22] E vii. 254.   [23] See above, p. 100.   [24] E iv. 272.
[25] See above, p. 54.

as the Germans' worldly Bible. His evocation of *West-östlicher Divan*, which follows, is justly renowned, and, clearly, different criteria are at work here from those by which he judged Schiller and Jean Paul. This is not engaged literature: it is the realization in poetry of the life and world of which Heine dreamed. In this quotation he speaks first of the notes with which Goethe accompanied his collection of poems:

Diese Prosa ist so durchsichtig wie das grüne Meer, wenn heller Sommernachmittag und Windstille und man ganz klar hinabschauen kann in die Tiefe, wo die versunkenen Städte mit ihren verschollenen Herrlichkeiten sichtbar werden; — manchmal ist aber auch jene Prosa so magisch, so ahnungsvoll wie der Himmel, wenn die Abenddämmerung heraufgezogen, und die großen Goetheschen Gedanken treten dann hervor, rein und golden wie die Sterne. Unbeschreiblich ist der Zauber dieses Buches: es ist ein Selam, den der Occident dem Oriente geschickt hat, und es sind gar närrische Blumen darunter: sinnlich rote Rosen, Hortensien wie weiße nackte Mädchenbusen, spaßhaftes Löwenmaul, Purpurdigitalis wie lange Menschenfinger, verdrehte Krokosnasen und in der Mitte, lauschend verborgen, stille deutsche Veilchen. Dieser Selam aber bedeutet, daß der Occident seines frierend mageren Spiritualismus überdrüssig geworden und an der gesunden Körperwelt des Orients sich wieder erlaben möchte.   (E v. 262 f.)

Thus Goethe re-emerges as the genius of *Die Nordsee* III, and as if to recapture the admiration he felt for Goethe at that time Heine uses images and scenes from his North Sea cycles. The association with Napoleon, even, is now restored, when he compares the divine serenity of Goethe's eyes with those of the Frenchman. Goethe was a veritable Jupiter. But writing in 1833 Heine could now see that, like Napoleon, Goethe also was doomed to die— 'Les dieux s'en vont'—and he completes this section of the essay with the speculation that perhaps Death has decided to assist democracy by enforcing spiritual equality. We understand that it is the equality of the lowest common denominator.

Heine's ambivalent attitude towards Goethe is brought out still more strikingly if we examine the other extant versions of the passage where he describes the Goetheans' theory of art for art's sake. Elster's variants from the manuscript of the first edition, *Zur Geschichte der neueren schönen Literatur in Deutschland*, speak for themselves: 'Ich (widerspreche daher) (huldige daher) stimme daher ganz überein mit jener erhabenen Ansicht, (von der Kunst,) (die der Kunst) welche die Goetheaner von der Kunst hegen, indem sie letztere, gleich einer unabhängigen zweiten Welt, so hoch stellen, daß . . .' The French version of the same year reads: 'Je me joins entièrement aux Goethéens, qui, dans ses [sic] vues élevées sur l'art le placent si haut, et en font comme un second monde.' *De l'Allemagne* of 1834 and its second edition of 1854 read, however: 'Je ne diffère pas entièrement des Goethéens . . .' (E v. 540.)[26]

We have seen that Heine's Utopianism and his scepticism both derive essentially from different attitudes to the flux of human history. What is vital is whether change is seen as part of a meaningful historical process or whether on the contrary it serves as proof that all human endeavour is destined to perish. Can there be any similar crux which explains this deep rift in Heine's view of art and the artist? Goethe's alleged indifference to history as opposed to Schiller's immersion in it is certainly one important factor which relates the problem to that of the optimist and the pessimist. But it is only one factor and the contradiction is not restricted to his view of Goethe. It accompanies him right through the Paris years, and no sooner has he reiterated the ideal of the engaged artist than another very different picture emerges.

B. *The poet and the party—Börne and the Republicans*

Again we must turn to that key essay, *Die Nordsee* III, for a solution to this remarkable anomaly in Heine's thought. At the heart of Heine's reflections in this work lies an overriding belief in the figure of the genius, an interest which places him firmly in a tradition of German aesthetics which has its roots as far back as in Bodmer and Breitinger's championing of Milton and the poetic imagination. In Kant's hypothesis of an archetypal intelligence, to which Heine refers in his essay,[27] we have a late Enlightenment counterpart to the *Sturm und Drang* proclamation of the genius as the 'second creator', a theory which culminated in the Romantic concept of the individual as the primary, unique, and irreplaceable *exemplum* of humanity. It was a tradition in which Heine had been

---

[26] See also Kurz, op. cit., pp. 222 f. Kurz's chapter 'Probleme der Einheit', pp. 198–230, is an intelligent if complicated attempt to present this and related discrepancies in Heine's conception of the artist.

[27] See above, pp. 29–31.

reared and which gained new and significantly different momentum
from the advent of that military and political genius, Napoleon.
Indeed, as I have shown, what Heine was particularly intent on
arguing for in *Die Nordsee* III was the concept of a genius whose
creations were not artistic but social, hence his additional words at
the end of the Kant quotation in this essay, which[28] assume the
existence of this hypothetical intelligence and 'explain' it in terms
of the genius's ability to understand and manipulate his age.[29] It
was Hegel who transformed the Romantic genius into the monumental creator of history, a theory which served to justify Heine's
youthful love of Napoleon. Thus it was an easy step for Heine and
the Left Hegelians to turn the genius of art into the genius of
history. But just as the Left Hegelian view of philosophy entailed
a profound change in the situation of the philosopher, so too their
aesthetic theory entailed a fundamental reappraisal of the artist
and his work. For the Romantics and Schiller alike, what the
genius created transcended any utilitarian or ephemeral purpose:
for the former the work of art strove to approach the Infinite, a
quasi-religious task, while for the latter art sought to come as close
as possible to the Ideal and therefore had to leave behind it the
immediate circumstances of the real world. This meant in effect
that for both the Romantics and the Weimar Classicists art could
not be measured by criteria drawn from the actual, historical
situation in which they happened to find themselves. But the view
which emerged in the 1820s of the artist as a warrior for a cause and
as the expression of his age radically altered all this. As we have
observed, the artist's realm is no longer that of *theoria*, of contemplation, but of *praxis*, of commitment, to which he must make his
art and even his person subservient. This element of service is
clearly reflected in Heine's own descriptions of the engaged poet.
In *Die romantische Schule*, written at the time of his Saint-
Simonian preoccupations, we have already seen that he is called
a tribune, or in other words a spokesman for the people, and an
apostle, one of a religious leader's select companions and witnesses.
In the fragmentary preface to *Neue Gedichte* the image is more
radical, and, appropriately perhaps, the artist is likened to a slave
labourer. Still more eloquent are Heine's victims of the *Idee*,
whipped and goaded into the gladiatorial arena,[30] or lashed naked

[28] E iii. 113 f.   [29] See above, p. 32.
[30] E iv. 14.

to a bareback runaway steed careering wildly across steppe and waste.[31]

But, as I have shown in my first chapter, all Heine had wanted to restore was the lost connection between life and art, which he believed had once been inseparable realms of experience—hence his longing for Ancient Greece and other non-Christian cultures such as those of India and Islamic Spain, where life itself seemed to have been poetic, and hence his love of the folk-song and the remnants of German peasant culture. This was an ideal that had little in common with the aims of the emergent Socialist ideologies which Heine espoused or which, in the case of Börne and the Republicans, wished to espouse him. Nevertheless such movements expected of their followers, including Heine, an allegiance of a kind that pointed forward to developments of a century later, if only in embryonic form. Just how remote Heine's concept of the engaged poet was from what political ideologies were later to demand of their adherents can be seen in his choice of Jean Paul as the herald of the post-aesthetic age. Admittedly he had good reason for thinking of this writer since both Menzel and, more significantly, Ludwig Börne had praised him as the epitome of everything that was different from Weimar Classicism. The fervour of Börne's *Denkrede auf Jean Paul* of December 1825 was no more restrained than his invective was to be against Goethe, and it anticipated in a remarkable manner Jean Paul's curious position as the ideal of Young Germany and the Biedermeier age alike when it proclaimed him as the liberator of the heart, the poet 'der Niedergeborenen', and the humorist in an age of slavery. But still more important in our context was Börne's appreciation of Jean Paul as a directly autobiographical writer, whose works reflected faithfully his own life, a life that was as moral and upright as the works themselves—in a phrase, 'er war ein sittlicher Sänger'.[32] But one wonders just how this eccentric and whimsical genius would have fared if he had actually served the German Republican cause for which Börne was posthumously conscripting him. When a living court jester and humorist in an age of slavery came to Paris in the form of Heine, eccentricity and genius were neither appreciated nor even tolerated by the acknowledged leader of the German Liberals in

---

[31] E vii. 375. Heine mentions Vernet's pictures of Mazeppa as the source of his image, not Byron direct.

[32] *Sämtliche Werke*, i. 794.

exile, and in Börne's outrage we witness the beginnings of an ideological intolerance that was later to have the power to deal more than verbally with the offender.

Heine first visited Börne in Paris in September 1831 and it is apparent from Börne's letters to Jeanette Wohl that he was then bent on winning Heine's support in launching a new journal.[33] Heine was not willing to participate in the venture. Börne, however, was not content to let Heine go his own way. Whether he liked it or not Heine was still one of the flock and Börne behaved, to use Heine's own term, as if he were the local 'Gemeinde-Versorger'.[34] He began to deplore Heine's private life as lewd,[35] vain,[36] and above all insincere—'es ist ihm nichts heilig, an der Wahrheit liebt er nur das Schöne, er hat keinen Glauben.'[37] If Börne could not use Heine directly for the cause then he probably planned to use him as an example in a book; certainly he recorded his impressions carefully in his letters to Wohl, asking her to keep them for some later purpose. On one occasion he went so far as to state: 'Der arme Heine wird chemisch von mir zersetzt, und er hat gar keine Ahnung davon, daß ich im geheim beständig Experimente mit ihm mache.'[38] What Börne expected of Heine as a Liberal was not simply his support in political debate and in his writings—he wanted a totally different man. Heine's private life and even his temperament were a matter of decisive concern to the party. It was little more than a year later that Börne's hostility towards Heine came into the open with the review of *Französische Zustände* in *Briefe aus Paris*. Heine's monarchism, and wavering monarchism at that, was the last straw for Börne. Adopting the usual sectarian approach he set out to destroy the poet who, since he was not for the Republican cause, must be against it. Heine was condemned as a political chameleon, an aesthete whose only value was beauty, and, significantly, as a man who believed too much in the power of the individual to achieve political ends.[39] No doubt Heine was right in part at least when, in his essay on Börne, he tried to analyse his hostility on a psychological level with the distinction between the Hellenes and the Nazarenes of this world, the fat and

---

[33] Cf. Houben, *Gespräche*, p. 195, and Friedrich Hirth, *Heinrich Heine. Bausteine zu einer Biographie*, Mainz, 1950, pp. 30 f.

[34] E vii. 105.   [35] Houben, op cit., pp. 196, 205, 211, etc.

[36] Ibid., pp. 197, 204.   [37] Ibid., p. 195.   [38] Ibid., p. 213.

[39] *Sämtliche Werke*, iii. p. 813.

the lean observed by Julius Caesar in Shakespeare's drama.[40] But this was only one factor. Equally important was Börne's insistence on loyalty to the cause, which was rather a symptom of the rise of ideological thinking.

Heine had not chosen to associate with Börne. It was the Saint-Simonian religion which had drawn him to Paris, but here, too, he had a foretaste of what was to become a common experience in the twentieth century. The Saint-Simonians were proscribed by royal decree not long after Heine reached Paris, and naturally he never had the opportunity to see what it would in fact be like as a poet in the strictly hierarchical scheme which the theorists of the movement proposed. What he did discover was that there was no room for a personal interpretation of the doctrine. We have seen that from its categories of analysis to its dedication to Enfantin *Zur Geschichte der Religion und Philosophie in Deutschland* was intended to contribute to the cause. But Enfantin found Heine's essentially Left Hegelian and revolutionary tone highly undesirable. The Saint-Simonian writer was required to adhere to the party line and 'Le Père' firmly rejected the work.[41]

c. *Marx and the Communists*

Heine's brilliant yet unscrupulous reply to Börne came in his essay, *Ludwig Börne. Eine Denkschrift*, published in 1840. And he continued the fight in 1841–2 with *Atta Troll*, the remarkable satirical epic in which he mocked the whole spectrum of contemporary German politics, parodied the clumsiness and unconsciously comic tone of *Tendenzdichter* like Freiligrath and Herwegh, and proclaimed the carefree independence of poetry. But as 'Die Tendenz' and 'Verheißung' of January 1842 suggest, Heine is not arguing for poetry that ignores political and social issues: rather he is mocking committed poetry that is abstract in tone and inept in execution. Circumstances were in any case steering him back into the world of politics. Early in 1840 he was able to resume his reports on the French political scene for the *Augsburger Allgemeine Zeitung*. The accession of Friedrich Wilhelm IV seemed to augur liberalization. But such hopes rapidly evaporated. In January 1842, the very month in which his two early *Zeitgedichte*

[40] E vii. 23, 39; see also *Shakespeares Mädchen und Frauen*, E v. 401.
[41] See above, pp. 83–4.

appeared, he learned that all works published by Campe had been banned in Prussia. This gave new impetus to Heine's political concern and he even wrote to Campe that he was now prepared to join forces with the 'shabbiest of demagogues' if that would deal a blow to the Prussian government.[42] His poem 'Bei des Nacht-wächters Ankunft in Paris', based on Dingelstedt's journey to Paris and which he included in the same letter to Campe, is already a miniature *Deutschland. Ein Wintermärchen*, a picture of anachronism and tyranny in Germany. A letter to Laube of November 1842[43] shows he knew and sympathized with the Young Hegelians and their principal organ *Hallische Jahrbücher*. Its editor, Ruge, came to Paris in the autumn of 1843 shortly before Heine returned to Germany for the first time in some thirteen years. What Heine saw there confirmed his worst fears. He reached Paris again in December 1843. There could hardly have been a more propitious moment for the young Karl Marx to meet Heine.

Heine's relationship with Marx was quite different from that with Börne. All the evidence points to their having been genuine friends during the year that both were in Paris.[44] Heine was a constant visitor to Marx's house and the two men contributed to the same left-wing journals, Ruge's *Deutsch-französische Jahr-bücher* and Bernays and Börnstein's *Vorwärts*. Unlike Engels,[45] Marx sided with Heine in the Börne dispute. Marx's daughter, Eleanor, reports that he judged 'auf das Nachsichtigste über seine politischen Schwächen. Dichter, erklärte er, seien sonderbare Käuze, die man ihre Wege wandeln lassen müsse. Man dürfe sie nicht mit dem Maßstabe gewöhnlicher oder selbst ungewöhn-licher Menschen messen.' This was Heine's view entirely, as he was to show so clearly in 'Jehuda ben Halevy':

> . . . In der Kunst,
> Wie im Leben kann das Volk
> Töten uns, doch niemals richten.   (E i. 443)

How is one to explain Marx's indulgent attitude, the patent opposite to that of Börne? Marx spared no other allies once he

[42] *Br* ii. 419.   [43] Ibid., p. 439.
[44] Cf. their correspondence: Heine to Marx, 21 Sept. 1844 (*Br* ii. 541 f.); Marx to Heine, 12 Jan. 1845 (MEW xxvii. 434), 24 Mar. 1845 (ibid., p. 435); 5 Apr. 1846 (?) (ibid., p. 441). See also Eleanor Marx's report in Houben, op. cit., p. 450 f. For full account see Reeves, 'Heine and the young Marx'.
[45] Cf. MEW i. 438 ff., Ergänzungsband ii., p. 23.

discovered significant differences of opinion—Proudhon, Heß, Bauer, all were mercilessly flayed as historical materialism took on definition. Certainly the young Marx admired Heine's work. I have shown elsewhere[46] in some detail that Heine exercised a significant influence both on Marx's early lyrical and satirical works and on key writings such as the 1844 *Einleitung zur Kritik der Hegelschen Rechtsphilosophie*, which marks the first decisive stage in the evolution of his mature philosophy. But intellectual influence did not save Heß or Bauer from Marx's scorn. Unlike them, however, Heine, who was now forty-seven, was less a threat to this ambitious young man than a mentor, and a mentor of European fame at that.

Of particular significance for Marx were Heine's views on the role of religion in suppressing political discontent and in divorcing men from a truly human state, a state of harmony. Heine's despair at modern man's *Zerrissenheit* fully anticipates Marx's anger at industrial man's alienation. Both men grew up in the tradition of German *Humanität* and though Heine came to express his ideals in more colourful terms, his gods on earth in *Zur Geschichte* and Marx's integrated and harmonious humans of the 1844 'Paris Manuscipts'[47] are very close. Again, Heine, as a Hegelian, believed that action was a concrete expression of ideas—'Die Welt ist die Signatur des Wortes'.[48] The German political revolution would follow on inexorably from the German philosophical revolution. Stubbornly, even after the 1848 débâcle, Marx retained this same faith long after Heine had abandoned hope.

These ideas recur both in Heine's *Deutschland. Ein Wintermärchen* and in Marx's 'Paris Manuscripts' and the *Einleitung zur Kritik der Hegelschen Rechtsphilosophie*. When Heine reaches his 'fairy-tale land' he interrupts

> . . . das alte Entsagungslied,
> Das Eiapopeia vom Himmel,
> Womit man einlullt, wenn es greint,
> Das Volk, den großen Lümmel. (E ii. 431)

It is time for the epoch of beauty, pleasure, and social justice

---

[46] 'Heine and the Young Marx'.
[47] Karl Marx, *Texte zu Methode und Praxis*, ed. Günther Hillmann, Hamburg, 1968 , ii. 81 f.
[48] E iv. 248. See above, p. 100.

which he had proclaimed ten years before in *Zur Geschichte* to be realized:

> Wir wollen auf Erden glücklich sein,
> Und wollen nicht mehr darben;
> Verschlemmen soll nicht der faule Bauch,
> Was fleißige Hände erwarben.
>
> Es wächst hienieden Brot genug
> Für alle Menschenkinder,
> Auch Rosen und Myrten, Schönheit und Lust,
> Und Zuckererbsen nicht minder. (432)

The narrator's contraband for which the customs officers vainly seek is in his mind, and he has not travelled far on German soil before his double appears, his lictor, whose task is to translate thought into action, to transform theory into practice:

> 'Ich bin von praktischer Natur,
> Und immer schweigsam und ruhig.
> Doch wisse: was du ersonnen im Geist,
> Das führ' ich aus, das thu' ich.' (444)

We have a taste of what the lictor intends to do when he follows the narrator into a chapel and smashes a sculpture depicting the Three Wise Kings. The end of kings recurs in the last canto, where the poet warns Friedrich Wilhelm that his verse can sentence him to a more infernal fate than that to which censors can condemn writers. And when in the preface Heine dreams of servility being eradicated from every nook and cranny of Germany so that his country can surpass what even the French have achieved, we have no doubt in what this infernal fate will consist. Marx puts the point still more forcibly in the concluding lines to *Zur Kritik*:

In Deutschland kann *keine* Art der Knechtschaft gebrochen werden, ohne *jede* Art der Knechtschaft zu brechen. Das *gründliche* Deutschland kann nicht revolutionieren, ohne *von Grund aus* zu revolutionieren. Die *Emanzipation des Deutschen* ist die *Emanzipation des Menschen*. Der *Kopf* dieser Emanzipation ist die *Philosophie*, ihr *Herz* das *Proletariat*. Die Philosophie kann sich nicht verwirklichen ohne die Aufhebung des Proletariats, das Proletariat kann sich nicht aufheben ohne die Verwirklichung der Philosophie.

Wenn alle innern Bedingungen erfüllt sind, wird der *deutsche Auf-erstehungstag* verkündet werden durch das *Schmettern des gallischen Hahns*.[49]

Heine had opened the essay in which he first evolved the idea of the German philosophical revolution as a parallel to the French Revolution, *Kahldorf über den Adel*, with the words: 'Der gallische Hahn hat jetzt zum zweiten Male gekräht, und auch in Deutschland wird es Tag.'[50]

In his *Kritische Randglossen* Marx greeted the Silesian weavers' uprising of June 1844 as the first informed working-class revolt in Germany. He saw it as the initial sign of the eventual German proletarian revolution, a revolution that would be nourished by theory in a way that not even the two revolutions in France had been nourished. The weavers' critical awareness of how they were being exploited as a class expressed itself in their song, the song incidentally that Hauptmann used in his drama. But the song that is remembered is not 'Das Blutgericht': it is Heine's brilliant verse prophecy of Old Germany's downfall, which, ironically, was based less on the Silesian model than on that sung by the silk weavers of Lyons during their uprising of 1831:[51]

> Im düstern Auge keine Thräne,
> Sie sitzen am Webstuhl und fletschen die Zähne:
> 'Deutschland, wir weben dein Leichentuch,
> Wir weben hinein den dreifachen Fluch,
> Wir weben, wir weben!' (E ii. 177)

Should we, then, consider Heine to be one of the first German Communists? Heine had repeatedly drawn the attention of the German public to the there virtually unknown French Communist groups in his new series of reports for the *Augsburger Allgemeine Zeitung*. He saw them as the greatest extra-parliamentary threat to Guizot's ministry, and his words betray a characteristic mixture of admiration, awe, and fear:

. . . wie immer, erwartet die Revolution eine parlamentarische Initia-tive. Das entsetzliche Rad käme dann wieder in Bewegung, und wir sähen diesmal einen Antagonisten auftreten, welcher der schrecklichste sein dürfte von allen, die bisher mit dem Bestehenden in die Schranken getreten. Dieser Antagonist bewahrt noch sein schreckliches Inkognito

---

[49] MEW i. 391. [50] E vii. 280.
[51] Cf. Hans Kaufmann, *Geistige Entwicklung und künstlerisches Werk*, pp. 239 ff.

und residiert wie ein dürftiger Prätendent in jenem Erdgeschoß der offiziellen Gesellschaft, in jenen Katakomben, wo unter Tod und Verwesung das neue Leben keimt und knospet. Kommunismus ist der geheime Name des furchtbaren Antagonisten, der die Proletarierherrschaft in allen ihren Konsequenzen dem heutigen Bourgeoisieregimente entgegensetzt. (E vi. 314 f.)

The Communists of whom Heine was thinking were the neo-Babouvist groups[52] that had existed in Paris since the early 1830s, and who based their philosophy on Buonarroti's influential *Conspiration pour l'égalité dite de Babeuf* (translated into French 1828). The catacombs evoked by Heine were probably the crypt in which the 'Panthéon' had met—certainly Buonarroti had described the 'Panthéon's' subterranean meeting-place in vivid terms.[53] It was from the 'Panthéon', proscribed by Napoleon in 1796, that Babeuf's conspiratorial directory had evolved. Babeuf had hoped to overthrow Napoleon in a tightly organized *coup d'état*. The insurrectionists would then introduce the rejected 1793 Constitution. At the heart of the philosophy was radical egalitarianism, which was hostile not only to political élitism but to any kind of intellectual or artistic eminence. Such sentiments were repulsive to Heine and a threat to his dearest values and ideals. These Communists, he feared, would reduce men to a 'gleichgeschorene, gleichblökende Menschenherde',[54] not elevate them to a 'Demokratie gleichherrlicher, gleichheiliger, gleichbeseligter Götter'.[55]

Significantly Marx and Engels were of the same opinion. Both condemned the Babouvists' egalitarianism, Engels in an account of Continental Socialism for a British public in 1843,[56] Marx in his 'Paris Manuscripts' of 1844,[57] and jointly in the Communist Manifesto of 1848.[58] This explains how Heine could collaborate with Marx and Engels and yet dissociate himself from the Communists. In an unfinished work of 1844, generally known by Strodtmann's title 'Briefe über Deutschland',[59] Heine succinctly summarized the revolutionary importance of the people's loss of

---

[52] Cf. Leo Kreutzer, *Heine und der Kommunismus*, Göttingen, 1970, and Reeves, op. cit., part II, pp. 78–84.

[53] Philippe Buonarroti, *Conspiration pour l'égalité dite de Babeuf*, ed. Georges Lefebvre, 2 vols., Paris, 1957, i. 75.

[54] E vi. 316.   [55] E iv. 223.   [56] MEW i. 485.

[57] Hillmann, op. cit. ii. 73 f.   [58] MEW iv. 489.

[59] E vi. 531–6. Cf. Eberhard Galley, 'Heines "Briefe über Deutschland" und die "Geständnisse". Eine Textgeschichte an Hand der Manuskripte des Heine-Archivs', *Heine-Jahrbuch 1963*, pp. 60–84.

religious faith and consequent rejection of its moral code, which was based on the acceptance of suffering.[60] He elucidates Hegel's role in the new social movement, interpreting him as an esoteric revolutionary, and speaks of the intellectuals who would lead the proletariat to victory, transforming doctrine into action. Their Communist programme, he claims, is his very own, the ideal of an Olympian world on earth, which he had depicted in *Zur Geschichte*.

But at the end of 1844 *Vorwärts* was suppressed. Marx and Engels were ordered to leave France. And in the same fateful month of January 1845 Heine learnt that he had been tricked out of an acceptable inheritance and pension from his uncle Salomon, who had just died. Even as he fought to obtain redress, his health took a disastrous turn for the worse. He was never to recover, and the abortive 1848 Revolution coincided with the paralysis of his legs. The Olympian could no longer sustain his hedonist philosophy. The revolutionary despaired. When Heine came to use his material from 'Briefe über Deutschland' for *Geständnisse* of 1854 it was for a very different purpose—to dissociate himself from the Hegelians, those 'fanatische Mönche des Atheismus', those 'Großinquisitoren des Unglaubens',[61] and to declare his solidarity with the Israel of Moses.[62] In the preface to the 1852 edition of *Salon* I he lists the Hegelians and they include Feuerbach, Bauer, 'der grimme Ruge', and his 'even more stubborn friend, Marx'.[63] He had already addressed his Communist colleagues in *Deutschland. Ein Wintermärchen* as his fellow wolves but they had listened attentively to his overtures. One of his *Letzte Gedichte* (1869) adopts a still more menacing image. 'Die Wanderratten'[64] pictures the Communists not as a party led by an élite of intellectuals but as a hungry, uncontrollable horde. However necessary, however justified their invasion of the smug burgher rats' township may be, there is something apocalyptic about the arrival of this anonymous, innumerable multitude, whose appearance is as uncompromising as its doctrine, 'ganz radikal, ganz rattenkahl'. Lean or fat? Cassius or Caesar? In the last years of his life Heine remained divided in his loyalties, for he faced a choice he had never wished to make—to choose, as he saw it, between a mass movement whose ideology was essentially Puritan and an establishment that alone could or would afford pleasure. One of those pleasures, one of

[60] E vi. 534 ff.   [61] Ibid., p. 41.   [62] Ibid., p. 55.
[63] E iv. 157.   [64] E ii. 202 ff.

those 'schöne Nebensachen', as he had called it so many years
before[65] and which he now knew to be an indispensable part of
life, was poetry. Shades of Börne! In his sickness and disenchantment Heine could no longer distinguish between Marx and the
Jacobin–Babouvist image with which Communism was indelibly
stamped for him. He confessed the unassailable logic that was
the motor force of the Communists, their 'Suppenlogik',[66] the
'schreckliche Konsequenz' of their doctrine,[67] 'cette prémisse:
"que les hommes ont tous le droit de manger"'.[68] But they were
the levellers who would not spare his work. To express his fear
of utilitarian banality, the Philistinism that characterized these
iconoclasts, Heine turned to images some of which may stem from
a friend who was in every way the opposite of Marx, Théophile
Gautier. Heine's celebrated passage in the 1855 preface to the
French edition of *Lutezia* reads:

Cet aveu, que l'avenir appartient aux communistes, je le fis d'un ton
d'appréhension et d'angoisse extrêmes, et hélas! ce n'était nullement
un masque! En effet, ce n'est qu'avec horreur et effroi que je pense à
l'époque où ces sombres iconoclastes viendront à la domination: de leur
mains calleuses ils briseront sans merci toutes les statues de marbre de la
beauté, si chères à mon cœur; ils fracasseront toutes ces babioles et
fanfreluches fantastiques de l'art, qu'aimait tant le poëte; ils détruiront
mes bois de lauriers et y planteront des pommes de terre; les lis qui ne
filaient ni ne travaillaient, et qui pourtant étaient vêtus aussi magnifique-
ment que le roi Salomon dans toute sa splendeur, ils seront arrachés
alors du sol de la société, à moins qu'ils ne veuillent prendre en main le
fuseau; les roses, ces oisives fiancées des rossignols, auront le même
sort: les rossignols, ces chanteurs inutiles, seront chassés, et hélas! mon
Livre des Chants servira à l'épicier pour en faire des cornets où il versera
du café ou du tabac à priser pour les vieilles femmes de l'avenir. Hélas!
je prévois tout cela, et je suis saisi d'une indicible tristesse en pensant à
la ruine dont le prolétariat vainqueur menace mes vers, qui périront avec
tout l'ancien monde romantique.   (E vi. 572)

In Gautier's preface to *Mlle de Maupin* of 1834 we find the tobac-
conists and grocers who use paper from books for their bags and
the utilitarians who would dig up flowers to plant potatoes. For
Gautier, God's commandment was not 'Ayez de la vertu, mais:
Ayez de l'amour . . .'[69]

[65] *Br* i. 51 f. See above, p. 1.   [66] E ii. 204.   [67] E vi. 45.
[68] Ibid., p. 572.
[69] *Mlle de Maupin*, ed. Adolphe Boschot, Paris, 1955, p. 24.

This was no sudden change in Heine, as we have seen. Even as he was formulating his ideal of the committed artist in the 1830s he had begun by a natural and almost instinctive process to defend poetry from the claims made on it by parties and causes. Gradually he evolved the theory that art exists solely for its own sake. He found the roots for this theory in his admiration for Goethe and the view of art for art's sake which he believed Goethe held, but which was largely his own creation—hence his contradictory desire both to execrate and to deify Goethe. In his year of collaboration with Marx he imagined that the genius and the people could rule together.[70] It was a fragile alliance.

[70] E ii. 429 f.

VI

KING AND MARTYR

A. *The sovereignty of the genius*

Alle Dinge sind uns ja nur durch ihren Gegensatz erkennbar,
es gäbe für uns keine Poesie, wenn wir nicht überall auch
das Gemeine und das Triviale sehen könnten, wir selber erkennen unser eignes Wesen nur dadurch, daß uns das fremd-
artige Wesen eines andern Menschen bemerkbar wird und zur
Vergleichung dient . . .

(To Immermann, June 1823; *Br* i. 83)

From the start Heine had found the relationship of poetry to the
real world problematic. As a poet he felt threatened by the ruthless
pressure and unashamed utilitarianism of the business world, of
which he had first-hand experience in Frankfurt and Hamburg;
yet even this experience paled before the mechanization of life
which confronted him in a chaotically expanding London. Heine
had seen through the fiction of the latter-day folk-song: now he
could see with his own eyes the nightingales and moonshine being
destroyed by industrialization. '. . . der Kohlendampf verscheucht
die Sangesvögel, und der Gasbeleuchtungsgestank verdirbt die
duftige Mondnacht.'[1] The criterion of *Zeitgemäßheit*, which he
increasingly applied to poetry in the years preceding the July
Revolution, was intended to close the gap between art and life,
between the activity of the poet and that of the revolutionary. It
was easy to forget when writing in the seclusion of Norderney and
of Germany's political backwaters that detachment, far from being
entirely negative, is a necessary part of the creative process. In
Germany there was nothing but stagnation: in Paris, he wrote
within a short time of his arrival, 'ertrinke ich im Strudel der
Begebenheiten, der Tageswellen, der brausenden Revoluzion'.[2]

In September 1831 Heine met Börne again and in the same month
produced the first work he wrote on French soil—a report on that
year's Salon. Börne repelled him, the paintings fascinated him.

[1] E vii. 418.   [2] *Br* ii. 5 (to Varnhagen, June 1831).

And even as he reflected on his impressions of the exhibition the clamour from the streets told him that Warsaw had fallen to Russia. Everywhere there were contradictions and conflicting experiences, experiences which inevitably helped to accentuate an inherent duality in his views on art and artists. He was divided between an essentially Romantic belief in the genius 'der kein Gesetz über sich leide'[3] and his new-won Left Hegelian conception of the engaged poet, just as in Die Nordsee five years before he had been divided between Goethe and Napoleon. This split emerges very plainly in his discussion of the Salon. We cannot regard it as a conscious reaction against Börne: the essay was written too early for that. But in subsequent years the pressure Heine felt from this and other political quarters drove him to explore his ideas on the autonomy of art further. One of the exhibition's most striking paintings was Delacroix's picture of the goddess of freedom leading the people of Paris to victory in the July Revolution.[4] Nothing could have served better to show the committed artist in action and Heine openly admits that in view of the 'Heiligkeit des Sujets' the critic is not empowered to censure its technical quality.[5] This is living history: the age of the gods seems to have returned—or almost:

Heilige Julitage von Paris! ihr werdet ewig Zeugnis geben von dem Uradel der Menschen, der nie ganz zerstört werden kann. Wer euch erlebt hat, der jammert nicht mehr auf den alten Gräbern, sondern freudig glaubt er jetzt an die Auferstehung der Völker. Heilige Julitage! wie schön war die Sonne und wie groß war das Volk von Paris! Die Götter im Himmel, die dem großen Kampfe zusahen, jauchzten vor Bewunderung, und sie wären gerne aufgestanden von ihren goldenen Stühlen und wären gerne zur Erde herabgestiegen, um Bürger zu werden von Paris! Aber neidisch, ängstlich, wie sie sind, fürchteten sie am Ende, daß die Menschen zu hoch und zu herrlich emporblühen möchten, und durch ihre willigen Priester suchten sie 'das Glänzende zu schwärzen und das Erhabene in dem Staub zu ziehn', und sie stifteten die belgische Rebellion, das de Pottersche Viehstück. Es ist dafür gesorgt, daß die Freiheitsbäume nicht in den Himmel hineinwachsen.

(E iv. 37 f.)

[3] Friedrich Schlegel, Kritische Schriften, ed. Wolfdietrich Rasch, Munich, 1964, p. 39.
[4] 'Liberty leading the People'. It still hangs in the Louvre. This and the paintings by Decamps and Delaroche to which I shall refer below are reproduced in Michael Mann's edition of Heine's Zeitungsberichte über Musik und Malerei, Frankfurt a. M., 1964; for Delacroix's painting see p. 64.
[5] E iv. 37.

Yet the next painter to be discussed, Decamps, is judged according to quite different criteria. Heine sets out to defend Decamps's paintings of Oriental scenes against the charge that they were not realistic and little more than caricatures. In art, Heine claims, the imagination is of primary importance: reason has only to keep fantasy from running riot. And it is entirely in the tradition of Herder and the Romantics that he now goes on to reject all *a priori* rules and norms in aesthetics. A genius is a rule unto himself:

> Der große Irrtum besteht darin, daß der Kritiker die Frage aufwirft: was soll der Künstler? Viel richtiger wäre die Frage: was will der Künstler, oder gar, was muß der Künstler? Die Frage, was soll der Künstler? entstand durch jene Kunstphilosophen, die, ohne eigene Poesie, sich Merkmale der verschiedenen Kunstwerke abstrahierten, nach dem Vorhandenen eine Norm für alles Zukünftige feststellten, und Gattungen schieden, und Definitionen und Regeln ersannen. Sie wußten nicht, daß alle solche Abstraktionen nur allenfalls zur Beurteilung des Nachahmervolks nützlich sind, daß aber jeder Originalkünstler und gar jedes neue Kunstgenie nach seiner eigenen mitgebrachten Ästhetik beurteilt werden muß.   (E iv. 42 f.)

The artist has one task and that is to give expression to his idea— 'die Veranschaulichung seiner Idee'. He needs symbols but these cannot be selected by conscious decision. They come to him mysteriously as if he were dreaming or sleep-walking:

> Ist der Künstler so ganz willensfrei bei der Wahl und Verbindung seiner geheimnisvollen Blumen? Oder wählt und verbindet er nur, was er muß? Ich bejahe diese Frage einer mystischen Unfreiheit. Der Künstler gleicht jener schlafwandelnden Prinzessin, die des Nachts in den Gärten von Bagdad mit tiefer Liebesweisheit die sonderbarsten Blumen pflückte und zu einem Selam verband, dessen Bedeutung sie selbst gar nicht mehr wußte, als sie erwachte.   (E iv. 43 f.)[6]

From here to Baudelaire's *correspondances* is clearly not far:

> La nature est un temple où de vivants piliers
> Laissent parfois sortir de confuses paroles;
> L'homme y passe à travers des forêts de symboles
> Qui l'observent avec des regards familiers.[7]

At least two sources have been suggested for Baudelaire's theory that 'everything in this world is merely the symbol of a hierogly-

---

[6] Heine also called Goethe's *Divan* a 'Selam' of flowers, cf. E v. 262 f.
[7] *Œuvres complètes: Les Fleurs du Mal*, p. 17.

phic language and . . . that it was the duty of the artist to decipher the hidden writing of nature and to interpret the mysterious book of the universe':[8] Swedenborg[9] and Hoffmann.[10] Nevertheless, it was precisely Heine's words a few lines later which fascinated first Sainte-Beuve and then Baudelaire himself in his *Salon de 1846*.[11] Heine argues that it is not reality in the raw which the artist seeks to reproduce. It is his vision of reality, and this vision draws on depths that are inexplicable in purely empirical terms:

In der Kunst bin ich Supernaturalist. Ich glaube, daß der Künstler nicht alle seine Typen in der Natur auffinden kann, sondern daß ihm die bedeutendsten Typen, als eingeborene Symbolik eingeborner Ideen, gleichsam in der Seele geoffenbart werden . . .

Dem Kritiker, der im Decampschen Bilde die Natur vermißt, und die Art, wie das Pferd des Hadji-Bey die Füße wirft, und wie seine Leute laufen, als unnaturgemäß tadelt, dem kann der Künstler getrost antworten: daß er ganz märchentreu gemalt und ganz nach innerer Traumanschauung. (E iv. 44 f.)[12]

It was not the first time Heine had suggested that the power of a poet's vision defies all rational explanation. Admittedly, in the description of the archetypal intelligence in *Die Nordsee* III Heine had resorted to the Kantian terms he had found conveniently quoted by Goethe in his *Morphologie*, but in the jotting he presumably made about the same time on Indian culture he speaks of the Indian muse as 'die träumende Prinzessin der Märchen'.[13] In the preface to *Reisebilder* IV (November 1830) he even suggests that in *William Ratcliff* he had himself captured the atmosphere of Britain without having been there thanks to 'jene wundersame Intuition, die einem Poeten die Anschauung der Wirklichkeit entbehrlich macht'.[14] Seven years later in the last part of the *Salon* Heine takes the argument one step further. Speaking of the

[8] Enid Starkie, ed. *Charles Baudelaire: Les Fleurs du Mal*, Oxford, 1942, p. xii.

[9] Ibid., p. 197.

[10] Cf. Crépet, *Œuvres complétes: Les Fleurs du Mal*, p. 412; Weinberg, op. cit., p. 251.

[11] See above, pp. 4 f., nn. 24, 25. Weinberg explores the relationship of the two poets at length, op. cit., pp. 157–203 and discusses the problem of *correspondances*, pp. 217 f. He relates Heine's vital passage on the 'Selam' to Mallarmé (pp. 46 f.). The most recent discussion of the topic is to be found in Boeck, op. cit., pp. 116 ff.

[12] Heine is referring to Decamps's painting of the night patrol in Smyrna, reproduced in Mann, op. cit., p. 80.

[13] See above, pp. 22 f. [14] E iii. 375.

theatre, he condemns audiences who expect the sort of naturalistic approach that Iffland had encouraged and which Goethe and Schiller had tried to combat.[15] Picking up the points he put in the mouths of the Goetheans in *Die romantische Schule* he now defends drama as a spectacle that is not concerned merely to reflect the real world. Reality is transformed, and while implicitly referring back in time to Schiller's idealist theory of drama, he also anticipates the view of later 'high priests' of poetry for whom the work of art was to be of a higher order than its creator:

. . . das Theater ist eine andere Welt, die von der unsrigen geschieden ist wie die Szene vom Parterre. Zwischen dem Theater und der Wirklichkeit liegt das Orchester, die Musik, und zieht sich der Feuerstreif der Rampe. Die Wirklichkeit, nachdem sie das Tonreich durchwandert und auch die bedeutungsvollen Rampenlichter überschritten, steht auf dem Theater als Poesie verklärt uns gegenüber. Wie ein verhallendes Echo klingt noch in ihr der holde Wohllaut der Musik, und sie ist märchenhaft angestrahlt von den geheimnisvollen Lampen. Das ist ein Zauberklang und Zauberglanz, der einem prosaischen Publikum sehr leicht als unnatürlich vorkommt, und der doch noch weit natürlicher ist als die gewöhnliche Natur; es ist nämlich durch die Kunst erhöhte, bis zur blühendsten Göttlichkeit gesteigerte Natur. (E iv. 523 f.)

The genius has a universality that goes beyond all pedestrian imitation of reality. In his essay of 1838 on the heroines of Shakespeare's dramas Heine describes the capacity of the genius to see the world not in fragments and partial relationships but as an undivided whole, and again he falls back on innate intuition to explain the poet's remarkable powers of perception:

In dem Dichtergeiste spiegelt sich nicht die Natur, sondern ein Bild derselben, das dem getreuesten Spiegelbilde ähnlich, ist dem Geiste des Dichters eingeboren; er bringt gleichsam die Welt mit zur Welt, und wenn er, aus dem träumenden Kindesalter erwachend, zum Bewußtsein seiner selbst gelangt, ist ihm jeder Teil der äußern Erscheinungswelt gleich in seinem ganzen Zusammenhang begreifbar: denn er trägt ja ein Gleichbild des Ganzen in seinem Geiste, er kennt die letzten Gründe

---

[15] Heine's source was probably Schiller's *Über den Gebrauch des Chors in der Tragödie* where we find the argument that precisely the artificiality of dramatic art enables it to transcend reality and approach the Ideal. The same passage also contains a direct declaration of war on 'dem Naturalismus in der Kunst'. Cf. Schiller, *Sämtliche Werke*, ed. Fricke, Göpfert, and Stubenrauch, Munich, 1965, ii. 817 ff.

aller Phänomene, die dem gewöhnlichen Geiste rätselhaft dünken und
auf dem Wege der gewöhnlichen Forschung nur mühsam oder gar
nicht begriffen werden . . . . Und wie der Mathematiker, wenn man ihm
nur das kleinste Fragment eines Kreises gibt, unverzüglich den ganzen
Kreis und den Mittelpunkt desselben angeben kann: so auch der
Dichter, wenn seiner Anschauung nur das kleinste Bruchstück der
Erscheinungswelt von außen geboten wird, offenbart sich ihm gleich
der ganze universelle Zusammenhang dieses Bruchstücks; er kennt
gleichsam Zirkulatur und Zentrum aller Dinge; er begreift die Dinge in
ihrem weitesten Umfang und tiefsten Mittelpunkt. (E v. 379)

These are the same qualities of vision which he had admired in
Goethe in *Die Nordsee*: the genius stands above the *Zerrissenheit*
of his age and of lesser men.[16] Here his example is Shakespeare and
we are not surprised to find the English dramatist accompanying
Goethe and the exiled gods in the Wild Hunt of *Atta Troll*.
Christianity can no more forgive genius than it can the Olympian gods.

Heine's thought is essentially associative. In the *Reisebilder* we
see Philistines killing poetry and stifling the imagination. For
Heine the most Philistine country of all was England, where
industrialization was completing the destruction of beauty that the
Puritans had began two centuries before. When Heine had half-
defended Goethe against Menzel's strictures he instinctively
thought of the politeness with which the executioners of Charles I
had proceeded. This brings us back to *Französische Maler*. In the
exhibition Heine found a painting by Delaroche depicting Cromwell looking at Charles's corpse as it lay in its coffin.[17] These
figures, Heine reflects, represent the two hostile principles that
dominate the world. He does not name these principles but the
passage marks a clear stage in the evolution of Heine's Hellene/
Nazarene antithesis. The dead king is seen to be 'verklärt von
dem eben erlittenen Märtyrtume, geheiligt von der Majestät des
Unglücks'. The Republican is just a 'rohe, derblebendige Purita-
nergestalt',[18] a contrast that reminds us of the comparison Heine
makes in the Italian *Reisebilder* between the ruddy, insensitive
English tourists and the subtle, sickly beauty of Italian women.

[16] But it is interesting to note that in *Die Bäder von Lucca* Heine had claimed
that his own heart was at the very centre of the world and this was why it was
so divided against itself. The age itself was dissonant. (E iii. 304. See also above,
pp. 27 f.) In a sense Goethe is thus anachronistic—like the gods in exile.
[17] Reproduced in Mann, op. cit., p. 160.   [18] E iv. 61.

There Heine had said in a passage that reads as a remarkable anticipation of Thomas Mann's early works:[19] '. . . kranke Menschen sind immer wahrhaft vornehmer als gesunde; denn nur der kranke Mensch ist ein Mensch, seine Glieder haben eine Leidensgeschichte, sie sind durchgeistet.' (E iii. 270.) These Englishmen are the products of the age that succeeded the reign of Charles. With his death Merry England also died, to be replaced by prosaic uniformity. Poetry vanished:

Da steht sie, die gefestete, erdsichere Gestalt, 'brutal wie eine Thatsache', gewaltig ohne Pathos, dämonisch natürlich, wunderbar ordinär, verfemt und zugleich gefeit, und da betrachtet sie ihr Werk, fast wie ein Holzhacker, der eben eine Eiche gefällt hat. Er hat sie ruhig gefällt, die große Eiche, die einst so stolz ihre Zweige verbreitete über England und Schottland, die Königseiche, in deren Schatten so viele schöne Menschengeschlechter geblüht, und worunter die Elfen der Poesie ihre süßesten Reigen getanzt; — er hat sie ruhig gefällt mit dem unglückseligen Beil, und da liegt sie zu Boden mit all ihrem holden Laubwerk und mit der unverletzten Krone; — unglückseliges Beil!   (E iv. 66 f.)

The essay on Shakespeare gave a further opportunity to touch on Charles, poetry's martyr.[20] The Puritans smashed the images in the churches and banned theatre. The subsequent persecution of actors and suspicion of the theatre, Heine states, is another example of the age-old struggle between the spirit of Greece and the spirit of Judaea, and when the actors were proscribed so also were the poets who had sought to give the gods of the Greeks asylum in their works. The threads of Heine's thought are simple and all-embracing: the conflict between Hellene and Nazarene is made to explain the mechanics of world history, and seen in this light the final reckoning with Ludwig Börne in 1840 seems almost inevitable.

In *Ludwig Börne. Eine Denkschrift* Heine makes clever use of association, half-suggestion, and reminiscence to weave together Börne, Republicans, Puritans, Nazarenes, the Bible, journalism, and political opportunities on the one hand and Heine himself (or more properly his public image), monarchism, Hellenes, Homer,

---

[19] Thomas Mann was particularly devious about his debt to Heine, who at the turn of the century, following the Dreyfus affair, was not entirely 'respectable' literary company. On one occasion (see above, p. 6) he did openly confess the profound impression made on him by Heine's essay on Börne—cf. T. J. Reed's intriguing account, 'Thomas Mann, Heine, Schiller; The Mechanics of Self-interpretation', *Neophilologus*, 47 (1963), 41–50.

[20] E v. 373 ff.

art, and artistic detachment on the other in a giant antithesis. The July Revolution is both the beacon that brings Heine und Börne together in Paris and subsequently the 'mountain'[21] that divides them or, as Heine would have us believe, divides the demagogue from the exiled poet. In this essay the polemic against Goethe in which Börne, Menzel, and Heine himself had participated stood Heine in good stead. By careful adjustment the very arguments Börne had levelled against others are turned against their own author or inverted. Börne had carried over his attack on Goethe to Heine, whom he also pictured as a chameleon-like talent lacking in all moral fibre. The terms character and talent used to describe two fundamentally different types of men originated from Goethe. In lines that anticipate the clash between Tasso and Antonio, Leonore Sanvitale tells the Duke:

> Es bildet ein Talent sich in der Stille,
> Sich ein Charakter in dem Strom der Welt.
> (*Torquato Tasso*, i. 2)[22]

Menzel had adopted this distinction in his history of German literature, labelling Goethe himself as the talent, the actor whose performance bears no relation to his own feelings. He is a mere virtuoso and entirely uncommitted:

> Es treibt ihn nicht, sein volles Herz auszuströmen, und ein Heiliges und Geliebtes, das er erkannt hat, äußerlich darzustellen, vielmehr ist ihm jede Empfindung und jeder Gegenstand an sich völlig gleichgültig, und gilt ihm nur etwas, sofern er ihn darstellt; nur die Darstellung gilt ihm, was auch immer das Dargestellte sey. Darum wird er auch durch keinen besondern Gegenstand beherrscht, er herrscht vielmehr über alle, und gefällt sich im Wechsel derselben, der seine Herrschaft beurkundet.[23]

Börne in turn accused Heine of loving truth only when it happened to be beautiful, which was, of course, uncomfortably accurate. Heine's ideal from *Almansor* onwards had been a world in which

---

[21] Laube persuaded Heine that as the essay stood it was too obviously a personal attack on Börne, though Heine still insisted that he was simply defending his own world-view. On his advice he inserted a 'mountain', the 'Briefe aus Helgoland', which would make the subsequent hostility towards Börne seem a direct consequence of the turn events had taken—cf. E vii. 4 ff. Laube considered Heine had deceived him; the *Briefe* were a mere valley.

[22] Cf. Kaufmann, *Heinrich Heine*, p. 64.

[23] Menzel, *Die deutsche Litteratur* (1st edn.), ii. 212 f.

truth and beauty were identical: the enemy was always the banal
and ugly. In a passage from the *Briefe aus Paris*, which Heine
quotes in his essay, Börne wrote:

> Man versetze Heine in das *Ballhaus*, zu jener denkwürdigen Stunde,
> wo Frankreich aus seinem tausendjährigen Schlafe erwachte und
> schwur, es wolle nicht mehr träumen — er wäre der tollheißeste Jako-
> biner, der wütendste Feind der Aristokraten und ließe alle Edelleute
> und Fürsten mit Wonne an einem Tage niedermetzeln. Aber sähe er
> aus der Rocktasche des feuerspeienden Mirabeau auf deutsche Studen-
> tenart eine Tabakspfeife mit rot-schwarz-goldener Quaste hervorragen
> — dann pfui Freiheit! und er ginge hin und machte schöne Verse auf
> Marie-Antoinettens schöne Augen.[24]

Heine's later poem 'Marie-Antoinette' serves as an amusing
counterblast to this particular charge: passing the Tuileries one
sunny morning the poet observes the now headless Queen and her
headless entourage performing their grotesque morning toilet, for
ever spared the bother of adjusting their coiffures.[25] Of more
gravity was Heine's presentation of Ludwig Börne as the ephemeral writer who is popular because he is carried away by the
tastes and causes of the moment. This marks a significant shift in
Heine's own position. Some ten years before, he accused Platen of
being a virtuoso on language as one might be on a musical instru-
ment—'Ungleich dem wahren Dichter, ist die Sprache nie Meister
geworden in ihm'.[26] In *Die romantische Schule* Goethe was un-
favourably compared to Schiller since he wrote about emancipation merely as a piece of prefigured material—'der Geist wurde
Materie unter seinen Händen, und er gab ihm die schöne, gefäl-
lige Form'.[27] But beautiful though the resultant works of art were,
they remained barren and childless. In *Ludwig Börne*, however,
Heine claims that the detached artist alone is honourable. Heine
himself had censured the coldness of Goethe's works.[28] Now it is
the short-sighted Börne:

> In seiner subjektiven Befangenheit begriff er nicht die objektive
> Freiheit, die goethische Weise, und die künstlerische Form hielt er für
> Gemütlosigkeit: er glich dem Kinde, welches, ohne den glühenden
> Sinn einer griechischen Statue zu ahnen, nur die marmornen Formen
> betastet und über Kälte klagt. (E vii. 18)

After his visit to Weimar in 1824 Heine had deplored Goethe's

---

[24] *Sämtliche Werke*, iii. 811 f.; E vii. 138.   [25] E i. 343 ff.
[26] E iii. 352.   [27] E v. 253.   [28] Ibid., p. 254.

hedonist way of life and his lack of enthusiasm for the *Idee*.[29] Now Heine speaks as a hedonist and pokes fun at Börne, who cannot even eat a meal without joining the company of an entire restaurant filled with political refugees, each with a price on his head. It is Börne who deplores that Heine spent his first day in Paris visiting not the graves of Voltaire and Rousseau but the *Bibliothèque Royale* to examine the poems of Walther von der Vogelweide in the Manesse Manuscript.[30] It is not the *Talent* who vacillates but the man who is acclaimed by the public to be a *Charakter*.

> Es ist immer ein Zeichen von Borniertheit, wenn man von der bornierten Menge leicht begriffen und ausdrücklich als Charakter gefeiert wird. Bei Schriftstellern ist dies noch bedenklicher, da ihre Thaten eigentlich in Worten bestehen, und was das Publikum als Charakter in ihren Schriften verehrt, ist am Ende nichts anders als knechtische Hingebung an den Moment, als Mangel an Bildnerruhe, an Kunst. (E vii. 134)

The true artist is now the man who reigns supreme *over* language and is *not* governed by the dynamic of words:

> Der Grundsatz, daß man den Charakter eines Schriftstellers aus seiner Schreibweise erkenne, ist nicht unbedingt richtig; er ist bloß anwendbar bei jener Masse von Autoren, denen beim Schreiben nur die augenblickliche Inspiration die Feder führt, und die mehr dem Worte gehorchen als befehlen. Bei Artisten ist jener Grundsatz unzuläßlich, denn diese sind Meister des Wortes, handhaben es zu jedem beliebigen Zwecke, prägen es nach Willkür, schreiben objectiv, und ihr Charakter verrät sich nicht in ihrem Stil.
>
> Ob Börne ein Charakter ist, während andere nur Dichter sind, diese unfruchtbare Frage können wir nur mit dem mitleidigsten Achselzucken beantworten. (E vii. 134)

Thus Heine makes Börne's deeply committed *Charakter* the sincere but sadly limited writer whose products last but a day. The *Talent* is now the critical intelligence who shapes his works for posterity from a position of masterly distance.[31]

---

[29] *Br* i. 216 f. [30] E vii. 103 f.

[31] Here were sentiments that one can imagine deeply appealed to Thomas Mann as he struggled with his Geist/Kunst antithesis in his projected but never finished essay of the same title. The *Notiz über Heinrich Heine* in which Mann points to Heine's 'tiefe Einsicht in den Gegensatz von Geist und Kunst (nicht etwa nur von Moral und Kunst)' in the Börne essay, dates from 1907—cf. Reed, op. cit., pp. 41 ff., and ibid., ' "Geist und Kunst". Thomas Mann's Abandoned Essay on Literature', *Oxford German Studies*, 1 (1966), 53–101.

At the time when the Börne essay was published the public were most shocked at Heine's reciprocal though distasteful attack on a dead man's morals. Karl Kraus, writing seventy years later, made sure that Heine's shifting arguments did not escape attention. Referring to the passage quoted above in his vitriolic critique 'Heine und die Folgen', Kraus claims that precisely the lack of involvement which Heine praises in the artist pinpoints his own essential dishonesty. Heine changes his ground as he pleases, Kraus argues, since he was never committed. Kraus does not miss the discrepancy between Heine's charge against Platen and that against Börne. Heine's *Artist* is nothing but a journalist.[32] This neatly reverses Heine's strictures on Börne and ironically implies, as Börne had stated, that a character does not alter his principles. Heine had certainly changed his view of poetry in the light of his experience. Nor can it be denied that in this essay he was consciously manipulating his categories in order to score a polemical victory: the sovereignty of the artist over his material is shared by the polemicist planning his tactics. But at bottom the Börne essay is, as Heine told Laube,[33] a defence of his own world view and thus a defence of creative freedom. During his nine years in Paris it had become evident to him that the enemies of the poetic age of which he dreamed were as much the revolutionaries as the feudal German *status quo* with its conspiracy of priesthood and aristocracy. What Heine dreaded was equality at the expense of quality. He longed for 'eine Demokratie gleichherrlicher, gleichheiliger, gleichbeseligter Götter'.[34] The people Börne appealed to were real—and far from beautiful: they were Philistine in their habits and only too proletarian in their hygiene. The same poet who was moved by the sight of appalling poverty and hunger in the back streets of London,[35] and who still was to write 'Die schlesischen Weber', was deeply shocked at the thought of fighting shoulder to shoulder with the industrial working classes:

Man muß in wirklichen Revolutionszeiten das Volk mit eigenen Augen gesehen, mit eigner Nase gerochen haben, man muß mit eignen Ohren anhören, wie dieser souveräne Rattenkönig sich ausspricht, um zu begreifen, was Mirabeau andeuten will mit den Worten: 'Man macht keine Revolutionen mit Lavendelöl'. Solange wir die Revolution

[32] Kraus, op. cit., pp. 226 ff.
[33] Cf. Laube's article of 1846, cited, E vii. 5.   [34] E iv. 223.
[35] E iii. 441 f.

in den Büchern lesen, sieht das alles sehr schön aus, und es ist damit wie mit jenen Landschaften, die kunstreich gestochen auf dem weißen Velinpapier, so rein, so freundlich aussehen, aber nachher, wenn man sie in Natura betrachtet, vielleicht an Grandiosität gewinnen, doch einen sehr schmutzigen und schäbigen Anblick in den Einzelheiten gewähren; die in Kupfer gestochenen Misthaufen riechen nicht, und der in Kupfer gestochene Morast ist leicht mit den Augen zu durchwaten!

War es Tugend oder Wahnsinn, was den Ludwig Börne dahin brachte, die schlimmen Mistdüfte mit Wonne einzuschnaufen und sich vergnüglich im plebejischen Kot zu wälzen? (E vii. 81)

Heine was by nature an aesthete: he was physically repelled by what was ugly, coarse, and indifferent to beauty. He could see with his own eyes in Paris that the new age would be the opposite of the one for which he had striven in Germany. '. . . der Parnaß', reads one of his jottings, 'soll geebnet werden, nivelliert, makadamisiert, und wo einst der müßige Dichter geklettert und die Nachtigallen belauscht, wird bald eine platte Landstraße sein, eine Eisenbahn, wo der Dampfkessel wiehert und der geschäftigen Gesellschaft vorübereilt.'[36] Or to use the terms of the Börne essay, the Puritans will have won the day, and just as the death of Charles I had spelt the end of Shakespeare's England, so here royalty of blood and royalty of mind will abdicate together:

Alle überlieferte Heiterkeit, alle Süße, aller Blumenduft, alle Poesie wird aus dem Leben herausgepumpt werden, und es wird davon nichts übrigbleiben als die Rumford'sche Suppe der Nützlichkeit. — Für die Schönheit und das Genie wird sich kein Platz finden in dem Gemeinwesen unserer neuen Puritaner, und beide werden fletriert und unterdrückt werden noch weit betrübsamer als unter dem älteren Regimente. Denn Schönheit und Genie sind ja auch eine Art Königtum, und sie passen nicht in eine Gesellschaft, wo jeder im Mißgefühl der eignen Mittelmäßigkeit alle höhere Begabnis herabzuwürdigen sucht bis aufs banale Niveau.

Die Könige gehen fort, und mit ihnen gehen die letzten Dichter. 'Der Dichter soll mit dem König gehen', diese Worte dürften jetzt einer ganz anderen Deutung anheimfallen. (E viii. 143 f.)[37]

---

[36] E vii. 419.

[37] The quotation is from Schiller's *Die Jungfrau von Orleans*, i. 2, where Charles VII tries to find some last remaining gift with which to reward his troubadours. He is more concerned with their welfare than that of his kingdom. For Mann's interest in this passage and theme, an interest he preferred to refer back to Schiller, see Reed, 'Thomas Mann, Heine, Schiller', cited above. Boeck, op. cit., p. 42, detects the influence of a passage in Gautier's preface to *Mlle de*

The essay ends with Heine's vision of a spectral bacchanal danced by the gods in exile, all that remains of the ideal world he believed had come to Paris when he heard the news of the July Revolution on Heligoland.

Heine may have been a cunning polemicist but he was not the pseudo-artistic journalist that Kraus held him to be. He was driven to the defence of poetry, even to the defence 'der absoluten Kunst' to which Börne had mockingly referred,[38] by the clash between the reality he encountered in Paris and a Utopian vision which originated in German Romanticism. Where Heine differed from the Romantics was in his desire to implement in the here and now what was for them an essentially metaphysical Golden Age. Heine set himself an impossible task: his 'programme' was just a dream. He anticipated this insuperable obstacle to his ambitions when he sensed he was a dreaming poet being thrust into battle[39] or a would-be warrior enchained with garlands of flowers.[40] As the 1830s wore on and Börne launched open attacks on Heine's aestheticism, Enfantin lambasted his principal 'Saint-Simonian' writing in private. The theory, at least, of a poetry that was subject to no external pressures and of the poet as a monarch who could know no spiritual master grew increasingly attractive to Heine. If

Maupin (1834), where Gautier speaks of the destruction of royalty and poetry at the hands of the utilitarians.

[38] Börne unwittingly anticipated the terminology of a genuine exponent of art for art's sake, Gottfried Benn. In his *Probleme der Lyrik*, Wiesbaden, 1951, p. 39, Benn speaks of 'das absolute Gedicht'—but more significant in our context is his use of the concept 'Artistik'. As in Heine it serves the purpose of defence against an inimical world. 'Artistik ist der Versuch der Kunst, innerhalb des allgemeinen Verfalls der Inhalte sich selber als Inhalt zu erleben und aus diesem Erlebnis einen neuen Stil zu bilden, es ist der Versuch, gegen den allgemeinen Nihilismus der Werte eine neue Transzendenz zu setzen: die Transzendenz der schöpferischen Lust' (p. 12). He derives the concept from Nietzsche, who, he claims, took it from France. But Heine was Nietzsche's favourite writer of prose and it would seem highly likely he was familiar with *Ludwig Börne*, especially considering that the Hellene/Nazarene antithesis was so close to his own critique of Christianity in the name of life. When Benn speaks of the origins of the modern lyric he mentions Nerval, who is 'only known at home as the translator of Goethe'. But Nerval was Heine's friend and also *his* translator. Benn goes on to mention Baudelaire. Again there is an affinity and a debt. Either Benn chose deliberately to omit Heine's name or the omission is symptomatic of an attitude in Germany which would prefer to forget Heine's existence. Certainly Mann was happy to conceal what he owed to Heine, as T. J. Reed has shown. Benn's case may be parallel.

[39] Cf. the preface to *Salon* I, E iv. 13–22.

[40] Cf. E i. 203 and above, p. 1.

he could not save his political ideals at least he could save the genius. It was a rearguard action which was to be of greater significance in the history of aesthetics than Heine himself could possibly have imagined.

We have seen Heine distinguish the enchanted world of the stage from that of reality in *Über die französische Bühne*. In the same passage he turned his analysis to account in rejecting the Saint-Simonian claim that poetry must serve to further the holy cause. Defending a Victor Hugo who was as yet far from the national hero of French literature we know today, Heine writes:

Sogar die unsichtbare Kirche der Saint-Simonisten, die überall und nirgends wie die christliche Kirche vor Konstantin, auch diese verwirft ihn; denn diese betrachtet die Kunst als ein Priestertum und verlangt, daß jedes Werk des Dichters, des Malers, des Bildhauers, des Musikers Zeugnis gebe von seiner höheren Weihe, daß es seine heilige Sendung beurkunde, daß es die Beglückung und Verschönerung des Menschengeschlechts bezwecke. Die Meisterwerke Victor Hugos vertragen keinen solchen moralischen Maßstab, ja sie sündigen gegen alle jene großmütigen, aber irrigen Anforderungen der neuen Kirche. Ich nenne sie irrig, denn, wie Sie wissen, ich bin für die Autonomie der Kunst; weder der Religion noch der Politik soll sie als Magd dienen, sie ist sich selber letzter Zweck, wie die Welt selbst. Hier begegnen wir denselben einseitigen Vorwürfen, die schon Goethe von unsren Frommen zu ertragen hatte, und wie dieser muß auch Victor Hugo die unpassende Anklage hören, daß er keine Begeisterung empfände für das Ideale, daß er ohne moralischen Halt, daß er ein kaltherziger Egoist sei u. s. w. (E iv. 524 f.)

In the following year of 1838 Gutzkow, who had previously been a great admirer of Heine,[41] and had been imprisoned for the alleged immorality of his novel *Wally, die Zweiflerin*, wrote to warn Heine against publishing further poems of 'niedere Minne', some of which had already appeared in *Salon* I. Heine, rarely over-modest, replied by comparing his erotic poems to the *Satyricon* and to *Römische Elegien*:

Wie letztere sind auch meine angefochtenen Gedichte kein Futter für die rohe Menge. Sie sind in dieser Beziehung auf dem Holzwege. Nur vornehme Geister, denen die künstlerische Behandlung eines frevelhaften oder allzu natürlichen Stoffes ein geistreiches Vergnügen gewährt, können an jenen Gedichten Gefallen finden. Ein eigentliches Urtheil können nur wenige Deutsche über diese Gedichte aussprechen,

[41] Cf. *Br* v. 261 ff.

da ihnen der Stoff selbst, die abnormen Amouren in einem Welttollhaus, wie Paris ist, unbekannt sind. Nicht die Moralbedürfnisse irgend eines verheuratheten Bürgers in einem Winkel Deutschlands, sondern die Autonomie der Kunst kommt hier in Frage. Mein Wahlspruch bleibt: Kunst ist der Zweck der Kunst, wie Liebe der Zweck der Liebe, und gar das Leben selbst der Zweck des Lebens ist. (*Br* ii. 278)

These are the anti-teleological arguments Heine had put in the mouths of Goethe's disciples in *Die romantische Schule*. There he had wavered in his allegiance. By 1838 he used them openly as his own. It was Gautier who perhaps felt the closest affinity with Heine at the time,[42] and in Hirth's view the term 'l'art pour l'art' derives directly from Heine's phrase.[43] Certainly Gautier's review of *Tableaux de voyage* (November 1837)[44] was more than just positive towards Heine: it retranslated him into the language of Gautier's own philosophy of art. But Heine's theory did not correspond to his practice. His art was inspired by life and fought for life. Gautier so refined beauty that it could exist only in poetry.

The one work Heine directly claimed to have written in the spirit of art for art's sake is *Atta Troll*. In the German preface of 1846 he states that its aim is to defend the inalienable rights of poetry.[45] In the French version he speaks more specifically of 'l'autonomie de l'art, l'indépendance souveraine de la poésie',[46] while in canto III of the poem itself we read the celebrated strophe:

> Traum der Sommernacht! Phantastisch
> Zwecklos ist mein Lied. Ja, zwecklos
> Wie die Liebe, wie das Leben,
> Wie der Schöpfer samt der Schöpfung! (E ii. 359)[47]

---

[42] For a full discussion of Heine and Gautier's mutual debt see Boeck, op. cit., pp. 40 ff.

[43] *Br* v. 264. But Hirth provides no further documentation, while in *Heine und seine französischen Freunde*, Mainz, 1949, p. 147, Hirth states the opposite and says that Gautier invented the term. However, according to *Geflügelte Worte, der Zitatenschatz des deutschen Volkes*, ed. Georg Büchmann, rev. Gunther Haupt and Winfried Hofmann, 32nd edn., Berlin, 1972, the phrase was first used by Victor Cousin in a lecture of 1818, entitled *Du vrai, du beau et du bien*, printed in 1836.

[44] Cited *Br* v. 231.   [45] E ii. 353.   [46] Ibid. 525.

[47] The last line is a reminiscence of Heine's *Schöpfungslieder* (E i. 252 ff.), of which no. 6 in particular takes up the theme of the primacy of form. Sandor, op. cit., pp. 134 ff., regards these poems as Heine's *ars poetica*, a view which overlooks the comic tone of all but perhaps the last two. As a cycle they seem rather

But a work of art that is written for the sake of its intrinsic beauty or as an independent aesthetic structure can only be impaired by such statements of intention. By the third strophe of the same canto it becomes plain that Heine's 'absence of purpose' is a fiction. He is anxious to deliver a blow against the party that had tried to infringe his own freedom and was now encouraging the wooden, and in Heine's eyes unwittingly funny, poetry of the *Tendenzdichter*. His poem, Heine asserts:

> Ist kein nützlich tugendhafter
> Karrengaul des Bürgertums,
> Noch ein Schlachtpferd der Parteiwut,
> Das pathetisch stampft und wiehert!

In structure *Atta Troll* resembles *Die Harzreise*, or more accurately an inverted *Harzreise*. In the earlier work the narrator sets off from polite society down on the plains to seek the simplicity of life in the mountains: in the mock epic the narrator sets out from a tourist resort in a valley of the Pyrenees to track down an escaped dancing bear. In the *Reisebild* he encounters as many Philistines as simple peasants: in *Atta Troll* the bear himself is a Philistine and the narrator's intention is to find him. What happens by mistake in the first, is deliberate in the second. Far from being without a purpose the story tells of a hunt, and the victim, Atta Troll, is an amalgam of Heine's favourite targets, the Philistine who proclaims his religiosity to the world and hides his sensuality behind a moral façade, the egalitarian revolutionary, the ham-fisted *Tendenzdichter*, the wretchedly limited *Charakter* who believes he is a genius. Moreover, Atta Troll's escape from captivity, his pursuit and final death are a parody of events in Freiligrath's *Der Mohrenfürst*, where the hero is captured, sold, and finishes up working as a drummer at the entrance to a circus arena.[48] Heine's poem suggests the following inscription should be put on Atta Troll's memorial in Walhalla:

> 'Atta Troll, Tendenzbär; sittlich
> Religiös; als Gatte brünstig;
> Durch Verführtsein von dem Zeitgeist,
> Waldursprünglich Sanskülotte;

to be a parody of an *ars poetica*: they could have been inspired by Gleim's mock song to the creator, 'Der Schöpfer', Deutsche National-Litteratur 45, ed. Franz Muncker, Stuttgart, undated, p. 224.

[48] Cf. Prawer, *The Tragic Satirist*, pp. 82 f.

'Sehr schlecht tanzend, doch Gesinnung
Tragend in der zott'gen Hochbrust;
Manchmal auch gestunken habend;
Kein Talent, doch ein Charakter!' (E ii. 415)

But if these obviously satirical parts of the epic are not art for
art's sake, what of the 'Midsummer Night's Dream' promised us in
the subtitle? This comes in the vision of the Wild Hunt, which the
narrator sees at midnight through the window of the witch's hovel
in the midst of the loneliest mountains. Like most of Heine's
'chance' dreams or encounters it is of symbolical significance:
these are the gods and goddesses, the geniuses of poetry, and the
great lovers who have been driven out of life into this frenzied
but ghostly existence by Christianity, Puritanism, Nazarenism. It
is the familiar vision of the Golden Age that has been reduced to
a shadowy underworld and so forms a sad and probably deliberate
counterpart to the bold optimism of Heine's 'Ritter des Geistes'
in the *Harzreise* 'Berg-Idylle'. As in the closing lines of *Almansor*
a moment of magic has yielded to an eternity of hell. *Atta Troll* is
perhaps 'das letzte freie Waldlied der Romantik'[49] in the sense that
Heine tries to come to terms with what remains of the youthful
Utopianism he derived from Schlegel. As S. S. Prawer so aptly
states: 'The true unity of *Atta Troll* must be sought in its evocation of a complex state of mind—a state of mind analogous to that
of its author in the early 1840s. For all its epic trappings, the work
has the confessional quality of a lyric poem.'[50] In this it also
resembles *Die Harzreise* and the other *Reisebilder* I have interpreted
in an earlier chapter—but confessional lyric and 'absolute Dichtung' are far from synonymous.

Seen against this backcloth Heine's increasing political concern
of the early 1840s, culminating in his association with Marx and
in *Deutschland. Ein Wintermärchen* seem all the more remarkable.
But Heine did not vacillate between extremes, as it might appear
on the surface. Of course, *Deutschland* vividly pinpointed the
principal weaknesses of German political life, censorship, chauvin-
ism, and inwardness as a justification for political indifference.
And as we have seen, a number of significant motifs corresponded
closely to ideas also treated in Marx's crucial *Einleitung zur Kritik
der Hegelschen Rechtsphilosophie* of the same year. Moreover, these
ideas on the German Revolution were Heine's own, presented

[49] E ii. 422.   [50] Prawer, op. cit., p. 84.

in a new garb perhaps, but ideas that had already influenced Marx in his earlier writings. None the less, Heine's work remains a poem and not a treatise. Even this broad-fronted attack on the anachronism of mid-nineteenth-century Germany hinges on a poetic vision—the vision of Barbarossa—and the narrator's hopes and fears of a German millennium, a millennium which was conceivable to a German only in terms of long-past and therefore feudal glories. In consciously assuming the role of a German dreamer Heine strikes home at the inherent flaw in a would-be nation state with only a loosely federal and now nebulous Imperial history on which to build. Yet these dreams of the Kyffhäuser were also his own dreams and again the remnants of more grandiose hopes. Heine is neither a satirist alone nor a lyric poet alone. Despite his Left Hegelian convictions and his relationship with Marx he continued to portray his political dislikes and aspirations as part of a subjective and reflective vision. Despite his pioneering ideas on an art whose sole justification is its beauty, he was too involved in the problems of his age ever to write *poésie pure*.

B. *Heine's* Todesgesang

Manchmal in meinen trüben Nachtgesichten glaube ich den armen Klerikus der Limburger Chronik, meinen Bruder in Apoll, vor mir zu sehen, und seine leidenden Augen lugen sonderbar stier hervor aus seiner Kapuze; aber im selben Augenblick huscht er von dannen, und verhallend, wie das Echo eines Traumes, hör' ich die knarrenden Töne der Lazarusklapper.

(*Geständnisse*, E vi. 74)

In its dates of composition, 1841–2 and 1846, *Atta Troll* straddles *Deutschland. Ein Wintermärchen* and indeed it points forward to Heine's late poetry more directly than the other epic.[51] In the same year as *Atta Troll* appeared in book form Heine published 'Karl I.' in a journal with which Marx had put Heine in touch.[52] In *Französische Maler*, it will be remembered, Heine had compared Delaroche's Cromwell to a woodcutter looking at the majestic oak that he had just felled. Here Heine pictures the

---

[51] The emphasis Kaufmann places on *Deutschland* both in his work on that poem and in his general study of Heine (cited above) is a distortion of the trend in Heine's production and of the poem's significance in the later poetry. It is patently misleading to imply that *Romanzero* and the last poems are a mere falling-off from a high-point of achievement.

[52] Cf. Hirth, *Bausteine*, p. 125. 'Karl I.': E i. 342 f.

martyr king and symbol of a poetic age, rocking to sleep the very woodcutter who will one day be his executioner. This apparently idyllic scene—the hut of simple peasant folk, a child sung to sleep with a popular lullaby, the sound of sheep, and the rustling of straw—conceals a sense of foreboding and death: 'Mein Todesgesang ist dein Wiegenlied.' Once again Heine does not allow the innocence of folk-song to reign supreme, but now his purpose is more complex than were his early parodies of false *naïveté*. The king is melancholy, his song monotonous, and the child seems positively menacing: he smiles horribly in his sleep and his forehead is disfigured by the mark of Cain. Why is it that the old lullaby about the mice that play while the cat is away should have such a disturbing ring?

> Der alte Köhlerglaube verschwand,
> Es glauben die Köhlerkinder —
> Eiapopeia — nicht mehr an Gott
> Und an den König noch minder.
>
> Das Kätzchen ist tot, die Mäuschen sind froh —
> Wir müssen zu schanden werden —
> Eiapopeia — im Himmel der Gott
> Und ich, der König auf Erden.

The charcoal-burners' children, the new generation of the proletariat, have lost their faith in God and with it their belief in the divine right of kings. The tom-cat is dead, God is dead, the king will die. The people have come to claim their kingdom on earth. But this message, which Heine had preached with such energy in *Zur Geschichte, Deutschland. Ein Wintermärchen*, and the unpublished 'Briefe über Deutschland', and which so obviously corresponds to a basic tenet of Marxist theory, is no longer positive. The mighty are destined to fall, the sheepish onlookers bleat, the mice squeak with delight, and a monarch rocks his executioner to sleep: 'Schlafe, mein Henkerchen, schlafe'—a line of rare tenderness.[53] No less disturbing is the closing stanza of *Schlachtfeld bei Hastings*. Edith Schwanenhals has at last found the corpse of King Harold, so mutilated that only she who had so loved him and had been so

---

[53] Lukács's interpretation of this poem in 'Heine als nationaler Dichter', pp. 144 f., is distorted. There are no grounds for his claim that 'die Melancholie des Vergehens unmittelbar ironisch in den Triumph der populären Revolution umschlägt, daß der Sieger über das vergehende Mittelalter nicht die Prosa des Kapitalismus, sondern die Poesie der Revolution ist.'

loved by him could recognize it. Yet, like Charles, she too for-
gives, and as she sings a litany 'In kindisch frommer Weise' the
contrast with the gruesome search on the battlefield is shocking.

In the latter half of the 1840s Heine's health had been steadily
deteriorating. In 1848 it finally broke down and paralysis kept him
confined to his apartment, then to his bed until his death eight
years later. Heine himself tells the story that in this year of revolutionary débâcle when any last political hopes were dashed he
collapsed in the Louvre at the feet of his beloved Venus de Milo.[54]
She could not help him for, as he remarks with characteristic
humour, she has no arms. As usual Heine's apparent frivolity
rests on serious ground. This is the humour which he had said
in *Das Buch Le Grand* twenty-five years before makes it possible
to survive in a senseless world.[55] The destruction of beauty by
Puritan iconoclasts comes to symbolize the way of the world, the
way it was, is, and ever shall be. In these last years the pessimism
which had repeatedly thrown shadows across Heine's Utopianism
wins the upper hand, and the fate of the poet and genius, of
royalty of the mind, illuminates life's inherent tragedy.

True, poetry is still magical in its power. Heine created no more
suggestive image for the imagination, complexity, and yet subtle
unity of his own works than in his description of the Haggadah in
'Jehuda ben Halevy'. Jehuda, the poet of Jewish exile, has been
reared on the Talmud. From the Halachah he learns the art of
polemic: he is thrust, as it were, into a school of fencing. But what
holds him spell-bound is the other part of the Talmud, the
Haggadah with its anecdotal illustrations of the Law and its
legends. This seems to the young Jehuda to be a world of fantasy
and enchantment which is not bound to the earth at all. The
Haggadah is a poetic wonder of the world to be likened to the
Hanging Gardens of Babylon:

> Hoch auf kolossalen Säulen
> Prangen Palmen und Cypressen,
> Goldorangen, Blumenbeete,
> Marmorbilder, auch Springbrunnen,
>
> Alles klug und fest verbunden
> Durch unzähl'ge Hängebrücken,
> Dic wie Schlingepflanzen aussahn
> Und worauf sich Vögel wiegten —   (E i. 441)

[54] E i. 487.   [55] E iii. 166.

In the letter to Friederike Robert of twenty-five years before which had provided the basis for the passage in *Das Buch Le Grand* on humour and tragedy, the sublime and the ridiculous, Heine had spoken of Aristophanes' comedy *The Birds*. In the city that the birds had wished to create in the air from which to rule over the gods Heine saw 'eine ungeheuere Weltanschauung; ich sehe darin den göttertrotzenden Wahnsinn der Menschen, eine echte Tragödie, um so tragischer, da jener Wahnsinn am Ende siegt und glücklich beharrt in dem Wahne, daß seine Luftstadt wirklich existire. . . .'[56] Heine never knew the consolation of such blindness or insanity. His own Utopian hopes of the following years, his belief that men could create the kingdom of heaven on earth, had proved illusory. Tied to his *Matratzengruft* Heine's imagination fled instead to the airy realm of poetry, from which he could survey the absurdity and cruelty of the world below. But he knew that the poet, who was privileged to observe and depict man's folly, could reign supreme in the mind alone. Jehuda may stand for all the geniuses and kings of *Romanzero* whom the viciousness and short-sighted banality of the world destroy physically but cannot judge spiritually; like Charles I they are still the divinely appointed sovereigns of humanity. If Heine abandoned Hegel's monumental scheme of world history, he tried to preserve his faith in the genius as the immortal creator of world poetry:

> Wie im Leben, so im Dichten
> Ist das höchste Gut die Gnade —
> Wer sie hat, der kann nicht sünd'gen
> Nicht in Versen, noch in Prosa.
>
> Solchen Dichter von der Gnade
> Gottes nennen wir Genie:
> Unverantwortlicher König
> Des Gedankenreiches ist er.
>
> Nur dem Gotte steht er Rede,
> Nicht dem Volke — In der Kunst,
> Wie im Leben kann das Volk
> Töten uns, doch niemals richten.   (E i. 443)

This is not a defence of poetry that is 'absolute' in the sense of neglecting moral or social responsibility. On the contrary, in

[56] *Br* i. 232.

Heine's case, the sovereign independence of poetry meant that nothing was out of bounds for examination or expression whether it was discovered in the maze of the poet's own complex mind or in the dark corners of world history. Heine's poetic freedom was a licence to explore, and his *Romanzero* is a veritable inventory of man's inhumanity to man whether it simply shows us the prosperity of an executioner in *Schelm von Bergen* or the grotesque end of the executioner's victim in *Spanische Atriden*, his head brought up from the dungeons to the banquet table by his dog, whether we witness the poet Firdusi's ironic funeral before the Shah could make good his deception or the apocalyptic end of the New World's promise in *Vitzliputzli*, the dance of death performed under torment by the god's Spanish prisoners.

An essential part of the poetic freedom which Engels, Ruge, and others[57] could not forgive was the freedom to look at oneself. This seemed to them senseless introspection—'die ewige Liebesnörgelei'.[58] But Heine was by nature a highly self-conscious poet. Prawer is right to stress the significance of the *Doppelgänger* motif in the *Buch der Lieder* as the symbol for Heine's loss of innocence and subsequent need to adopt roles and then ironize them.[59] In his late poetry Heine was too honest to allow any beautiful 'Luftstadt' which his imagination might create as a last bastion against the world to go unchallenged. It was not enough that his heroes died martyrs' deaths, that Jehuda was slaughtered within sight of his beloved Jerusalem. The power of the imagination is itself revealed as a sad delusion. In the prologue to 'Bimini' the magic of poetry transforms Heine's song into an enchanted boat carrying his readers back to the days when America was discovered and men still believed in miracles. We hardly need to be told that his ship bears the black-red-gold colours of Romanticism or that this age of faith and of miracles that came true was the blue flower for which the poet longed in his own modern prosaic world. But once his passengers are safely on board and the vessel is well out in the fairy-tale ocean of the Age of Discovery the poet declares his ship is a ship of fools, a ship of fools like the one in which Juan Ponce de Leon, the governor of Cuba, set out in old age to seek his long-lost

[57] But with the notable exception of Marx. See, for example, his daughter's remarks in Houben, *Gespräche*, p. 451 and above pp. 152 f.   [58] Houben, p. 467.
[59] S. S. Prawer, *Buch der Lieder*, pp. 36 ff., *The Tragic Satirist*, pp. 2 ff. This is essentially the starting-point for Sammons's important investigation (*Heinrich Heine*, cited above).

youth on the legendary island of everlasting life, Bimini. Standing on the beach the old man looks at his reflection in the water and recalls painfully the glories of his past. Here the *Doppelgänger* motif of the early lyric appears literally for what it really is—self-observation, reflection. Juan Ponce de Leon's Indian maid-servant has sung of a mysterious land, however, where youth is eternal, and he resolves to find it in one last voyage of discovery. Like Mann's Gustav von Aschenbach, Juan Ponce de Leon dresses his enfeebled body and frames his emaciated face in the finery of a youthful dandy, ready for the non-existent paradise where he fondly imagines he will recapture the life that he has already lived. But:

> Während er die Jugend suchte,
> Ward er täglich noch viel älter,
> Und verrunzelt, abgemergelt
> Kam er endlich in das Land,
>
> In das stille Land, wo schaurig
> Unter schattigen Cypressen
> Fließt ein Flüßlein, dessen Wasser
> Gleichfalls wunderthätig heilsam —
>
> Lethe heißt das gute Wasser!
> Trink daraus, und du vergißt
> All dein Leiden — ja, vergessen
> Wirst du, was du je gelitten —
>
> Gutes Wasser! gutes Land!
> Wer dort angelangt, verläßt es
> Nimmermehr — denn dieses Land
> Ist das wahre Bimini.   (E ii. 146)

The discovery of Cuba had been real: poetry can provide new worlds only in the fantasy. Thus deception governs the day in poetry and in reality alike—Bimini is no more real than the sunken city had been in 'Seegespenst' of the *Nordsee* cycle. Eternal youth is found in death, in the eternal absence of memory, of reflection and the quest for heaven on earth, in short, in release from the major preoccupations of Heine's own lifetime. Here is Heine's sad retraction of the belief in the magic of poetry fostered by art for art's sake, a movement he had himself in a modest capacity helped to create.

Poetic worlds are as illusory as life is transient. The living poetry Heine observes in Pomare's dance (dance, it will be remembered, was a form of expression that seemed to promise direct communication unhindered by language) is as ephemeral as the girl's new-found riches. This latter-day Herodias, whose every gesture is a command to her infatuated admirers, is accompanied to her grave by her dog and her hairdresser.[60] Heine is equally merciless to the very god of the arts, Apollo. The divine figure who travels down the Rhine with his entourage of goddesses and who bewitches a nun watching from her cell is a defrocked rabbi and as handy at cards as at the lyre. His companions are the inmates of an Amsterdam brothel out for a touring holiday.[61] So much for the Lorelei and *Rheinromantik*. Heine has found no answers: the young man who pleaded with the North Sea to solve for him the riddle of life's ways reappears as Lazarus who has known death and is not in the least interested in the exotic costumes of the Orient that so fascinated his dreamy predecessor. Life is unjust and cruel. Philosophical theories, Hegelian schemes have proved nothing:

> Laß die heil'gen Parabolen,
> Laß die frommen Hypothesen —
> Suche die verdammten Fragen
> Ohne Umschweif uns zu lösen.
>
> Warum schleppt sich blutend, elend,
> Unter Kreuzlast der Gerechte,
> Während glücklich als ein Sieger
> Trabt auf hohem Roß der Schlechte?
>
> Woran liegt die Schuld? Ist etwa
> Unser Herr nicht ganz allmächtig?
> Oder treibt er selbst den Unfug?
> Ach, das wäre niederträchtig.
>
> Also fragen wir beständig,
> Bis man uns mit einer Handvoll
> Erde endlich stopft die Mäuler —
> Aber ist das eine Antwort? (E ii. 91 f.)

But for Heine there was not even the peace of Lethe's waters, to which Juan Ponce de Leon had succumbed. In a last Midsummer

---

[60] E i. 345 ff. [61] Ibid. 348 ff.

Night's Dream—'Für die Mouche'—he imagines his future
resting-place, a sarcophagus round which are entwined bas-relief
figures from the Old Testament and from Greek mythology. Over
his head hangs the passion flower, where there lie metamorphosed
the instruments of Christ's death. The martyrdom of poets here
receives its most extreme expression: Heine dies not as royalty of
mind but as divinity of mind—at least until the two hostile cultures
that have so long vied for possession of his loyalties shatter the
quiet with their fierce, unending altercations. We now learn there
will be no millennial victory of Hellene over Nazarene:

> O, dieser Streit wird enden nimmermehr,
> Stets wird die Wahrheit hadern mit dem Schönen,
> Stets wird geschieden sein der Menschheit Heer
> In zwei Partein: Barbaren und Hellenen.   (E ii. 49)

Yet, though his dreams of a better world now seemed mere
hallucinations, the poet obstinately, masochistically almost, continued to explore and to record the bitter-sweet agonies of slow
death.

> Wie langsam kriechet sie dahin,
> Die Zeit, die schauderhafte Schnecke!
> Ich aber, ganz bewegungslos
> Blieb ich hier auf demselben Flecke.
>
> In meine dunkle Zelle dringt
> Kein Sonnenstrahl, kein Hoffnungsschimmer;
> Ich weiß, nur mit der Kirchhofsgruft
> Vertausch' ich dies fatale Zimmer.
>
> Vielleicht bin ich gestorben längst;
> Es sind vielleicht nur Spukgestalten
> Die Phantasieen, die des Nachts
> Im Hirn den bunten Umzug halten.
>
> Es mögen wohl Gespenster sein,
> Altheidnisch göttlichen Gelichters;
> Sie wählen gern zum Tummelplatz
> Den Schädel eines toten Dichters. —
>
> Die schaurig süßen Orgia,
> Das nächtlich tolle Geistertreiben,
> Sucht des Poeten Leichenhand
> Manchmal am Morgen aufzuschreiben.   (E ii. 92 f.)

The affinities with Baudelaire are patent.[62] Here is the experience of *spleen*, of the world transformed into a giant dungeon, the brain into a cobwebbed vault, aspirations into silent funeral processions.[63]

Admittedly the tone is not always so desperate, so utterly without hope. There is a moment of tenderness in 'Ich war, o Lamm, als Hirt bestellt',[64] which seems to bear out Heine's own claim that he had turned back to God.[65] There are also moments of humour at the most unlikely times—certainly piety was never one of Heine's qualities:

> Ob deiner Inkonsequenz, o Herr,
> Erlaube, daß ich staune;
> Du schufest den fröhlichsten Dichter, und raubst
> Ihm jetzt seine gute Laune.

> Der Schmerz verdumpft den heitern Sinn
> Und macht mich melancholisch,
> Nimmt nicht der traurige Spaß ein End',
> So werd' ich am Ende katholisch.

> Ich heule dir dann die Ohren voll,
> Wie andre gute Christen —
> O Miserere! Verloren geht
> Der beste der Humoristen! (E ii. 90)

But the lasting impression with which the late poetry leaves us is dark. These are the works of a disappointed idealist. The pessimism and historical resignation that he so hated in others because he recognized its power in himself finally catch up with both the humorist and the Utopian. Not even the 'unabhängige zweite Welt' of art can console the dying poet. Heine leaves us as he came in. In the early 1820s he had torn away the pastoral trappings which so prettily adorned the *Kunstlied*, leaving its theatricality naked for all to see. Thirty years later he confesses that poetry itself is theatre, that his own life's work has been a passing

---

[62] Cf. Weinberg's related account, op. cit., esp. pp. 157 ff. The circumstances surrounding the common experience were, of course, very different. Heine was reduced to his Lazarus condition by ill-health; he did not choose to be subjected to drugs and the similar extreme effects induced by sleeplessness. Nor did he share Baudelaire's ultimate religiosity and profound sense of guilt. See also Boeck's section on Heine and Baudelaire, op. cit., pp. 116 ff.

[63] Baudelaire, *Œuvres complètes: Les Fleurs du mal*, p. 118.

[64] E ii. 42 f.   [65] E i. 485; vi. 49 f.

entertainment. This is the last performance but here the actor is
not free to go:

> Der Vorhang fällt, das Stück ist aus,
> Und Herrn und Damen gehn nach Haus.
> Ob ihnen auch das Stück gefallen?
> Ich glaub' ich hörte Beifall schallen.
> Ein hochverehrtes Publikum
> Beklatschte dankbar seinen Dichter.
> Jetzt aber ist das Haus so stumm,
> Und sind verschwunden Lust und Lichter.
>
> Doch horch! ein schollernd schnöder Klang
> Ertönt unfern der öden Bühne; —
> Vielleicht daß eine Saite sprang
> An einer alten Violine.
> Verdrießlich rascheln im Parterr'
> Etwelche Ratten hin und her,
> Und alles riecht nach ranz'gem Öle.
> Die letzte Lampe ächzt und zischt
> Verzweiflungsvoll und sie erlischt.
> Das arme Licht war meine Seele.   (E i. 428 f.)

CONCLUSION

THE CREATIVE PERSONALITY

Um meine Wiege spielten die letzten Mondlichter des achtzehnten und das erste Morgenrot des neunzehnten Jahrhunderts.   (E vii. 400)

OUR study has turned full circle. Heine dreamed of a world
where innocence, simplicity, and wholeness would be
restored. He did not succeed in reaching it and the tensions
remained. But we can no longer accept Heine's own picture of
himself as two separate men, the dreaming lyrical poet and the
warrior in the cause of freedom. This was a feeling engendered by
the constant resistance which he met when he tried to realize his
ideals—when, like his lictor in *Deutschland. Ein Wintermärchen*,
he tried to transform his thought into practice. But despite his
theory action did not follow the idea as thunder does lightning.

The song that parodies the *Kunstlied* and sings of lost innocence,
the satire of the Philistine, the war against Christianity and then
against the Puritanism of even the revolutionary parties, the defence of the genius and of poetry's autonomy, the elegy on the disappearance of nobler ages and the lurking despair at the world's
senseless round—all these are born of the clash Heine experienced
between the poetic and the real, the beautiful and the banal. Heine
was entirely justified when he claimed that all his work, whatever
its mode, was inspired by one great 'gottfreudigen Frühlingsidee'.[1]
We have traced this ideal to Schlegel's view of the Greeks and to
Herder's and the Romantics' visions of the poetic childhood of
civilization. Heine soon abandoned his attempt to recreate *naïveté*
in the song: instead he turned to dreams of a revolution which
would implement his ideal in a real Golden Age for mankind. This
was Heine's hope and ambition until he was struck down by fatal
disease in early middle age. He stated that aim quite specifically in
the preface to *Deutschland* of 1844, the year of his active involvement with Marx:

... wenn wir den Gott, der auf Erden im Menschen wohnt, aus seiner

---

[1] E iv. 13. See also i. 497 f.

Erniedrigung retten, wenn wir die Erlöser Gottes werden, wenn wir das
arme, glückenterbte Volk und den verhöhnten Genius und die ge-
schändete Schönheit wieder in ihre Würde einsetzen, wie unsere großen
Meister gesagt und gesungen, und wie wir es wollen, wir, die Jünger —
Ja, nicht bloß Elsaß und Lothringen, sondern ganz Frankreich wird uns
alsdann zufallen, ganz Europa, die ganze Welt — die ganze Welt wird
deutsch werden! Von dieser Sendung und Universalherrschaft Deutschlands träume ich oft, wenn ich unter Eichen wandle. Das ist mein
Patriotismus. (E ii. 429 f.)

This was the ideal to which Heine held so tenaciously, so obstinately. This was his brand of Hegelianism, Romantic Left Hegelianism, or if that sounds too clumsy, poetic Socialism. Marx and
Engels sought the roots of industrial man's alienation and misery in
the mechanics of early capitalist systems and hoped to turn the
same utilitarian functions to the advantage of the proletariat:
Heine chose to forget the utilitarian and to think only of the good
life it could produce, while as far as parties went, he wished to
drink the juice of the fruit and to leave the skins:

> 'Mein liebes Kind! Wie denkst du jetzt?
> Treibst du noch immer aus Neigung
> Die Politik? Zu welcher Partei
> Gehörst du mit Überzeugung?'

> 'Die Apfelsinen, lieb Mütterlein,
> Sind gut, und mit wahrem Vergnügen
> Verschlucke ich den süßen Saft
> Und ich lasse die Schalen liegen.'   (E ii. 473)

Heine was an idealist. His life circled around his ideal: he interpreted his experience in the light of ideas. The lightning cartoons,
the seemingly chance encounters and spontaneous *Kleinmalerei* that
characterize so much of his work from the *Reisebilder* on are not a
form of early impressionism.[2] Heine's vivid satire and often minute
observation derive from the same source. He reflects the world
in the distorting mirror of his philosophy. His impressionism is
symbolical. How much is contained in a tiny scene such as the one
Heine 'observed' in Ala! It gives us a critique of Christianity and

---

[2] Günther Tschich in *Der Impressionismus im Prosastil von Heines 'Reisebildern'*, Diss., Kiel, 1928, follows Alexander Pache (*Naturgefühl und Natursymbolik bei Heinrich Heine*, Berlin, 1904) in claiming Heine as the father of modern
Impressionism, cf. esp. pp. 42 ff. This view was already dismissed by Weckmüller (op. cit., pp. 30 ff.). Weckmüller suggests the term 'konstruktiver
Realismus'.

of the conspiracy between aristocrat and priest that oppresses Italy, it reveals hidden tokens of a Bacchic spirit nourished by nature itself, supplies, in its admiration for the non-reflective life and for children, the proof that vitality and beauty have survived and will triumph—while the narrator's own wry humour gently ironizes the entire complex:

Ala ist schon ein echt italienisches Nest. Die Lage ist pittoresk an einem Berghang, ein Fluß rauscht vorbei, heitergrüne Weinreben umranken hie und da die übereinander stolpernden, zusammengeflickten Bettlerpaläste. An der Ecke des windschiefen Marktes, der so klein ist wie ein Hühnerhof, steht mit großmächtigen gigantischen Buchstaben: *Piazza di San Marco.* Auf dem steinernen Bruchstück eines großen, altadligen Wappenschilds saß dort ein kleiner Junge und notdürftelte. Die blanke Sonne beschien seine naive Rückseite, und in den Händen hielt er ein papiernes Heiligenbild, das er vorher inbrünstig küßte. Ein kleines, bildschönes Mädchen stand betrachtungsvoll daneben und blies zuweilen akkompagnierend in eine hölzerne Kindertrompete. (E iii. 254)

Heine's satire cannot be separated from his dreams of a more harmonious world: the present is measured against the ideal and found wanting. But the world proved impervious to his vision and Heine could not escape the fear that the Golden Age was past and its disappearance could only be mourned—'Les dieux s'en vont'.

The one god whom Heine actually met and whom, if we may adopt Thomas Mann's words, he loved 'mit einer sehnsüchtigen Feindschaft' was Goethe. In this study we have had to turn repeatedly to Heine's interpretation of Goethe as a yardstick of his own poetic and philosophical development. In *Schwere Stunde* Thomas Mann was referring to Schiller's ambivalent relationship to Goethe. One could almost imagine Heine in his place. Certainly a passage from Schiller's famous letter to Goethe of 23 August 1794 could have been subscribed by Heine. Schiller wrote:[3]

Über so manches, worüber ich mit mir selbst nicht recht einig werden konnte, hat die Anschauung Ihres Geistes (denn so muß ich den Totaleindruck Ihrer Ideen auf mich nennen) ein unerwartetes Licht in mir angesteckt. Mir fehlte das Object, der Körper, zu mehreren spekulativischen Ideen, und Sie brachten mich auf die Spur davon. Ihr beobachtender Blick, der so still und rein auf Dingen ruht, setzt Sie nie in

---

[3] *Briefwechsel zwischen Schiller und Goethe in den Jahren 1794 bis 1805*, Stuttgart and Tübingen, 1828–9, Part I, pp. 12 f. This was the first edition so that Heine could hardly have known the letter when writing *Die Nordsee*.

Gefahr auf den Abweg zu geraten, in den sowohl die Speculation als die willkürliche und bloß sich selbst gehorchende Einbildungskraft sich so leicht verirrt.

Schiller now proceeds to evolve the distinction between the speculative and the intuitive mind in much the same way as Heine distinguishes some thirty years later in *Die Nordsee* between Goethe's 'archetypal intelligence' and the divided minds of his contemporaries: the intuitive mind, Schiller argues, sees things in their entirety while speculative minds have to resort to analysis. This letter was to form the nucleus of his essay *Über naive und sentimentalische Dichtung*, and no one has analysed more acutely than Schiller in that treatise the intellectual and emotional crisis from which his era was suffering. The reflective poet—'der sentimentalische Dichter'—had been estranged from primary experience, seeing and feeling only through the filter of ideas and self-awareness. Of the Greeks Schiller could say: 'Sie empfanden natürlich'; of his own age: 'wir empfinden das Natürliche'.[4] The reflective poet longs for the *naïveté* of a civilization that has long since vanished and mourns its disappearance: he writes elegy. He looks up admiringly to Goethe, for him the naïve genius of the modern age. The reflective poet finds in the present a world that can only disgust him, a perverse and distorted place which he seeks to portray and punish in satire. And if he can still free his imagination from the dross of reality he may create in poetry what Schiller calls the ultimate aim of culture—the idyll, not a rosy recreation of pastoral innocence but a new, vivid world where sophistication and spontaneity coexist, not Arcadia but Elysium.[5]

Elegy, satire, idyll; past simplicity, present dissonance, future harmony—Schiller's analysis of the reflective poet reveals and relates the tensions and component parts of Heine's creative personality with an astounding precision and with only one exception: Heine's voyage to Elysium led him only to Bimini. This is the unity which we have sought to uncover, a unity in diversity, a unity of tension that springs from one central, overriding experience, an experience which affects all subsequent experience, loss of innocence—'der Teufel, der "Gedanke" wird genannt' as he called it in his early Byron translation.[6] Heine lived as an intellectual and political Messalina, to use his own term,[7] not because he

---

[4] Schiller, *Sämtliche Werke*, v. 711.   [5] Ibid., p. 750.   [6] E ii. 234.
[7] E vi. 54.

was insincere but because he was desperately hunting for a new spiritual home. His homelessness, his rootlessness was occasioned most obviously by his social situation—an enlightened Jew with a French education and poetic temperament growing up outside the ghetto in Restoration Germany and relying financially on his uncle's commercial success. But to argue that these external circumstances made Heine the great exception of German literature, the man without tradition, as one celebrated Marxist critic has done, is facile.[8] Heine's external circumstances made him doubly receptive to precisely the feeling of rootlessness which was the inspiration and goad of the entire *Goethezeit*, of the Classicists and the Romantics alike. Heine so imbibed the cultural climate of his age, he was so steeped in the German intellectual tradition, so sensitive to the spiritual changes of the present, that his work is a focus-point for nineteenth-century European cultural history. His roots lie ultimately not in Romanticism itself but back in the seventeenth and eighteenth centuries, which Schiller portrayed in his essay. The reflectiveness which Heine conveniently found symbolized in the Romantic *Doppelgänger* motif, Schiller discovered in Haller.[9] *Die Alpen* was already inspired by the purer way of life found in the mountains, and which Heine sought in the Harz. The visions of a long-lost paradise Schiller found above all in Milton.[10] That Heine's satire is of older provenance than the Romantic mockery of the Philistine hardly needs to be stated. As we have seen, he claimed himself that the first book he read was *Don Quixote*, while his description of Fielding in *Die romantische Schule* is in effect a shrewd summary of his own achievement:

. . . er führt uns gleich hinter die Kulissen, er zeigt uns die falsche Schminke auf allen Gefühlen, die plumpesten Springfedern der zartesten Handlungen . . . kurz, er zeigt uns jene ganze innere Maschinerie, die große Lüge, wodurch uns die Menschen anders erscheinen,

[8] Cf. Hans Mayer, 'Ahnen und Erinnern Heinrich Heines', *Literatur der Übergangszeit*, Wiesbaden, 1951, pp. 31 ff; id., 'Die Ausnahme Heine', *Von Lessing bis Thomas Mann. Wandlungen der bürgerlichen Literatur in Deutschland*, Pfullingen, 1959, pp. 273 ff.   [9] Schiller, *Sämtliche Werke*, v. 731 f.
[10] Ibid., p. 749. Milton was also Wordsworth's inspiration in *The Prelude*, which is the starting-point of M. H. Abrams's fascinating study of the secularized eschatology underlying both English and German Romanticism, *Natural Supernaturalism*, New York, 1971. Though Abrams does not refer to Heine, his book reveals many of the same patterns of thinking and feeling which I have been concerned to illuminate here as central to the *Goethezeit* (including its philosophers) and to the English Romantics.

als sie wirklich sind, und wodurch alle freudige Realität des Lebens verloren geht. (E v. 339)

Romanticism provided him with poetic forms with which to express his vision, the vision of a Schillerian reflective poet. That they were only forms, stage properties and a backcloth, emerges nowhere more clearly than from his parodies of the Romantic *Kunstlied*.

In Berlin Heine moved towards a new conception of engaged art and to a new version of the historical philosophy he had inherited from Herder and the Romantics. In his simplified, popular, and therefore significant way he became a pioneering Left Hegelian. In Paris an intellectual love-affair with Saint-Simonism inspired him to write his anti-spiritualist history of German religion and philosophy, a writing that influenced both Marx and the Young Hegelians. But Heine did not pursue the implications of the Saint-Simonian economic analysis and strategy: instead he turned to the defence of the Romantic concept of the genius and of inspired art. He helped to give the 'art for art's sake' movement and even French Symbolism a vital impulse with his brilliant flashes of insight into the mystical origins of the creative process.

But Heine's struggle with Romantic materials and his anticipation of future political and artistic movements and theories were only parts of what was for him a more central process—his search for an adequate poetic medium in which to portray his mind and so his age, 'die adäquate Klangfigur' to use one of Heine's terms.[11] Heine made the tensions that constitute the emotional and intellectual world of the reflective poet the substance of his poetry. A Utopian vision yields to grotesque reality, a happy childhood memory gives way to an elegy for the disappearance of more perfect times; the mood of tragic despair is relieved by laughter, the bitter laughter aroused by satire of the present. The song with its *Stimmungsbrechung*, the travel picture, the mock epic, the narrative lyric of *Romanzero*,[12] and in a certain degree even the critical reports and treatises of the *Salon*, all capture those shifts in tone and preoccupation, those inner pressures which characterized his own psyche. His greatest debt in this quest for an appropriately

---

[11] E iv. 342. See also ibid. 559. Heine employed this term specifically to refer to the visions which music conjured up in him.

[12] Cf. Hofrichter's argument, op. cit., pp. 113 ff., that in his later poetry Heine transforms external narrative forms into lyrical mood.

flexible and sensitive medium was to another eighteenth-century writer, Sterne. In this medium the distinction between the epic and lyric genres, which so bothered Heine in the later 1820s and the 1830s,[13] and which has led to such one-sided appreciations of Heine in later years, becomes superfluous. What better illustration of Staiger's argument that the distinction should be sought in the poet's attitude and approach to the world, not in external forms,[14] than Heine's mature work—as a comparison of *Atta Troll* and *Die Harzreise* could show. In Sterne, then, Heine found a mentor who had also been too open to the ambivalence of human thought and endeavour to tie himself down to a single unyielding viewpoint. Börne could only insist that integrity of character implied unchanging principles because he did not share the essential *disponibilité* of poetic awareness. He could not understand what Hofmannsthal has termed the poet's 'seismographic' sensibility.[15] Heine's satirical talent, which Börne hoped to employ, is only an element in the ultimately psychological self-portrait which Heine has left us in his major works. Heine provides us with a penetrating characterization of his art in *Memoiren*, the work he intended to be his final, all-embracing masterpiece but which his family preferred to destroy almost in its entirety:

Alles Bedeutsame und Charakteristische ist hier treuherzig mitgeteilt, und die Wechselwirkung äußerer Begebenheiten und innerer Seelenereignisse offenbart Ihnen die Signatura meines Seins und Wesens. Die Hülle fällt ab von der Seele, und du kannst sie betrachten in ihrer schönen Nacktheit. (E vii. 459)

But this 'Paßepartout zu meinem Gemüthslazarethe', as Heine called his *Lyrisches Intermezzo* cycle,[16] is not just subjective, arbitrary, or private. Subjectivity was the medium, the perspective from which Heine viewed and depicted his age. It was an age of transition and therefore of tension. Unlike so many of his fellow poets in Germany Heine did not possess 'ein prosaisches weitabgelegenes Winkelherz'.[17] The dreams and the melancholy, the frustrations and the anger which Heine uncovered in his breast showed 'the very age and body of the time, his form and pressure'.[18]

---

[13] Cf. E i. 9 f., 496 ff., E vii. 153 ff.; *Br* i. 270.
[14] Emil Staiger, *Grundbegriffe der Poetik*, Zürich, 1961.
[15] Hugo von Hofmannsthal, 'Der Dichter und diese Zeit', *Selected Essays*, ed. Mary Gilbert, Oxford, 1955, p. 135.
[16] *Br* i. 51 (to Immermann, Dec. 1822).   [17] E iii. 304.
[18] *Hamlet*, Act III, Sc. ii—cf. E v. 377.

BIBLIOGRAPHY

I. HEINRICH HEINE

i. *Primary Literature*

Sämtliche Werke, ed. E. Elster, 7 vols., Leipzig, 1887–90 (referred to in text as E).

Sämtliche Werke, ed. O. Walzel, J. Fränkel, L. Krähe, A. Leitzmann, and J. Petersen, 10 vols., Leipzig, 1910–15; Index volume, 1920.

Werke in Einzelausgaben, ed. G. A. E. Bogeng with introductions by G. Brandes, O. Loerke, E. Loewenthal, *et al.*, 12 vols., Hamburg and Berlin, 1921–6.

Werke, ed. E. Elster, 4 vols. (incomplete), Leipzig, 1925.

Werke und Briefe, ed. H. Kaufmann, 10 vols., Berlin, 1961–4.

Briefwechsel, ed. F. Hirth, 3 vols., Munich, 1914–20.

Briefe, ed. F. Hirth, 6 vols., Mainz, 1950–1 (referred to in text as *Br*).

Gespräche, Briefe, Tagebücher, Berichte seiner Zeitgenossen, ed. H. Bieber, Berlin, 1926.

Gespräche mit Heine, ed. H. H. Houben, Frankfurt a. M., 1926.

ii. *Studies*

ADORNO, T., 'Die Wunde Heine', in *Noten zur Literatur*, vol. i, Frankfurt, 1958.

ANDLER, C., 'Le *Romanzero* de Heine', *Études germaniques*, 2 (1947), 152–72.

—— *La Poésie de Heine*, Lyons and Paris, 1948.

ARENDT, H., 'Heinrich Heine: Schlemihl und Traumweltherrscher', in *Sechs Essays*, Heidelberg, 1948.

ARNOLD, M., 'Heinrich Heine', in *Lectures and Essays in Criticism, Complete Prose Works*, ed. R. H. Super, Ann Arbor, 1962, iii. 107 ff.

AYRAULT, R., 'Le symbolisme du décor dans le *Lyrisches Intermezzo*', *Études germaniques*, 11 (1956), 105–13.

BARBEY D'AUREVILLY, J., 'Heine' in *Littérature étrangère* (XIXᵉ Siècle. Les Œuvres et les Hommes. Deuxième série, xii.), Paris, 1890, 153–81.

BARTO, P. S., 'Sources of Heine's *Seegespenst*', *Modern Language Notes*, 32 (1917), 482–5.

BELART, U., *Gehalt und Aufbau von Heinrich Heines Gedichtsammlungen*, Berne, 1925.

BERENDSOHN, W. A., 'Heine's "Buch der Lieder". Struktur- und Stilstudie', *Heine-Jahrbuch 1962*, pp. 26–38.

BERNHARD, M., *Welterlebnis und gestaltete Wirklichkeit in Heines Prosaschriften*, Diss., Munich, 1962.

BEYER, Paul, *Der junge Heine*, Berlin, 1911.

BLOEMERTZ, W., *Die Personenschilderung in Heines journalistischen Berichten*, Diss., Bonn, 1909.

BOECK, O., *Heines Nachwirkung und Heine-Parallelen in der französischen Dichtung*, Göppinger Arbeiten zur Germanistik 52, Göppingen, 1972.

BORRIES, M., *Ein Angriff auf Heinrich Heine. Kritische Betrachtungen zu Karl Kraus*, Stuttgart, Berlin, Cologne, Mainz, 1971.

BOUCKE, E. A., 'Heine im Dienste der "Idee"', *Euphorion*, 16 (1909), 116–131, 434–60.

BRANDES, G., 'Das junge Deutschland', in *Die Hauptströmungen der Literatur des neunzehnten Jahrhunderts* (9th edn.), Berlin, 1904, vol. vi.

BRAUWEILER, E., *Heines Prosa, Beiträge zu seiner Wesensbestimmung* (Bonner Forschungen ix), Berlin, 1915.

BRECH, J., *Heinrich Heine und die jungdeutsche Reiseliteratur in ihren Hauptvertretern*, Diss., Munich, 1922.

BROD, M., *Heinrich Heine. The Artist in Revolt*, London, 1956.

BRUMMACK, J., 'Heines Entwicklung zum satirischen Dichter', *Deutsche Vierteljahrsschrift*, 41 (1967), 98–116.

BÜRGER, P., *Der Essay bei Heine*, Diss., Munich, 1959.

BUTLER, E. M., 'Heine and the Saint-Simonians. The Date of the Letters from Heligoland', *Modern Language Review*, 18 (1923), 68–85.

—— *The Saint-Simonian Religion in Germany. A Study of the Young German Movement*, Cambridge, 1926.

—— *Heinrich Heine. A Biography*, London, 1956.

CLARKE, M. A., *Heine et la Monarchie de Juillet. Étude critique sur les 'Französische Zustände'*, Paris, 1927.

CLOSS, A., *Die freien Rhythmen in der deutschen Lyrik*, Berne, 1947 (Heine, pp. 131 ff.).

CUMINGS, E. C., 'Echoes in Heine's *Gedanken und Einfälle*', *Germanic Review*, 13 (1938), 48–55.

—— 'Parallel Passages in Heine's Poetry and Prose', *Germanic Review*, 14 (1939), 284–90.

DIETZE, W., *Junges Deutschland und deutsche Klassik. Zur Ästhetik und Literaturtheorie des Vormärz*, Berlin, 1957.

EBERT, M., *Der Stil der Heineschen Jugendprosa*, Diss., Berlin, 1903.

ECKERTZ, E., *Heine und sein Witz* (Literarhistorische Forschungen 36), Berlin, 1908.

EISNER, P. H., 'Unbekannte Beiträge Heines zum "Morgenblatt" und zur "Allgemeinen Zeitung"', *Weimarer Beiträge*, 4 (1958), 72–87.

—— 'Ein Aufsatz Heines in "Le Globe", Februar 1832?', *Weimarer Beiträge*, 5 (1959), 421–5.

—— 'Neues zu "Heine und die politischen Annalen"', *Weimarer Beiträge*, 5 (1959), 425–7.

—— 'Echtes, Unechtes und Zweifelhaftes in Heines Werken. Ergebnisse der Heine-Philologie seit 1924', *Heine-Jahrbuch 1962*, pp. 50–69.

ELIOT, G., 'German Wit: Heinrich Heine', in *Essays and Leaves from a Note-Book*, Edinburgh, 1884, pp. 79–144.

ELSTER, E., 'Aus Heinrich Heines Nachlaß. Ein bisher ungedrucktes

Bruchstück der Harzreise', *Tägliche Rundschau. Unterhaltungsbeilage*, 15 Mar. 1901, no. 63.

—— 'Das Vorbild der freien Rhythmen Heinrich Heines', *Euphorion*, 25 (1924), 63–86.

EMMERICH, K., *Heinrich Heines 'Reisebilder'*, Diss., Berlin (Humboldt), 1965.

ENDERS, C., 'Heinrich Heines Faustdichtungen. Der Tanz als Deutungs- und Gestaltungsmittel seelischer Erlebnisse', *Zeitschrift für deutsche Philologie*, 74 (1955), 364–92.

EVANS, E. L., 'Heinrich Heine's Attitude to Tradition', Diss., Swansea, 1954.

FAIRLEY, B., 'Heine's Vaudeville', *University of Toronto Quarterly*, Jan. 1934.

—— *Heinrich Heine. An Interpretation*, Oxford, 1954.

—— 'Heine, Goethe and the *Divan*', *German Life and Letters*, 9 (1956), 166–70.

FEISE, F., 'Form and Meaning of Heine's Essay "Die Nordsee"', in *Xenion: Themes, Forms and Ideas in German Literature*, ed. W. Neuse, Baltimore, 1950, pp. 90–104.

—— 'Typen Heinescher Balladen', ibid., pp. 105–10.

FEUCHTWANGER, L., *Heinrich Heines Fragment 'Der Rabbi von Bacherach'. Eine kritische Studie*, Diss., Munich, 1907.

FINKE, F., 'Heine als Lyriker des Übergangs', *Heine-Jahrbuch 1963*, pp. 33–42.

—— 'Zur Datierung des "Rabbi von Bacherach"', *Heine-Jahrbuch 1965*, pp. 26–32.

FRAENKEL, J., *Heinrich Heine. Ein Vortrag*, Biel, 1960.

GALLEY, E., 'Heinrich Heines Privatbibliothek', *Heine-Jahrbuch 1962*, pp. 96–116.

—— 'Heines "Briefe über Deutschland" und "Die Geständnisse". Eine Textgeschichte an Hand der Manuskripte des Heine-Archivs', *Heine-Jahrbuch 1963*, pp. 60–84.

—— 'Der "Neunte Artikel" von Heines Werk "Zur Geschichte der neueren schönen Literatur in Deutschland". Eine ungedruckte Vorarbeit zur "Romantischen Schule"', *Heine-Jahrbuch 1964*, pp. 17–36.

—— *Heinrich Heine* (3rd edn.), Stuttgart, 1971.

GAUTIER, T., 'Œuvres de Heine. Reisebilder — Tableaux de voyage', *La Presse*, 30th Nov. 1837: reproduced in full in Hirth, *Briefe*, Mainz, 1951, v. 229–33.

—— 'Henri Heine', in *Portraits et Souvenirs littéraires*, Paris, 1875, pp. 105–28.

GOETZE, R., *Heinrich Heines 'Buch der Lieder' und sein Verhältnis zum deutschen Volkslied*, Diss., Halle, 1895.

GOTTSCHALK, A., *Heinrich Heine. 'Der Doktor Faust. Ein Tanzpoem nebst kuriosen Berichten über Teufel, Hexen und Dichtkunst.' Eine Bibliographie*, Berlin, 1934.

HASS, H. E., *Heinrich Heine. Ein Vortrag* (Akademische Vorträge und Abhandlungen 11), Bonn, 1949.

HERMAND, J., 'Werthers Harzreise', in *Von Mainz nach Weimar, 1793–1919. Studien zur deutschen Literatur*, Stuttgart, 1969, pp. 129–51.

HESSEL, K., *Heinrich Heines Verhältnis zur bildenden Kunst*, Marburg, 1931.

HIRTH, F., *Heine und seine französischen Freunde*, Mainz, 1949.

—— *Heinrich Heine, Bausteine zu einer Biographie*, Mainz, 1950.

HOFRICHTER, L., 'Heines Entwicklung als Dichter', Diss., Toronto, 1954.

—— 'Heines Kampf gegen die Tradition', *Modern Language Notes*, 75 (1960), 507–14.

—— *Heinrich Heine*, Oxford, 1963.

HÖLLERER, W., 'Heinrich Heine. Entschleierung und Erneuerung', in *Zwischen Klassik und Moderne*, Stuttgart, 1958, pp. 58–99.

HOLZHAUSEN, P., *Heinrich Heine und Napoleon I.*, Frankfurt, 1903.

HOUBEN, H. H., 'Heine', *Verbotene Literatur von der klassischen Zeit bis zur Gegenwart*, Berlin, 1924, pp. 385–429.

IGGERS, G. G., 'Heine and the Saint-Simonians: a Re-examination', *Comparative Literature*, 10 (1958), 289–308.

JACOBS, J., 'Zu Heines "Ideen. Das Buch Le Grand"', *Heine-Jahrbuch 1968*, pp. 3–11.

JENNINGS, L. B., 'The Dance of Life and Death in Heine and Immermann', *German Life and Letters*, 18 (1965), 130–5.

JESPERSEN, U., 'Heinrich Heine. "Abenddämmerung"', in *Die deutsche Lyrik. Form und Geschichte*, ed. B. v. Wiese, Düsseldorf, 1956, ii. 134–143.

—— 'Heinrich Heine. "Das Fräulein stand am Meere"', ibid., pp. 144–9.

—— 'Heinrich Heine. "Ich weiß nicht, was soll es bedeuten"', ibid., pp. 128–33.

KAUFMANN, H., *Politisches Gedicht und klassische Dichtung. Heinrich Heine: Deutschland. Ein Wintermärchen*, Berlin, 1958.

—— *Heinrich Heine. Geistige Entwicklung und künstlerisches Werk*, Berlin and Weimar, 1967.

KILLY, W., '"Mein Pferd für 'n gutes Bild." Heine und Geibel', in *Wandlungen des lyrischen Bildes* (2nd edn.), Göttingen, 1958, pp. 94–115.

—— 'Nachwort' to Heine: *Buch der Lieder*, Frankfurt a. M., 1961, pp. 182–8.

KRAUS, K., 'Heine und die Folgen', in *Untergang der Welt durch schwarze Magie*, Vienna and Leipzig, 1922, pp. 200–35.

KRÜGER, H., *Die freie Kunst als ästhetisches Prinzip bei Heinrich Heine*, Diss., Würzburg, 1949.

KURZ, P. K., *Künstler, Tribun, Apostel. Heinrich Heines Auffassung vom Beruf des Dichters*, Munich, 1967.

LASHER-SCHLITT, D., 'Heine's Unresolved Conflict and "Der Rabbi von Bacherach"', *Germanic Review*, 27 (1952), 173–87.

LAUBE, H., 'Heine', *Geschichte der deutschen Literatur*, Stuttgart, 1840, iv. 213–27.

—— *Erinnerungen, 1810–1840, Gesammelte Werke*, ed. H. H. Houben, Leipzig, 1909, vol. xl.

LEGRAS, J., *Henri Heine poète*, Paris, 1897.

198   BIBLIOGRAPHY

LEHRMANN, C., *Heinrich Heine. Kämpfer und Dichter*, Berne, 1957.
LICHTENBERGER, H., *Henri Heine penseur*, Paris, 1905.
LINDE, O. ZUR, *Heinrich Heine und die deutsche Romantik*, Diss., Freiburg, 1899.
LINK, M., *Der Reisebericht als literarische Kunstform von Goethe bis Heine*, Diss., Cologne, 1963.
LOEWENTHAL, E., *Studien zu Heines 'Reisebildern'*, (Palaestra 138), Berlin, 1922.
—— 'Heines Gumpelino-Roman. Mit unveröffentlichten Stücken aus der Urschrift', *Bimini*, 19 (1924), 9–10.
—— 'Heines Fragment "Der Rabbi von Bacherach"', *Der Morgen. Zeitschrift der Juden in Deutschland*, 12 (1936), 168–75.
—— '"Der Rabbi von Bacherach"', *Heine-Jahrbuch 1964*, pp. 3–16 (reprint from 1937).
LUKÁCS, G., 'Heinrich Heine als nationaler Dichter', in *Deutsche Realisten des 19. Jahrhunderts*, Berlin, 1951, pp. 89–146.
MACHÉ, U., 'Der junge Heine und Goethe', *Heine-Jahrbuch 1965*, pp. 42–7.
MAGILL, C. P., ed., *Heinrich Heine: Zur Geschichte der Religion und Philosophie in Deutschland*, London, 1947.
MALINIEMI, I., 'Über rhythmische Satzkadenzen in Heinrich Heines Prosaschriften', *Heine-Jahrbuch 1965*, pp. 33–7.
MANN, M., ed., *Heinrich Heine: Zeitungsberichte über Musik und Malerei*, Frankfurt a. M., 1964 (introduction pp. 5–20).
MARCUS, F., *Jean Paul und Heinrich Heine*, Diss., Marburg, 1919.
MARCUSE, L., 'Heine and Marx: A History and a Legend', *Germanic Review*, 30 (1955), 110–24.
—— *Heinrich Heine in Selbstzeugnissen und Bilddokumenten*, Hamburg, 1960.
MARSHALL, A., 'Heine's Verse Satire, 1831–1845', Diss., Birmingham, 1964.
MAYER, H., 'Ahnen und Erinnern Heinrich Heines', in *Literatur der Übergangszeit*, Wiesbaden, 1951, pp. 31–50.
—— 'Die Ausnahme Heine', in *Von Lessing bis Thomas Mann. Wandlungen der bürgerlichen Literatur in Deutschland*, Pfullingen, 1959, pp. 273–296.
MELCHIOR, F., *Heinrich Heines Verhältnis zu Lord Byron*, Diss., Leipzig, 1902.
MENDE, F., 'Bekenntnis 1837. Heinrich Heines "Einleitung zum Don Quixote"', *Heine-Jahrbuch 1967*, pp. 48–61.
MOTEKAT, H., 'Hegel and Heine', in *A Hegel Symposium*, ed. D. C. Travis, Austin, Texas, 1962, pp. 65–79.
MÜLLER, J., 'Über Heines "Harzreise"', in *Wirklichkeit und Klassik*, Berlin, 1955, pp. 443–54.
—— 'Heines Nordseegedichte. Eine Sprach- und Stilanalyse des ersten Teils', *Wissenschaftliche Zeitschrift der Universität Jena*, 1965, 191–212.
MURAT, J., 'A propos d'un poème de Heine. Notes sur la création poétique', *Bulletin de la Faculté des Lettres de Strasbourg*, 35 (1956), 151–9.

MUTZENBECHER, H., *Heine und das Drama*, Diss., Bonn, 1914.

NIEHAUS, M., *Himmel, Hölle und Trikot. Heine und das Ballett*, Munich, 1959.

NOLLEN, J. S., 'Heine und Müller', *Modern Language Notes*, 17 (1902), 207–19; 261–76.

OCHSENBEIN, W., *Die Aufnahme Lord Byrons in Deutschland und sein Einfluß auf den jungen Heine*, Diss., Berne, 1905.

PACHE, A., *Naturgefühl und Natursymbolik bei Heinrich Heine*, Berlin, 1904.

PFEIFFER, H., *Begriff und Bild. Heines philosophische und ästhetische Ansichten*, Rudolstadt, 1958.

PRAWER, S. S., *Heine: 'Buch der Lieder'*, London, 1960.

—— *Heine, The Tragic Satirist. A Study of the Later Poetry, 1827–1856*, Cambridge, 1961.

RAHMELOW, W., *Zu den Anfängen des feuilletonistischen Stils. (Untersuchungen an Heine)*, Diss., Freiburg, 1936.

RANSMEIER, J. C., 'Heines "Reisebilder" und Laurence Sterne', *Archiv für das Studium der neueren Sprachen und Literatur*, 118 (1907), 289–317.

REEVES, N. B. R., 'The Art of Simplicity: Heinrich Heine and Wilhelm Müller', *Oxford German Studies*, 5 (1970), 48–66.

—— 'Heine and the Young Marx', *Oxford German Studies*, 7 (1972–3), 44–97.

REMER, P., *Die freien Rhythmen in Heinrich Heines 'Nordseebildern'. Ein Beitrag zur neuen deutschen Metrik*, Diss., Rostock, 1889.

ROSE, W., *Heinrich Heine: Two Studies of his Thought and Feeling*, Oxford, 1956.

—— 'Ein biographischer Beitrag zu Heines Leben und Werk', *Weimarer Beiträge*, 3 (1957), 586–97.

—— *The Early Love Poetry of Heinrich Heine. An Inquiry into Poetic Inspiration*, Oxford, 1962.

SAEDLER, H., 'Die Urform von Heines "Nordseebildern". Eine Lesartenstudie', in *Festschrift für Berthold Litzmann*, Bonn, 1920, pp. 277–302.

SAINTE-BEUVE, C. A., 'Henri Heine: De la France', *Premiers Lundis*, vol. ii, Paris, 1874, pp. 248–59.

SAMMONS, J. L., 'Heine's "Rabbi von Bacherach": The Unresolved Tensions', *German Quarterly*, 37 (1964). 26–38.

—— 'Heine's Composition: "Die Harzreise" ', *Heine-Jahrbuch 1967*, pp. 40–7.

—— *Heinrich Heine. The Elusive Poet*, New Haven and London, 1969.

SANDOR, A. I., *The Exile of Gods. Interpretation of a Theme, a Theory and a Technique in the Work of Heinrich Heine*, The Hague and Paris, 1967.

SANTKIN, P., *Ludwig Börnes Einfluß auf Heinrich Heine*, Diss., Bonn, 1913.

SCHEUER, O. F., *Heinrich Heine als Student*, Bonn, 1922.

SCHMITZ, G., *Über die ökonomischen Anschauungen in Heines Werken*, Weimar, 1960.

SEEGER, H., *Der Erzähler in Heines Balladen und Romanzen*, Diss., Bonn, 1953.

200 BIBLIOGRAPHY

SIEBERT, W., *Heinrich Heines Beziehungen zu E. T. A. Hoffmann*, Marburg, 1908.

SIEGRIST, C., 'Heines Traumbilder. Versuch einer Gliederung', *Heine-Jahrbuch 1965*, pp. 17–25.

SILZ, W., 'Heine's Synaesthesia', *Publications of the Modern Language Association of America*, 57 (1942), 469–88.

SIMON, E., 'Heine und die Romantik', in *Essays presented to Leo Baeck*, London, 1954, pp. 127–57.

STERN, J. P., 'History and Prophecy: Heine', in *Re-interpretations*, London, 1964, pp. 208–38.

STERNBERG, K., *Heinrich Heines geistige Gestalt und Welt*, Berlin, 1929.

STERNBERGER, D., *Heinrich Heine und die Abschaffung der Sünde*, Hamburg and Düsseldorf, 1972.

STIEFEL, R., 'Heine's Ballet Scenarios. An Interpretation', *Germanic Review*, 44 (1969), 186–98.

STRICH, F., 'Heine und die Überwindung der Romantik', in *Kunst und Leben*, Berne and Munich, 1960, pp. 118–38.

STRODTMANN, A., *Heinrich Heines Leben und Werke*, 2 vols. (1st edn.), Berlin, 1867.

TABAK, I., *Judaic Lore in Heine*, Baltimore, 1948.

TEICHGRÄBER, S., *Bild und Komposition in Heines 'Buch der Lieder'*, Diss., Freiburg, 1964.

TSCHICH, C., *Der Impressionismus im Prosastil von Heinrich Heines 'Reise-bildern'*, Diss., Kiel, 1928.

UHLENDAHL, H., *Fünf Kapitel über Heinrich Heine und E. T. A. Hoffmann*, Diss., Münster, 1919.

VACANO, S., *Heine und Sterne. Ein Beitrag zur vergleichenden Literatur-geschichte*, Diss., Berne, 1907.

VERMEIL, E., 'Heine als Politiker', *Sinn und Form*, 8 (1956), 407–24.

WADEPUHL, W., *Heine-Studien*, Weimar, 1956.

WALZEL, O., 'Henri Legras: "Henri Heine poète" ', *Euphorion*, 5 (1898), 149–60.

—— *Heines Tanzpoem 'Der Doktor Faust'*, Weimar, 1917.

WEBBER, K., 'Heine's Imagery in its Relationship to his Personality and Thought', Diss., Oxford, 1943.

—— ed., *Heinrich Heine: Poems*, Oxford, 1952.

WEBER, D., ' "Gesetze des Standpunkts" in Heines Lyrik', *Jahrbuch des freien deutschen Hochstifts*, 1965, pp. 369–99.

WECKMÜLLER, A., *Heines Stil* (Sprache und Kultur der germanischen und romanischen Völker. Germanistische Reihe 11), Breslau, 1934.

WEIDEKAMPF, I., *Traum und Wirklichkeit in der Romantik und bei Heine* (Palaestra 182), Leipzig, 1932.

WEINBERG, K., *Henri Heine, 'Romantique défroqué'. Héraut du symbolisme français*, New Haven and Paris, 1954.

WEISS, G., 'Heines Englandaufenthalt (1827)', *Heine-Jahrbuch 1963*, pp. 3–32.

—— 'Die Entstehung von Heines "Doktor Faust" ', *Heine-Jahrbuch 1966*, p. 41–57.

WELZIG, W., *Heine als Dichter der Sentimentalität. Ein Beitrag zur Wort-geschichte der Romantik*, Diss., Vienna, 1957.
WINDFUHR, M., 'Zu einer kritischen Gesamtausgabe von Heines Werken. Auswertung der Sammlung Strauß', *Heine-Jahrbuch 1962*, pp. 70–95.
—— 'Heine und der Petrarkismus. Zur Konzeption seiner Liebeslyrik', *Jahrbuch der deutschen Schillergesellschaft*, 10 (1966), 266–85.
—— 'Heines Fragment eines Schelmenromans "Aus den Memoiren des Herren von Schnabelewopski"', *Heine-Jahrbuch 1967*, pp. 21–39.
—— *Heinrich Heine. Revolution und Reflexion*, Stuttgart, 1969.
WOOD, F., *Heine as a Critic of his Own Works*, New York, 1934.
WORMLEY, S. L., *Heine in England*, Chapel Hill, 1943.

OTHER AUTHORS

i. *Primary Literature*

ADELUNG, J. C., *Grammatisch-kritisches Wörterbuch der hochdeutschen Mundart*, 4 vols., Vienna, 1811.
ARISTOPHANES, [*Werke*], transl. J. H. Voß, 3 vols., Brunswick, 1821.
ARNIM, L. A. v., and BRENTANO, C., *Des Knaben Wunderhorn. Alte deutsche Lieder*, ed. W. A. Koch, Darmstadt, 1963.
BAUDELAIRE, C., *Œuvres complètes*, ed. J. Crépet, Paris, 1922–53.
BÖRNE, L., *Sämtliche Werke*, ed. I. and P. Rippmann, Düsseldorf, 1964 ff.
BRENTANO, C., *Gesammelte Schriften*, ed. C. Brentano, Frankfurt a. M., 1852.
BYRON, G. G., Lord, *Poetical Works*, ed. E. H. Coleridge, London, 1905.
CERVANTES SAAVEDRA, M. DE, *Leben und Thaten des scharfsinnigen Edlen Don Quixote . . .*, transl. L. Tieck, (2nd edn.) 4 vols., Berlin, 1810–16.
DOBENECK, F. L. F. v., *Des deutschen Mittelalters Volksglauben und Heroensagen*, with an introduction by Jean Paul, 2 vols., Berlin 1815.
GLEIM, J. W. L., *Gedichte*, in Deutsche National-Litteratur 45, ed. F. Muncker, Stuttgart, undated, pp. 207–317.
GOETHE, J. W. v., *Werke* (Weimarer Ausgabe), Weimar, 1887–1919.
—— *Gedenkausgabe der Werke, Briefe, Gespräche*, ed. E. Beutler, Zürich, 1949 ff.
GRILLPARZER, F., *Die Ahnfrau* in *Sämtliche Werke*, ed. A. Sauer, Vienna, 1909, vol. i.
GRIMM, J. and W., *Kinder- und Hausmärchen in ihrer Urgestalt*, ed. F. Panzer, Hamburg–Bergedorf, 1948.
—— *Deutsche Sagen*, Berlin, 1816–18.
GRIMM, W., *Altdänische Heldenlieder, Balladen und Märchen*, Heidelberg, 1811.
—— *Kleinere Schriften*, ed. G. Hinrichs, 4 vols., Berlin and Gütersloh, 1881–7.
HAGEDORN, F. v., *Werke*, in Deutsche National-Litteratur 45, ed. F. Muncker, Stuttgart, undated, pp. 41–176.
HALLER, A. v., '*Die Alpen*' *und andere Gedichte*, ed. A. Elschenbroich, Stuttgart, 1965.

HEGEL, G. W. F., *Sämtliche Werke*, ed. H. Glockner, Stuttgart, 1927–40.

HERDER, J. G., *Sämtliche Werke*, ed. Bernhard Suphan, Berlin, 1877–1913.

HOFFMANN, E. T. A., *Gesammelte Werke*, ed. C. G. v. Maasen, Munich and Leipzig, 1912 ff.

IRVING, W., *The Sketch Book of Geoffrey Crayon, Gent*, with an introduction by Van Wyck Brooks, London and New York, 1963.

KERNER, J., *Die Reiseschatten*, ed. W. P. H. Scheffler, Stuttgart, 1964.

KLEIST, E. v., *Werke*, in Deutsche National-Litteratur 45, ed. F. Muncker, Stuttgart, undated, pp. 129–98.

KORNMANN, H., *Mons Veneris, Fraw Veneris Berg . . .*, Frankfurt a. M., 1614.

MANN, T., *Gesammelte Werke*, Frankfurt a. M., 1960.

MARX, K., and ENGELS, F., *Werke*, ed. at the 'Institut für Marxismus/Leninismus beim ZK der SED', Berlin, 1957 ff. (referred to in text as MEW).

MENZEL, W., *Die deutsche Litteratur*, (1st edn.) Stuttgart, 1828; (2nd edn.) Stuttgart, 1836.

MÜLLER, W., *Vermischte Schriften*, ed. G. Schwab, Leipzig, 1830.

—— *Gedichte*, ed. J. T. Hatfield, Deutsche Literaturdenkmale 137, Berlin, 1906.

MÜLLNER, A., *Die Schuld*, in *Das Schicksalsdrama*, ed. J. Minor, Deutsche National-Litteratur 151, Berlin and Stuttgart, undated.

NOVALIS, *Schriften. Die Werke Friedrich von Hardenbergs*, ed. P. Kluckhohn and R. Samuel, (2nd edn.) Stuttgart, 1960 ff.

SAINT-SIMON, C.-H. DE, and ENFANTIN, P., *Œuvres*, Paris, 1865–78.

SCHILLER, F. v., *Sämtliche Werke*, ed. G. Fricke, H. Göpfert, and H. Stubenrauch, Munich, 1965–7.

—— and GOETHE, J. W. v., *Briefwechsel zwischen Schiller und Goethe in den Jahren 1794 bis 1805*, Stuttgart and Tübingen, 1828–9.

SCHLEGEL, A. W. v., *Sämmtliche Werke*, ed. E. Böcking, Leipzig, 1846–7.

—— *Vorlesungen über schöne Litteratur und Kunst*, ed. J. Minor, Deutsche Literaturdenkmale 19, Heilbronn, 1884.

SCHLEGEL, F. v., *Kritische Schriften*, ed. W. Rasch, Munich, 1964.

SCOTT, Sir W., *The Waverley Novels*, London, 1906 ff.

STAËL, Mme de, *De l'Allemagne*, ed. La Comtesse J. de Pange, Paris, 1958.

STERNE, L., *The Life and Opinions of Tristram Shandy, Gentleman*, with an introduction by G. Saintsbury, London, 1912.

—— *A Sentimental Journey; The Journal to Eliza*, with an introduction by D. George, London, 1960.

STOLBERG, F. L., Graf zu, *Gedichte*, in *Der Göttinger Dichterbund*, Part III, ed. A. Sauer, Deutsche National-Litteratur 50, II, Stuttgart, undated.

UHLAND, L., *Gedichte*, ed. E. Schmidt and J. Hartmann, Stuttgart, 1898.

WERNER, Z., *Der vierundzwanzigste Februar*, in *Das Schicksalsdrama*, ed. J. Minor, Deutsche National-Litteratur 151, Berlin and Stuttgart, undated.

ZISKA, F., and SCHOTTKY, J. M. (ed.), *Österreichische Volkslieder*, Pest, 1819.

ii. Secondary Literature

ABRAMS, M. H., *Natural Supernaturalism. Tradition and Revolution in Romantic Literature*, New York, 1971.

ALLEMAGNE, H.-R. D', *Les Saint-Simoniens, 1827–1837*, Paris, 1930.

BARNARD, F. M., *Herder's Social and Political Thought*, Oxford, 1965.

BENN, G., *Probleme der Lyrik*, Wiesbaden, 1951.

BERLIN, I., *Karl Marx. His Life and Environment*, London, 1963.

BODE, K., *Die Bearbeitung der Vorlagen in 'Des Knaben Wunderhorn'*, Palaestra 76, Berlin, 1909.

COTTRELL, A., *Wilhelm Müller's Lyrical Song-cycles, Interpretations and Texts*, Chapel Hill, 1970.

CZERNY, J., *Sterne, Hippel und Jean Paul. Ein Beitrag zur Geschichte des humoristischen Romans in Deutschland*, Berlin, 1904.

DILTHEY, W., *Das Erlebnis und die Dichtung* (10th edn.), Leipzig and Berlin, 1929.

EHRENZELLER-FAVRE, R., *Loreley. Entstehung und Wandlung einer Sage*, Zürich, 1948.

FISCHER, K., *Hegels Leben, Werke und Lehre*, Heidelberg, 1963 (reprint of 1911 edn.).

FRIEDRICH, H., *Die Struktur der modernen Lyrik von Baudelaire bis zur Gegenwart*, Hamburg, 1956.

GILLIES, A., *Herder*, Oxford, 1945.

HAUFLER, H., *Kunstformen des feuilletonistischen Stils. Beiträge zur Ästhetik und Psychologie des modernen Zeitungsfeuilletonismus*, Diss., Tübingen, 1928.

HELLER, E., *The Disinherited Mind*, Cambridge, 1952.

HIGHET, G., *The Anatomy of Satire*, Princeton, 1962.

HOFMANNSTHAL, H. v., *Selected Essays*, ed. M. E. Gilbert, Oxford, 1955.

HOLBORN, H., *A History of Modern Germany, 1648–1840*, London, 1965.

JOST, K., 'Wilhelm Müllers Liederzyklen "Die schöne Müllerin" und "Die Winterreise"', *Zeitschrift für deutsche Philologie*, 82 (1964), 452–71.

KALFF, G., *De Sage van den Vliegenden Hollander. Naar behandeling, oorsprong en zin onderzocht*, Zutphen, 1923.

KAUFMANN, W. (ed.), *Hegel's Political Philosophy*, New York, 1970.

KAYSER, W., *Geschichte der deutschen Ballade*, Berlin, 1936.

—— *Das sprachliche Kunstwerk*, Berne and Munich, 1961.

KLUCKHOHN, P., *Die Auffassung der Liebe in der Literatur des 18. Jahrhunderts und der deutschen Romantik* (3rd. edn.), Tübingen, 1966.

—— 'Biedermeier als literarische Epochenbezeichnung', *Deutsche Vierteljahrsschrift*, 13 (1935), 1–43.

KOHN, H., *The Mind of Germany. The Education of a Nation*, London, 1961.

KORFF, H. A., *Geist der Goethezeit*, 4 vols. and index vol. (6th and 7th edns.), Leipzig, 1964.

LANGE, V., 'Erzählformen im Roman des achtzehnten Jahrhunderts', *Zur Poetik des Romans*, ed. V. Klotz, Darmstadt, 1965.

LÖWITH, K., *Von Hegel zu Nietzsche* (2nd edn.), Stuttgart, 1950.

—— *Die Hegelsche Linke*, Stuttgart, 1962.

McLELLAN, D., *The Young Hegelians and Karl Marx*, London, 1969.

—— *Marx before Marxism*, London, 1970.

MAINLAND, W. F., Introduction and Notes to Schiller: *Über naive und sentimentalische Dichtung*, Oxford, 1957.

MEINECKE, F., *Die Entstehung des Historismus*, 2 vols., Munich and Berlin, 1936.

MÜLLER, G., *Geschichte des deutschen Liedes*, Munich, 1925.

MUNDT, T., *Die Kunst der deutschen Prosa*, Berlin, 1837.

—— *Geschichte der Literatur der Gegenwart*, Berlin, 1842.

MUSTARD, H. M., *The Lyric Cycle in German Literature*, New York, 1946.

RAMM, A., *Germany, 1789–1919. A Political History*, London, 1967.

REED, T. J., 'Thomas Mann, Heine, Schiller: The Mechanics of Self-interpretation', *Neophilologus*, 47 (1963), 41–50.

—— ' "Geist und Kunst". Thomas Mann's Abandoned Essay on Literature', *Oxford German Studies*, 1 (1966), 53–101.

REICHARD, W. A., *Washington Irving and Germany*, Michigan, 1957.

RIESER, F., *'Des Knaben Wunderhorn' und seine Quellen*, Dortmund, 1908.

ROSE, W., *From Goethe to Byron. The Development of Weltschmerz in German Literature*, London, 1924.

SENGLE, F., *Arbeiten zur deutschen Literatur, 1750–1850*, Stuttgart, 1965.

STAIGER, E., *Grundbegriffe der Poetik*, Zürich, 1961.

STARKIE, E., Introduction and Notes to Baudelaire: *Les Fleurs du mal*, Oxford, 1942.

STRICH, F., *Die Mythologie in der deutschen Literatur*, Halle, 1910.

—— *Deutsche Klassik und Romantik oder Vollendung und Unendlichkeit* (2nd edn.), Munich, 1924.

WIEDMANN, F., *G. W. F. Hegel in Selbstzeugnissen und Bilddokumenten*, Hamburg, 1965.

INDEX